OUR SCANDINAVIAN HERITAGE

OUR SCANDINAVIAN HERITAGE

A COLLECTION OF MEMORIES BY
THE NORDEN CLUBS
JAMESTOWN, NEW YORK, USA

EDITED AND INTRODUCED BY
BARBARA ANN HILLMAN JONES

Copyright © 2012 by Barbara Ann Hillman Jones.

Library of Congress Control Number: 2012906294
ISBN: Hardcover   978-1-4691-9618-3
            Softcover   978-1-4691-9617-6
            Ebook   978-1-4691-9619-0

All rights reserved. No part of this book may be reproduced or transmitted in any form or by any means, electronic or mechanical, including photocopying, recording, or by any information storage and retrieval system, without permission in writing from the copyright owner.

Requests for information should be addressed to:

Barbara Ann Hillman Jones
1811 Brandywine Trail
Fort Wayne, Indiana 46856-1577
E-mail: *bajfw7@frontier.com*
Website: *www.phalanxassociatesinc.com*

This book was printed in the United States of America.

To order additional copies of this book, contact:

Xlibris Corporation
1-888-795-4274
www.Xlibris.com
Orders@Xlibris.com
109327
Or visit my website for special discounts.

Contents

TITLE	AUTHOR	PAGE
Introduction	Barbara Hillman Jones	13
Letter from Stephen E. Sellstrom, Honorary Consul of Sweden		17
Who Are The Scandinavians?	Arland O. Fiske	19
The Swedes In America	Barbara Hillman Jones	23
The Swedes In Jamestown, New York	Barbara Hillman Jones	25
The Norden Clubs Of Jamestown, New York		28
From There To Here	Maj-Britt Traynor	34
How Swede It Is	Elizabeth (Beth) Richetti	45
Queen Margaret I—Ruler Of All Scandinavia	Arland O. Fiske	47
Two Different Worlds Meet In The New World	Martha E. Lindner	50
Living With An Immigrant Father And Mother Who Were Swedish	C. Philip Thorsell	52
The Stave Churches Of Norway	Arland O. Fiske	53
Preserving Some Of The "Old Country" In A New World	Dennis Shows	56
Jackson's Dairy	Chuck Jackson	60
What's In A Name?	Barbara Hillman Jones	62
One Of Our Swedish Miracles	Sandra Sandy	65
Visiting Sweden	Jean Wistean Seastedt	67
Finland—Land Of Surprises	Arland O. Fiske	69
Leonard Edward Faulk's Story	Written by "Himself" Sub. by Leonard E. Faulk, Jr.	71
My Trip To The United States	Nels Nelson	78

Knut—The Dane Who Ruled England	Arland O. Fiske	80
Family Story	Julie Lindblom Boozer	83
Reindeer Boots	Katie (Cathy) Peterson	85
Like Comparing Oranges To Oranges	Celeste Nelson Kerns	86
Snorri Sturluson: Iceland's "Royal Storyteller"	Arland O. Fiske	87
Hofstedts Och Jonassons Från Östergötland	Newkirk L. Johnson	90
My Family Stuga	Donald K. Sandy	97
Åltomtabro	Barbara Hillman Jones	101
Pancakes And Pepparkakor	Norma Carlson Waggoner	103
August Erickson Came To Be An American!	Erickson Family	105
Sweden—Its People And Royalty	Arland O. Fiske	108
1976 Royal Visit	Carol Lind Kindberg	110
104 Hazeltine Avenue	Gordon Henry Mattson	111
The Scandinavian "Oscars" And The "French Connection"	Arland O. Fiske	117
Swedish Memories	Sharon Lofgren Garrison	120
J. Henry Carlson	Tanya Bilicki	122
"Prillar-Guri": The Country Girl Who Saved Norway	Arland O. Fiske	124
It's A Small World After All	Sandra Sandy	127
I Wish I Had Asked Questions Sooner	Lamae Ahlgren McCullor	129
Dad's Flag	Barbara Hillman Jones	132
Swedish Covenant Hospital, Chicago, Illinois	Karin Hillman Oeffling	134
On My Swedish Heritage	Gladys Carlson Peterson	136
Jean Sibelius And The Music Of Finland	Arland O. Fiske	140
School Daze	Carol Lind Kindberg	142

Title	Author	Page
The Emigration Of Anders And Anna Larson And The Reuniting Of Their Descendents 141 Years Later	Denise Nichols	143
Soren Kierkegaard—A Dane Whose Ideas Outlived Him	Arland O. Fiske	146
Nobody Speaks Swedish To Me Anymore	Yvonne Thorstenson McNallie	148
The Haglund/Nelson Experience In Jamestown	Margaret Mae Haglund Lynch	151
Erik The Red	Arland O. Fiske	156
Homemade Swedish Root Beer	Gregory Jones	159
A Letter From America In 1850 (Erik Johan Pettersson)	Sub. by Julie Lindblom Boozer	160
Karin's Swedish Picnics	Barbara Hillman Jones	164
My Grandparents	Karin Carlson Flynn	166
Latent Scandinavianity	Jay T. Stratton	168
Discovering The "Vasa Ship"	Arland O. Fiske	187
Swedish Hospitality	Carol Lind Kindberg	189
Rullepølse	Judith Erlandson Cowles	190
Who Are The "Lapps"?	Arland O. Fiske	192
Renewing An Old Friendship	Norma Carlson Waggoner	194
Youngberg—Martinson Families	Mary Wright	195
Edvard Grieg And "Troldhaugen"	Arland O. Fiske	198
Cousin Nia	Jean Wistean Seastedt	200
Looking Forward, Looking Back	Jane Samuelson	202
Vaxholm	Barbara Hillman Jones	206
Mother's Legacy	Carolyn Gustavson Johnson	208
The Spinning Wheel	Lois Jones Oster	209
The Saarinens: Finland's Architectural Gift To America	Arland O. Fiske	211
My Dad	Dolores Carlson Jackman	213
My Father's Family	John E. Anderson	215
Grundtvig—The Most Danish Of The Danes	Arland O. Fiske	218

Title	Author	Page
Tastes Of Home	Norma Carlson Waggoner	220
Searching For The Ghost Of My Grandfather	Loren G. Carlson	221
Leif Erikson Discovers America!	Arland O. Fiske	233
My Grandmother: Mrs. Arvid J. Thorsell	James Swan	236
A Chance Meeting	Susann Sparrman Gustafson	238
Niagara	Barbara Hillman Jones	241
Our Crossing Story	Joan Peterson Shevory	243
Brostroms And Ulanders	Janice Ulander Johnson	246
Raoul Wallenberg—"Righteous Gentile"	Arland O. Fiske	250
Our Swedish B&B	Carilyn Larson Wright	252
G. Elving Lundine, A Brief Biography	Stan Lundine And Barbara Lundine Goldman	254
'Syttende Mai'—Norway's Constitution Day	Arland O. Fiske	257
Johan August Hallin	C. David Jones	260
My Story	Rheba Brumberg Carlson	262
Mannerheim—A Name The Finns Trust	Arland O. Fiske	263
The Swedes In Zion	Russell N. Chall Sub. by Cynthia Chall Holt	265
A Swedish Family's History	Arthur (Pete) Thorstenson	267
The Herring Festival	Barbara Hillman Jones	272
Hard Times In The New World	Tom Erlandson	275
Simply Scandinavian	Ann Nelson Quackenbush	279
H. C. Andersen—Denmark's Beloved Storyteller	Arland O. Fiske	282
Carrying On The Tradition	Donna Nelson Johnson	284
Moster Anna	Karen Thorstenson Canfield	289
Dag Hammarskjold: Sweden's "Apostle Of Peace"	Arland O. Fiske	291
The Heavy Coats	Katie (Cathy) Peterson	293
"A Letter To My Dear Ones"	John A. Anderson	295

"St. Olaf"—Norway's Best Remembered King	Arland O. Fiske	303
A Coal Miner's Granddaughter	Karin Hillman Oeffling	306
Early Swede Hill Families	Carolyn Pearson Volk	307
The Doggie Box	Barbara Hillman Jones	310
Anna Lawson	Larry Koplik	312
Return To Sweden—2012	Donna Close Johnson	314
Berry Berry Swedish: Swedish Berry Lore	Jay T. Stratton	316
Carl Larsson's Home	Arland O. Fiske	321
My Mom, The Cook	Yvonne Thorstenson McNallie	324
Jamestownian Remembers Norway Under Siege	James Sorg Sub. By His Family	326
Gustavus Adolphus— "Lion Of The North"	Arland O. Fiske	328
Heritage And Good Memories	Karen E. Livsey	330
"Jul Mönster"	Barbara Hillman Jones	332
My Emigration From Norway	Vorin Hansen Johnston	334
Letters From Sweden To Andrew Sandberg In America	Sub. By Sallie A. Olson	337
Afterword		363
Acknowledgments		365
Index Of Contributing Authors		367
Bibliography		371

DEDICATION

This collection of our memories of the emigration of the Scandinavians to Jamestown, New York, the character of those family members, and the beginning of their life in the New World is lovingly dedicated to the generations who follow us. It is our hope that you will more fully understand and appreciate the depth of strength, determination, and sacrifice made by those who left family and country in order to make a new and better life for you in the United States of America.

INTRODUCTION

The Norden Men's Club, Jamestown, New York, had just celebrated its 100th anniversary. As the capstone of that celebration on Saturday, October 22, 2011, they were honored by the presence of King Carl XVI Gustaf and Queen Silvia of Sweden. Jamestown had previously been privileged to be visited by the young, unmarried king thirty-five years earlier in 1976, when he had been Sweden's monarch for only three years. As part of that 1976 celebration he was given honorary membership in The Norden Men's Club.

I remember well the king's visit on Sunday, April 25, 1976, albeit vicariously, because my father, Arnold Hillman, was president of The Swedish Society in Jamestown at that time, and in that capacity he was invited to participate in the festivities held in the king's honor. Special plans and preparations were put into motion months in advance of the king's visit, and there was great excitement. I have my father's special invitation, the program, and some photographs which appeared in the local newspaper. The memento I like the most is a photograph from the Jamestown Post-Journal showing my father and Mrs. Carl Peterson, a neighbor of ours on Elam Avenue, washing and drying one hundred place settings of Spode china that would be used for the luncheon the next day.

On his visit in October 2011, the king returned as a full, *bona fide* member of The Norden Men's Club, this time accompanied by his wife, Queen Silvia. The festivities were wonderful. The high school band played as the honored guests arrived by private plane and landed at the Jamestown Airport. The royal couple walked the red carpet that had been rolled out for them, they waved to the crowd that had gathered to welcome them, and there were greetings from community dignitaries. The king and queen and their entourage were driven in style to Jamestown Community College where an elegant luncheon had been prepared. The blue and yellow colors we love so much permeated the room in flags, flowers, and table decorations. There were more greetings and music before the luncheon, and afterwards Donna Johnson and her young dancers in their folk costumes performed beautifully for the honored guests. Queen Silvia got caught up in the celebration, and she spontaneously joined the children in a folk dance. The king watched intently, clapping as the children performed so delightfully the folk dances Donna had taught them.

Gifts and awards were given and received, and it was a grand, never-to-be-forgotten occasion. As I watched the video on my computer, I was proud of the Swedish community in Jamestown and of Jamestown's leaders. The occasion was as dignified but warm and lovely as any larger city with more resources could possibly have put together. It was delightful!

One of the awards given by the king was for civil service to an elderly gentleman who told the king a story after the medal had been presented to him. It seems that as a young man he had fallen in love with a pretty young *flicka* and they wanted to get married. However, there were rules about getting married many years ago, and he was too young. In order to be able to get married, he had to get permission from the King of Sweden, so he wrote a letter to the then king, Gustaf V, grandfather of present King Carl XVI Gustaf. In due time, permission was received, and the young couple were able to be married. That story touched me and remained in my memory.

A couple of weeks later, when my husband and I were driving to church on a Sunday morning, we talked about the visit of the royal couple to Jamestown and of the story about having to get permission to get married. Out of the blue I had an idea—if there is such a wonderful story as that, how many more must there be? Some of the local residents emigrated from Scandinavia themselves as children or young adults. For others, it may have been their parents or even their grandparents. Each person has a unique story to tell, one that belongs to no one else. As we get older and new generations come, things change. At first, Scandinavians married Scandinavians, but later on some Scandinavians married people of other ethnic origins. Now there are fewer and fewer persons who are one hundred percent Scandinavian, and we find it takes time and great effort to keep our heritage and customs alive for our children and grandchildren.

My husband's mother's family, the John Hallins, lived on Chapin Street on Swede Hill in Jamestown. His mother used to tell us that her grandfather Peterson had two requirements for anyone who wanted to date his daughter (my husband's grandmother): first, the young man must be a Swede and, second, he must be a Methodist (apparently in that order).

Something that I already knew from my own family history, but something that impressed me again when I read the stories and family histories of the contributors is the pride the emigrants took in becoming assimilated into their new country. This new life was not something they took for granted nor something they felt was owed them. Living in America and becoming a citizen here was a privilege, something they highly revered. They wanted to learn the language, they wanted to learn the customs, they wanted to be woven into the fabric of their new land—and they worked very hard to make sure that happened. It was all part of their dream.

From what I know of my own family, these emigrants were not only proud to become Americans, but they never lost their love for their homeland. I have no doubt that their mixed emotions seemed to some more than they could bear, but nevertheless, they felt compelled to press onward. Many never again saw the loved ones they had left behind. There must have been many tear-stained letters between them exchanging news from the place of their birth and from their adopted new country. Some wanted to return to Sweden because they were homesick or for other various reasons. My great-grandfather, who was a widower, came to Dagus Mines, Pennsylvania (near Ridgeway), bringing with him at least two of his daughters. A couple of his family of ten children had emigrated previously, one settling in Cicero, Illinois. After a couple of years, my great-grandfather returned to Sweden, leaving the daughters he had brought with him in Pennsylvania. He went back to marry my grandmother's Sunday School teacher! However, Grandma said she was happy because she loved her Sunday School teacher. Some of those left behind were fortunate enough at some point to be able to visit their relatives who had moved across the Atlantic, and some decided to stay in America. But for many, leaving the old country to start a new life in America was a sad occasion, and there must have been many tears, especially between parents and children who were being separated for probably the rest of their lives. My grandmother never again saw her father or the siblings who stayed in Sweden.

In our family, we celebrated with Swedish customs—the smörgåsbord, opening our presents on Christmas Eve, Julotta on Christmas morning, entertaining other Scandinavians, singing hymns in Swedish in church, displaying in their homes a treasure or two they had been able to bring with them. My grandparents learned to speak English as quickly as possible, but Swedish continued to be spoken in their home, and both of my grandmothers continued to cook and bake those scrumptious dishes and pastries that are the best in the world.

Although my dad was born in America, he spoke perfect Swedish as taught to him by his parents. When I visited Sweden with him in 1974, people who did not know him thought he was a native because his Swedish was impeccable. I'm extremely grateful to my father who was proud of his heritage and went to considerable effort to educate my sister and me about our family, and we were instilled with a love for our Swedish roots. In my kitchen I have a little shelf over a dry sink, and those two pieces comprise my "Swedish corner" where all manner of Swedish items I have collected over the years are permanently displayed. At Christmas, I happily unpack other Swedish memorabilia—my Jul bok (Swedish goat), ornaments that have been carefully carved from wood, beautifully painted and decorated candle holders, and of course, my tomten (the good little gnome).

My sister, my only first cousin, and I are the last one hundred percent Swedes in our family, and we are concerned that our heritage be kept alive. We observed many Swedish customs in our home and in our extended family in Jamestown, and we now try to pass those on to our children and grandchildren. Unfortunately, as we get ever farther away from the emigration of our relatives, that aspiration becomes more difficult.

This book is a result of the flash of inspiration I had driving to church that Sunday morning, and each contributor has written his or her own story. The stories are theirs—they are all unique and wonderful, now preserved for posterity and as part of the important historical records of the Scandinavians in Jamestown, New York, United States of America. I'm honored to have had the privilege of editing and introducing their memories to you.

In our family when a meal was ready, my grandmothers would say, *"Var så god,"* indicating that it was time to eat and we should find our places at the table. So the authors of this book say to you readers, *"Var så god"*—find a comfortable spot, get some *kaffe med dopp* (coffee and a roll, cookie, or whatever), kick off your shoes, sit back, and savor every story. Read every word because even the shortest one has hidden gems not to be missed!

Barbara Ann Hillman Jones
Editor

Consulate of Sweden
Stephen E. Sellstrom, Consul

April 26, 2012

Ms. Barbara A. Jones
1811 Brandywine Trail
Fort Wayne, IN 46845-1577

Dear Ms. Jones:

I am honored as the Honorary Consul for Sweden in Jamestown, New York to convey my best wishes for the success of your new book *"Our Scandinavian Heritage"*.

Your book will provide an important connection for us as Americans to the honorable history of our past. As time passes, and we drift farther and farther away from the Scandinavian culture and traditions of our predecessors, your memorialization of our historical roots will remind us of the richness of our lineage.

Scandinavian-Americans have helped shape our new home in so many positive ways. We can be proud of the substantial contributions we have made and will continue to make to our country.

My warmest regards,

STEPHEN E. SELLSTROM
Honorary Consul of Sweden

SES:cr

Address:
9-11 East Fourth Street
P.O. Box 50
Jamestown, New York 14702-0050

Telephone:(716)484-7195
Fax:(716)484-2133
Cable:SwedishConsulate

WHO ARE THE SCANDINAVIANS?

by Arland O. Fiske

Editor's Note: The Rev. Dr. Arland O. Fiske, a native of Colfax, ND is a fourth-generation Norwegian-American. He is a retired Lutheran pastor of The Evangelical Lutheran Church in America. Dr. Fiske is a Scandinavian historian and writer, having authored several books on Scandinavian history. For several years he wrote a syndicated column on Scandinavia. He is a graduate of the Norwegian-American educational system: Oak Grove High School, Fargo, ND; Concordia College, Moorhead, MN; and Luther Northwestern Theological Seminary, St. Paul, MN. He did his doctoral studies at Concordia Seminary, St. Louis, MO and clinical pastoral studies at Swedish Covenant Hospital, Chicago, IL. Fiske has served numerous Scandinavian organizations in various capacities over the years. His wife, Gerda, a native of Racine, WI, was a second-generation Danish-American and together they made several visits to Scandinavia. He now makes his home in Texas. Arland O. Fiske is a long-time friend of ours, and for many years he and my husband served together as officers of the Academy of Parish Clergy. I am extremely grateful to him for his *carte blanche* offer to me to reprint anything from any of his books that I deemed useful for this project, and so I took him up on it! Therefore, several of his articles are interspersed throughout, providing additional Scandinavian history for the reader.

The people of five nations make up the Scandinavian heritage. These are: Denmark, Finland, Iceland, Norway, and Sweden. The Scandinavians, however, have been a travelling people and now live in all parts of the world. Their greatest concentration is found in the USA with large numbers in the upper Midwest states and on the West Coast.

The Scandinavian lands, with the exception of Iceland, are known to have been inhabited since before the last Ice Age. People have lived in Denmark since about 10,000 BC and in Norway, Sweden and Finland since 8000-7000 BC. Iceland was not settled until the ninth century AD, though Irish monks had arrived two centuries earlier. Iceland was settled by Norwegians fleeing from the tyranny of King Harald Haarfagre (Finehair). The Icelandic people of today still speak the Old Norse of that period. The Danes, Norwegians and Swedes are a distinct Teutonic language group and share a common heritage with the North Germans and Dutch. This Germanic immigration to the Scandinavian lands began about 2000 BC and covered a lengthy period of time.

There are, of course, no pure races. In addition to the typically blonde and blue-eyed Scandinavians, there are many with darker complexions that settled especially in western Norway. Many flaxen-haired Celts were taken as slaves from Ireland and blended in with the Norwegians. They were given their freedom after Norway became Christian.

The term *Scandinavia* was originally *Scatinavia*, and was a misspelling in the writings of Pliny the Elder. In AD 5, Emperor Augustus sent his Rhine fleet to explore the region and then it became forgotten from the pages of history for almost 400 years.

The people of Finland are a part of a migration that passed through Hungary and Estonia. Because Finland was under Swedish rule from 1216 to 1809, there are many Finns of Swedish origin, especially in the southwestern part of the country, around Turku, the old Swedish capital. Swedish is the official language of Finland today, together with Finnish. In 1809, Russia occupied Finland and it did not gain its independence until 1917. The Russians made Finland a Grand Duchy and chose Helsinki for their capital. This was closer to St. Petersburg, the home of the Czars.

During the ninth through the eleventh centuries, the Germanic Scandinavians spread out in a series of conquests and colonizations to England, Scotland, Ireland, the North Sea islands, Russia and the Baltic areas. They carried on trade in a much larger area and were given possession of that part of France called Normandy (Northmandy). If you find some French people with blonde hair and blue eyes, ask if they are Normans.

But where have all the Vikings gone? Are they only in the movies and comic strips? And what kind of people were they really like? These hardy people who knew no fear in war or on the high seas, whose cruelty earned them a fearsome reputation, became eager settlers in the lands where they waged war. Once they became colonists, they became traders instead of raiders. They also became peaceful patriots, often joining in defensive wars against their former countrymen. Though war was a part of their culture, their main interests were trading and finding places to live for the people of their overcrowded homelands. Primogeniture was the law of the land. This meant that only the oldest son was entitled to inherit the family farm and other property. He also had to care for his parents for so long as they lived.

In America, the Scandinavian immigrants became fiercely patriotic to the cause of the New World. They were a willing part of the melting pot. My parents would not speak a word of Norwegian to me. That was left to one of my grandmothers who refused to speak a word of English to anyone. Education was of highest priority to these immigrants. Parents would sacrifice all luxuries and conveniences so that their children could get a high school diploma and a college degree. They also established many fine colleges which are still flourishing. The result was that a high proportion of the Scandinavian immigrant families became leaders in politics, science, education, the church and in the arts.

Scandinavianism as a modern movement began after the fall from greatness of the two powers, Denmark and Sweden, early in the 19th century. Students led the way. Meeting in Copenhagen, they pledged to be true to each other "in life and in death in their loyalty to our great common fatherland." Since the superpowers of the day feared the political rise of a Scandinavian kingdom, the alliance was kept to the bounds of culture and trade. There was also a strong nationalism in each country that wanted to support the special interests of each nation.

Peace, not war, is the trademark of the Scandinavians today. This is evident in the fact that the first two secretaries-general of the United Nations came from Scandinavia: Trygve Lie of Norway and Dag Hamarskjold of Sweden.

Small countries need good memories. The people of Scandinavia have learned well how to live as close neighbors to the Warsaw Pact nations and still preserve their heritage of freedom. It was a long-time dream of my family to visit Scandinavia. It was quite a surprise to our children to learn that it was the dream of Scandinavian children to go to America. Without doubt, they are some of the best friends America has in the world. Long live the lands of the Northmen and their children everywhere!

THE SWEDES IN AMERICA

by Barbara Hillman Jones

The Swedes first came to Delaware in 1638, just 18 years after the Pilgrims, but the biggest influx was in the mid-to late-1800s when at least one out of four immigrants came from Sweden. The peak was in 1882 when 68,000 Swedes came to America.

Why did they come? Many came for economic reasons. Much of the land in Sweden was not able to be farmed, and as the population grew and the small farms went to the eldest son, there was not much left for the remaining sons. Crop failures also contributed to their determination to go to America where it was reported that everyone was rich. In his 1983 book about the Swedes in Jamestown entitled *Saga From the Hills*, M. Lorimer Moe said the following was the general belief of life in America: "In America there were only two classes: the rich and the newcomers who had not been in America long enough to become rich!"

Many came for other reasons:
- There was a very sharp class distinction between the privileged and the non-privileged.
- Many wanted to avoid the military with its harsh discipline.
- Some came for political reasons. The right to vote was based on how much land a person held, and so some had no right to vote at all.
- Many came for religious reasons. In Sweden there was a State church supported by taxes, and there was indifference and cold formalism in many parishes. Churches were supported voluntarily here in America, and the Swedes quickly accepted that and built over 2,000 schools and colleges in America, many of which are still thriving today.
- Then, like many other immigrants, some Swedes were merely looking for adventure.

If you are interested in the immigration of the Swedes to America, a must read is Vilhelm Moberg's four-volume set of historical novels written in Swedish in the 1950s and translated into English. A TV series based on Moberg's books called *Unto a Good Land* was popular in the 1960s.

THE SWEDES IN JAMESTOWN, NEW YORK

by Barbara Hillman Jones

Jamestown, New York was settled by James Prendergast in 1810, named after him, and incorporated as a village in 1827. Prendergast was part of a 29-person party who were from Eastern New York bound for Tennessee. However, they became dissatisfied with their original destination and Tennessee's loss was Western New York's gain. The local land clerk encouraged them to settle in the Chautauqua Lake region which he called *"The Paradise of the New World."* So the Prendergasts bought 3,337 acres on the west side of Chautauqua Lake near Mayville. But while searching for horses that had wandered off, James discovered an area near the Chadakoin River. He was so taken with the potential for waterpower and the hardwood forests that he immediately envisioned mills, factories and a transportation route that would accommodate a lumbering and milling village. According to one historian, he found not only his horses but his "fortune and fame." He married, built a home, and by 1814 there were sawmills and gristmills, shops, and small businesses of all kinds. The pioneers developed a sense of community. Most of them were well educated, of high character, and of excellent reputation in the communities from where they had come. They came with a fixed purpose—"to transform the wilderness into a community of comfortable Christian homes for themselves and their posterity." Jamestown would soon become known for its furniture industry, an outgrowth of lumbering.

Many Swedish immigrants were headed for the Midwest where relatives or friends may have already settled. Their route took a number of them through Western New York, and seeing the countryside which reminded them so much of their homeland, they went no further. They stopped and settled in Jamestown and the surrounding area. Western New York and

Chautauqua County's trees, lakes, rolling hills, and climate were just like home.

The greatest number of Swedes came to Jamestown between 1865 and 1900. Having been wood and metal artisans in Sweden, they were skilled cabinetmakers, artists, carvers, and finishers, and they were credited with the tremendous growth of the furniture industry in a relatively short period of time. They invested savings and formed small factories and furniture cooperatives. The Furniture Expo Building was constructed in 1917, and after World War II, there might be as many as 3,000 buyers annually from the United States, Canada, and Mexico. It's said that even Lucy (Lucille Ball was born and raised in Celeron and Jamestown) and Desi bought Jamestown furniture and had it shipped to their home in Hollywood. Furniture made in Jamestown was recognized throughout the United States as quality furniture of outstanding design. Jamestown's finished products had a wide reputation and were unexcelled anywhere. My Uncle Bill Carlson was one of those skilled craftsmen and designed and made such furniture in his own shop, Lakeview Cabinet Company, in Celeron. My husband David's grandfather John Hallin was president of Elk Furniture in the 1920s.

Our friend, Arland O. Fiske, relates the following about Jamestown:

> "My friend, Paul Settergren, stopped by for a visit before he moved to Jamestown, New York. He brought a book for me to read, entitled *Saga from the Hills: A History of the Swedes of Jamestown*. Its 700 pages offer insight on all Swedes who came to America... I asked Settergren (himself a Swede) how many Swedish people live in the Jamestown area. At that time, he estimated about 35,000. That rivals Rockford, Illinois, another strong Swedish-American community.
>
> "The Swedes were considered desirable settlers because they had a reputation for honesty. They were noted for being hard workers and having respect for the law. They were also strong community builders.
>
> "Christian faith was important to Swedish immigrants. They built over 2000 churches in America, the largest being First Lutheran in Jamestown. One Swedish farmer near Jamestown

came to pay his bill at the store after harvest and was asked by the storekeeper if he wanted a receipt. 'No, God knows I have paid my bill,' he replied. The storekeeper sneered, 'Do you still believe in God?' Confessing to be a believer, the farmer asked, 'Don't you?' When the storekeeper replied 'Naw!' the farmer said, 'Then you'd better give me a receipt.' He wasn't taking any chances."

Note: An expansive history of the Swedes in Jamestown is carefully documented in the book, *Saga From the Hills: A History of the Swedes of Jamestown*, by M. Lorimer Moe, Fenton Historical Society, 1983.

THE NORDEN CLUBS OF JAMESTOWN, NEW YORK

Because Scandinavian people are by their very nature persons with strong family and ethnic loyalties, it was a natural inclination that drew Scandinavian immigrants to gather in communities where they could associate with others who came from the same "homeland," knew and spoke the same familiar languages of the lands from which they had come, shared the same or similar backgrounds, remembered and cherished the much beloved customs and celebrated the same holidays and holy days as they had before they came to America.

Since a significantly large number of Swedish immigrants settled in Jamestown, NY and the surrounding areas of Chautauqua County, it was a natural and predictable sociological phenomenon that Swedish families formed businesses, churches, social and civic clubs where the Swedish language was spoken, and Swedish customs were observed and preserved for posterity. Thus it was that around the turn of the last century, men from the Swedish community gathered together and officially formed a number of Scandinavian social clubs.

In the epic book *Saga From the Hills* which chronicles "A History of The Swedes of Jamestown," local historian and contributing author Jennie Vimmerstedt lists a number of the early Scandinavian Societies and Lodges. (*Saga From The Hills*. Fenton Historical Society, Jamestown, New York, 1983, pp. 624-64.)

Among these organizations are listed the following: (1) a *Scandinavian Society of Swedes and Danes*, formed circa 1868 and disbanded in 1871. (2) The Swedish Singing society *Brage*, which emerged in 1871, which initially admitted only men but eventually accepted women as well. (3) In 1872 the *Scandinavian Temperance and Benevolent Society* was founded to engage Scandinavians in promoting the temperance movement. (4) The *Vega Society* was established in 1880 as a life insurance and sick benefit society. Between

1880 to 1899 Vega distributed $27,000 to the relatives of deceased members. (5) The Good Templers Order was a prominent group in Sweden, and as might be expected, there emerged in 1883 the *Skandia Lodge, I.O.G.T.*, which is recognized as the eldest of fraternal groups among the Swedes in Jamestown. (6) The Jamestown Lodge, *Knights of Pythias* was founded in 1886 as an almost exclusively Swedish organization. (7) A rival second Jamestown "Tent" (lodge), *Knights of Maccabees*, was started in 1887 and both lodges thrived into the 20th Century. (8) Several benefit groups including the Swedish Brotherhood, which was organized March 1, 1885, and continued until 1964. (9) The parallel *Swedish Sisterhood* provided a benevolent role for many years as a sick benefit group for women. (10) The *Swedish Hundred Members Society*, formed in 1896, also provided significant help in times of illness and economic and civil stress. (11) The *Leif Erickson Lodge, No. 26*, established in 1897 was the first S.F.A. (Scandinavian Fraternity of America) lodge outside of the State of Pennsylvania and became part of the national *Scandinavian Brotherhood of America*. (12) The *Enighet Lodge* (Unity) for women grew quickly following its formation in 1898.

In 1937 five of the Scandinavian lodges—*Leif Erickson* and *Unity* of the S.F. of A., *Thule Lodge, Hercules* and *Flora* lodges of the *Order of Vasa* joined in the formation of (13) the *Nordic Temple Corporation* to purchase the building which they shared as a clubhouse. The Nordic Temple was razed in 1969 to make way for the new City Hall which now occupies that site.

One of the largest fraternal orders (14) the *Thule Lodge, Order of Vasa*, was established in Jamestown in 1907. Over the years the international Order of Vasa has grown to a membership of over 35,000 members, and has become the largest of all Swedish-American fraternal organizations. Its membership is open to anyone of Swedish descent (or anyone married to a Swedish person) who has an interest and desire to preserve the Swedish cultural heritage. On April 10, 1947 the *Thule Lodge* merged with the *Hercules Lodge, No. 399*, and with *Flora Lodge No. 143*, on August 14, 1965.

Although the international fraternal Order of Odd Fellows is not exclusively a Scandinavian or Swedish society, (15) the Monitor Lodge, Independent Order of Odd Fellows, organized in Jamestown 1911, was practically exclusively composed of Swedes and conducted its ritual in the Swedish language until 1919. (16) The Jamestown Star Rebekah Lodge was organized in 1931 with the assistance of the Monitor Lodge.

The largest Swedish-American organization in Jamestown, with 1,500 members is (17) the *Ingjald Lodge, Independent Order of Vikings*, founded in 1925. (18) The *Ingrid Lodge of the Viking Order* played a vital role as a sick benefit organization prior to the establishment of the Social Security System and group hospital plans. It continues today primarily as a social organization.

In 1914 the Swedish-American of Jamestown started (19) *The Frances Willard branch of the Women's Christian Temperance Union* (WTCU). This organization worked diligently for enactment of national prohibition in 1920 and to promote scientific temperance in the public schools. It is interesting that the WCTU was born in nearby Fredonia, NY in 1873 and became a national movement in 1874.

Begun in the early 1920s as a men's club in the First Lutheran Church of Jamestown, (20) the *Swedish Society* over the following decade this organization evolved into a community group composed of members representing many different churches, lodges and other Swedish organizations, all of whom were attracted by the use of the Swedish language which was spoken almost exclusively until 1981. [The father of this book's editor, Arnold E. Hillman, served as President of the Swedish Society for several years during the 1970s and was an active participant among Jamestown civic and fraternal leaders who were hosts to King Carl XVI Gustaf when he visited in Jamestown in 1976.]

A social group motivated by sentimental ties to Sweden's North Sea coastal province, (21) the *Halland Klub*, stemmed from a picnic on Lake Erie held by five couples in August 1943. The club's members use the Swedish language almost exclusively and enjoy Swedish food and customs which dominate its programs. Though primarily a social club, it has actively cooperated with other Swedish-oriented organizations in community activities promoting the Scandinavian heritage.

Because of its prominent role within the Swedish-American community in the Jamestown area, (22) **The Norden Club(s) of Jamestown** are given an entire chapter in *The Saga From the Hills* (Ibid., pp. 641-646; cf. p. 671-672.) The Norden Club of Jamestown began on April 4, 1911 with just six men in attendance at a meeting "for the purpose of promoting social intercourse and developing a higher . . . standard of culture among residents of Jamestown who are either of Swedish birth or heritage." The membership of this club grew rapidly and read like a "Who's Who" of the community's Scandinavian business, professional and civic leaders (see Jennie Vimmerstedt, Ibid, pp. 671, 672.) Just two years after its first meeting, the newly formed club laid the cornerstone for its impressive clubhouse building on East Second Street just East of Prendergast Avenue, at the site where the present U.S. Post Office now stands. The new building became a community cultural center for many years, and was regarded as one of the stellar clubs of its kind in America. When Prince Wilhelm of Sweden visited the city in 1927, he praised the club's impressive building, saying that he knew of no comparable building in Sweden. Through the years since its inception the Norden Club has filled an important leadership role in promoting our Scandinavian Heritage.

Following the pattern of many other voluntary organizations, (23) **The Norden Women's Club of Jamestown** grew out of the interest and involvement of the wives of the Norden Men's Club members. The men's spouses were invited to some of the special events sponsored by the club, especially those events where food and dining were involved.

Even though women's suffrage had not yet gained for women the right to vote in local and national elections, these energetic, industrious and gregarious ladies also were drawn together by their common interests, some of which were not necessarily shared by their husbands. Because at that time in our nation's history it was still "a man's world," the women were welcomed and expected to participate and provide food and dinners when the men requested such assistance; however, the ladies were not allowed to become members of the Norden Club.

But not to be outdone by male chauvinism, these Swedish matrons exercised their own initiative and began to meet together, at first informally, but soon decided to form themselves into the Norden Club Ladies' Auxiliary. Quite often the women met at the same time their husbands were meeting at the Norden Club. Apparently, even before the Ladies Auxiliary was formally organized, notes had been kept and the historic minutes record that at one of the ladies' meetings in 1914 a Swedish play written by Mrs. Emily Sellstrom had been presented. Entitled *Then and Now* the play was presented in the Swedish language and "provoked much mirth and interest." Mrs. Sellstrom's play was later repeated for the public, at a charge of 25 cents and the proceeds were used for "patriotic work," as reflected in the minutes of the Ladies' Auxiliary.

Two years later, when the women saw a need to formalize the social gatherings they had had for some time, the Norden Ladies' Auxiliary was formed and Mrs. Sellstrom was elected their first President. Mrs. Sellstrom also saw to it that the women worked "in harmony with the Norden Men's Club and assisted them whenever possible" according to minutes from long ago.

Mrs. Sellstrom served as the President from the Auxiliary's inception in 1916 until 1922, and after that was made honorary president, remaining a driving influence behind the Club. Mrs. Sellstrom died in 1940, after spending an active life locally as part of various area organizations.

When the Norden Ladies Auxiliary and its successor the Norden Women's Club were begun, any woman who was a wife, mother, sister or daughter of a member of the Norden Men's Club was eligible to join the Auxiliary, as was any widow whose husband would have been eligible for membership in the Norden Club. The women originally met in the clubhouse of the Norden Club, which was located on East Second Street, where the U.S. Post Office now stands. The Club's original building was of an impressive Swedish architectural design and was described as "a community cultural center." The women would often sit in the parlors of the club before gathering in the dining room for afternoon coffee.

Much later, in 1948, the Norden Ladies' Auxiliary became the wholly independent Norden Women's Club and that is the name by which the organization has since been known. As the old by-laws of the club state, the club was originally formed for social purposes. The Club adopted as its motto one that was suggested by its first President, Emily Sellstrom: "*Låt oss tänka högt och göra stort*" = "Let us think high and do nobly." Sometimes it's translated, "*Aspire* high and do nobly." Now, the club continues to have social functions and also works to promote the preservation of the Scandinavian heritage. In pursuing this goal, the club supports Swedish organizations with contributions of funding and membership. The list of such organizations includes the Council of America, the American Swedish Historical Foundation, the Scandinavian Studies Endowment Fund and the Fenton Historical Museum.

The Norden Clubs currently support organizations that promote Swedish heritage, and members and the community benefit from that through the literature obtained from these organizations promoting the Scandinavian and Swedish heritage. The Norden Clubs also entertain Swedish exchange students and often are hosts for Swedish youth visiting in America.

The Norden Clubs have for many years been staunch supporters of the annual Scandinavian Folk Festival held in the Jamestown area in July.

Editor's Note: This article is based in part on a news story by A. Tyler Settle entitled *Norden Women Maintain Scandinavian Culture* which appeared in the Jamestown POST-JOURNAL, Oct. 12, 1991, page 9T, on the occasion of their 75th anniversary. Thanks to Sandra Sandy for sending it to me.

FROM THERE TO HERE

by Maj-Britt Traynor

Playing house on my big Boulder located on the hill behind our house, my Boulder was my friend, even though it was a glacial mass of rock and dirt which had been formed and then erupted to the location in which it had now been planted for probably thousands of years. Through the years the center had eroded due to the elements of the weather. It was perfect for me to fashion a kitchen and living room in the concave areas.

The geological records show that at least three times in the last third of the geological history extensive glacial activity occurred in many parts of the world where no glaciers exist today. The earliest widespread glacial activity occurred during Precambrian times, about 570,000,000 years ago. The evidence for this lies mainly in glacially derived sedimentary materials called *Tillites,* and in glacial markings such as large grooves and scratches in the older boulders. Scientists assert the presence of an ice sheet covered several thousand square miles during the middle Precambrian time. They were found in Scandinavia, Greenland, Northern Germany and the Baltic area. A friend of Papa's who was a Geology Professor in Uppsala University visited one time and told me all about the formation and remaining evidence that my Boulder could well have some Tillites in its composition.

My home was just outside of the little village named Valberg in the province of Värmland, Sweden. I grew up with two boy cousins, Johann and Hilmer. Both were two years older than I and tolerated me, I guess because my Aunts told them they had to play with me, but when it came to playing house on my boulder, the boys said no. Instead, during those times Mama would hand each of us a pail and tell us to go pick blueberries up on the hill. I would dutifully bring my pail of fruit home, but the boys would either eat them or end up throwing them at each other.

In the winter, Johann and Hilmer would ride me on my *Sparkstuttning.* This is an elongated sled on which I would sit and they would ride and push on the runners. We also ice skated on a pond directly across the way from our house. Johann and Hilmer were very good skaters, and of course they played hockey on the ice all the time. I was just learning, so I went timidly over the ice. Then one particular day when we were on the pond, Johann stopped me and with a very serious tone to his voice, said "Now, Maj-Britt, you don't have to go to America if you don't want to. I'll go in your place. Heaven only knows what would happen to you because of the Indians over there." I stood there with my mouth wide open because I really did not know what the boy was talking about. "What are you talking about, Johann?" I asked in alarm. "I'm not going to America, am I?" Then Hilmer broke in. "Yes, you are, and Mor Mor and Mor Far are going with you and your parents." I felt weak with excitement and fear all at the same time as I stood there. "America, America, I'm going to America?" Hilmer caught me by my arm as I was in the process of falling down and said "I'll be willing to take your place too, because I have heard children have to work on rice paddies. Being a girl I know you wouldn't be able to do that." I just heard the tail end of Hilmer's suggestion because I was half way up the slope of the pond and across the road to my house. "Don't come in with your skates on, Maj Britt," Mama called as she had heard me rush into the kitchen. "Mama, Mama are we going to America?" Mama came into the kitchen and put her arms around me. "How did you hear this?" she asked. "Johann and Hilmer just told me." "Well, as long as they have told you some of it, I will tell you all of it," she said. "We do want to go to America, but we were told the quota for this passage was all filled up, so we will have to wait until the next census."

I did not know what *quotas* were or meant, and I suppose at five years of age a little girl wouldn't know about those things, although I had heard my parents and grandparents talk about quotas and they sounded very concerned. They were discussing the fact that we now would have to wait another three months to be able to leave Sweden and go to America. It seems we had just missed the numeration of quota for the last quarter which meant the United States had completed the immigration census for that period. We were assured that we would be able to be accepted into the United States in the following period. This created a problem for us as the King of Sweden had released us from Swedish protection in January.

My father, Carl Anderson, was the head of the Equestrian Corps of the Swedish Royal Army, serving as a specialized trainer for the Corps of men who rode with the Royal couple to appearances at Senior Citizens affairs and all other functions pertaining to the Equestrian Corps. Sometimes, if the route was close to our home, Mama and I went to see the presentations Papa and his men put on for the public. I was always so proud when I was allowed to be at one of the events to watch Papa command the performance.

As I grew older I could understand the anguish Papa had, knowing he had reached the highest position he would hold in the Army. The benefits would not be enough to give us the kind of life he wanted for us. That was the reason for his retirement from the Corps. As he said later on, his job was a lot of fun and glamorous when he was young, but now he had a family and needed more benefits. Going to America was the dream of a lifetime for us all. Mama's brother, Axel Dawson had signed our security papers, promising to care for us financially if we ran into trouble when we arrived. Of course, we never had any problems like that when we finally arrived.

When the time of departure arrived, I was so excited I could not sleep the night before our leaving. Many relatives and friends came to see us off and our arms were full of all kinds of presents and chocolates as we walked up the ramp to the first level of the SS Gripsholm, which would become our home for ten days during the crossing of the Atlantic Ocean. The SS Gripsholm was like a large city to me as we walked about to find our berths. My maternal grandparents, Sarah and Oscar Gustafsson, joined us on our trip to America. They had never been away from their home in Sweden although, of course, Mor Far had been a commercial fisherman when he was working and was away for weeks on end. They were all smiles to think that they were also going to America. I put my hand into Mor Far's mammoth hand and felt secure and happy that these dear people were going with us to this new country of "streets paved with gold."

Mor Far and Mor Mor retired to their room as soon as we found it for them. Mor Mor's arthritis was bothering her a little bit and Mor Far was beginning to feel tired too after all the excitement as we all waved goodbye from the deck of the ship. Papa took Mama and me to meet the Captain. He noticed me and at once made sure someone would take me to the playground. I found out that the playground was built over the bilge of the ship with large planks and then large mats placed upon them. This area served a double purpose. In the bilge, the ship carried vehicles belonging to the passengers and, of course, all the produce of foods that would sustain us during our voyage. Then quickly attendants came with teeter-totters, swings and slides. Everything was provided for the children of the passengers to make the trip go well and give us time to play and make friends with one another.

Often Papa would take me for walks on deck and a favorite thing we did was look for whales. After meal times, the attendants would toss the leftover food into the ocean and we would see the whales following the ship and zoom in for the food. We could count anywhere from five to ten whales always following our ship for food. It was wonderful to realize these huge mammals were right there in the wake of the ship breaching for us and several times Papa pointed out the baby whales all gliding effortlessly along our ship.

Time really went quickly and on the ninth day Papa informed us that tomorrow we would be landing in America. Mama made herself busy readying us for the departure from the SS Gripsholm that had been our home for the crossing of that huge ocean. Papa emphasized I was not to leave them because of the rush of people leaving the ship all at once. When I saw the rush of people trying to get off the ship, pushing and shoving everyone, I realized I would not let go of Mor Far's huge hand until we were on the ground. The sun was shining brightly and I felt as though the weather knew I was here and wanted to make me feel especially welcome. And indeed it did.

I of course had a vision of disembarking immediately onto those "streets of gold"; rather, we were taken to Ellis Island and into the medical building. I saw many of the friends I had made during the crossing on the SS Gripsholm. We were each given a number and told to find a seat. Mor Mor Sarah was very tired and we all looked for a seat for her. Then Mama opened a box with biscuits that were given each passenger as we left the ship. Because everyone had to do precisely what we were doing, it was very kind of the Steamship Company to provide nourishment for their former passengers.

Soon our numbers came up, and first Mor Far and Mor Mor were told to enter the doctor's examining room. After about forty-five minutes my grandparents came out of the doctor's office with large smiles on their faces. The doctor who spoke Swedish was very complimentary to Mor Mor and complimented her on her nice personality and said she would indeed be an asset as a visitor to America.

Then Papa's name was called, and after him, Mama and I were called into the doctor's office. He beckoned me to him and he took my arms and held them out and then dropped them. I was not used to being treated so briskly and when he pulled me over to him and began parting my hair and looking closely at my scalp, I whimpered a little bit. He laughed and said to my mother, "We have to be sure she isn't bringing any unwanted guests into the country." In Swedish he asked me to open my mouth and he then checked my tonsils. After considerable time both Mama and I were given a clean bill of health. The doctor shook my hand as we left and told me to enjoy every day of my new life and to make America proud of me. I curtsied to him and nodded my head and smiled.

Papa and Mor Mor and Mor Far were waiting for us in the reception center and when they saw us, big smiles broke over their faces. Papa said they had begun being a little worried because we were so long in the Doctor's office. Mama laughed and said she and I were in very good health by decree of the doctor.

Uncle Axel and Aunt Selma Dawson were waiting for us in the reception center in the Disembarkation area. In those days no immigrant was allowed to enter the United States without being sponsored by a friend or relative. Being sponsored meant the United States was in no way to be financially responsible for the new immigrants. Uncle Axel had signed a financial security on our behalf, which meant if we were to become ill or in need of money, he would have to provide those needs. Of course, as time went by there was never a need for that. I had never met my Uncle and Aunt so I was very excited to think that more of our family was here to meet us. The first thing my Aunt Selma asked if I would like was an ice cream cone. For some reason, I had never had ice cream in Sweden, and when I brought it up to my mouth I was frightened because of its very cold feel to my lips. Everyone laughed when they realized it was indeed a new experience for me. All of a sudden life seemed to become exciting and wonderful here in this strange new world.

We were in Uncle Axel's automobile and we were riding through streets and my eyes and mind could not comprehend the rushing traffic and beautifully dressed people were everywhere I looked. To me, it was just like a dream.... We were to stay overnight in a hotel in New York City and drive on to Jamestown, New York the following day. Everything was like a dream to me, the gorgeous sculptured carpeting and high ceilings in the lobby of the hotel. The lift that could soar us up to our rooms in merely seconds, and then entering our rooms that were adjoining with Mor Mor and Mor Far's. Papa urged me to try to go to sleep, but how could I feel sleepy when a whole new world was unfolding right in front of me? Papa of course was right and all of a sudden the excitement and strangeness of this day melted away for me, yet awaiting another full and I was sure exciting day tomorrow. Mama and Papa tucked me into bed, and I asked them if maybe we were in heaven. They pulled the covers over me, kissed me good night, and soon I was fast asleep.

After I woke, it took me a minute to collect my thoughts and come back to the busy and unusual day I had experienced yesterday. Then I looked around and saw Mor Mor and Mor Far talking in Swedish about the trip to Jamestown. They were very excited to arrive as there were another son and two daughters waiting to see my grandparents.

Before we began our long trip to Jamestown, Uncle Axel wanted to fill the gasoline tank, so we drove to a station where he began filling the tank. It was at that time that I saw a young boy walk by with the darkest complexion I had ever seen in my life. I don't know what got into me, but I just had to see the boy up close. I opened the door and out I ran after the boy. He noticed he was being chased and began running very fast and just then I felt a tug at my arm and Papa was holding me hard by my arm. I heard panic in his voice as he told me never to do that again. I had never seen so many different-looking people in all of my five years. There were aspects of my personality creeping out that I had never really had before. Of course, curiosity was an element I had never had before, my life had been regulated, seeing and knowing everyone around me. In a way I felt I was outside my body, seeing, experiencing, feeling and doing things not me.

When we finally got started we all agreed the day was beautiful to travel and the landscape was so different from the granite rock boulders and white birch trees in my part of Sweden. Here there were large maple trees just budding and beautiful borders of fir trees. There were so many large rounded mountains that were so tall. My grandparents were talking about their children (my aunts and uncles and cousins) in Jamestown and how excited they were to see them after so many years of being apart. I was likewise excited to meet all my cousins and relatives. Would they like me? What would they say to me? What should I say to them? Mama and I had often spoken of these thoughts and she would say it would all take care of itself. We were joining our loved ones in America. We were to stay with Uncle and Aunt for a while. It was about six o'clock in the afternoon when we arrived at 18 Durant Avenue in Jamestown. There were so many people waiting in the yard as we arrived. Large signs of "*Valkommen*" and several Swedish flags were waving in the breeze, all for us. Mor Mor was so happy to leave the car and walk around with her children who were all talking at once. Kissing and hugging was being done amongst everyone. Cousins were all around me and chattering was going on and, out of habit, I curtsied to them. At once the cousins became silent and then laughed. Being someone different, I was well aware that it must have been something I did or said. My Aunt Selma had seen the situation and came to my rescue in explaining to my cousins that a curtsy in Sweden was a sign of great appreciation to the others. After this was understood the cousins all wanted me to teach them how to curtsy. It was a wonderful time and I was so happy to be there with all my family finally. I did find it interesting that throughout those first few months my background differed with those around me. My curiosity was fed almost daily by different situations arising from my Swedish customs and those of America.

Papa quickly found a job building houses. By chance he was told about a five-bedroom house at 27 Dearing Avenue that was up for rent. Those were the days when anything was possible. So many of the young Swedish boys who had come about the same time we did also found work in Jamestown and Mama quickly rented a bedroom to two of the youths. Mama was a wonderful cook and baker, and these boys told her they would never leave as long as she was doing the cooking.

In about a week my parents visited school #7 on Falconer Street and enrolled me there.

Attending my Parochial school in Sweden and having studied English for one year I was able to comprehend a fair amount of what was being taught. Math was my favorite subject, and I began to enjoy reading quite well by the end of the school year. Summer that year was so much fun because I was taken to so many places and of course everything was new to me. On weekends we would usually go to Celeron Park for the afternoon. Mama would bring a basket of food for our group on all the rides. If time allowed, we would ride on one of the steamships that were going back and forth on Lake Chautauqua all summer long. So many of the children who went to school at #7 lived on my street and therefore we had our own little group. Most of the families were Swedish and had come from Sweden as we did. It was a lot of fun for my friends to come to our house because Mor Far loved to show the children different tricks.

As soon as we were settled in Jamestown, Mama and Papa wanted to begin our Citizenship to the United States. Mr. George Winslow, Sr. taught the Americanization classes at night for immigrants. Uncle Axel had signed up for seven years of night school for a high school equivalency diploma. Mama and Papa said they would go for the three years to get their citizenship diploma. Being under age, I would automatically become a citizen at the time my parents obtained their certification. It would take three years every Monday, Tuesday and Wednesday evening from 7:00 PM to 9:30 PM. Aunt Selma decided on the three years, as well, but she had graduated the previous year, and was now a citizen.

This of course made her very special in my eyes, as to be a citizen of the United States was a much cherished achievement. Uncle Carl Dawson became a citizen upon completing all seven years of instruction from Mr. Winslow, Sr. His wife, Anna, was born in America and met Uncle Carl when she was 18 years old. She was automatically a citizen, having been born in America. Aunt Cecelia and Aunt Anna had already gone through the Americanization process because they came to America a few years earlier.

During those three years, it was fun to study my day school work while Mama and Papa sat at the kitchen table studying all the information needed to pass their tests each week. When I was eight years old, Mama and Papa had their graduation. The three of us, along with Uncle Axel and Aunt Selma (who had been our sponsors), went to Mayville, New York. I was a little shy because I had never seen any place so stern as one walked down the corridors. Perhaps it was the shiny marble floors, or the high ceilings, or the echo of our footsteps as we proceeded to the proper courtroom.

Then at three o'clock, April 14, 1935, Judge Hugh Bodine sat down in a high leather chair behind his high desk. We were asked to rise. Judge Bodine was so nice. First, he welcomed Mama, Papa and me and said, "Good afternoon, Mr. and Mrs. Anderson, I am happy you are here today as I can guarantee you that today will be the best day of the rest of your life." I will never forget his words as he looked down at a paper and said, "Maj Britt, you are blessed to be a child of good people who wish to become Americans. They are giving you a gift that money cannot buy." Then the court person came over to us and quietly asked us to stand in the presence of Judge Bodine. We quickly took our positions with Mama on one side and Papa on the other side of me. Then Judge Bodine stood up and said, "Please raise your right hand." We raised our hands, and then he said, "As applicants for certification of citizenship to the United States, please repeat after me: 'I promise to uphold the Constitution of the United States; to forgo any other country and solely protect and defend the United States of America to the best of your ability.' If so, say 'I do'." We all said, "I do." Then he said, "I hereby on this date do so declare: you, Carl Oscar Anderson, Linnea Sarah Anderson, and Maj Britt Solveig Anderson, to be citizens of our great land. The ownership doesn't come lightly, because you, along with all our citizens, are asked to be true to your new country. Remember always, America is only as strong as her people. In a democracy such as ours, TOGETHER WE RISE—BUT ALSO TOGETHER WE CAN FALL. May we never fall, but rise to greater heights for all our citizens."

Judge Hugh Bodine came down from the bench and shook hands with all three of us—first Mama, then Papa, and then me. When he shook my hand, I automatically curtsied and when I felt his huge hand envelope mine, a mental picture flashed in my mind. He had to be "Uncle Sam." For me, that was one of the most solemn experiences I would ever have or remember. It was a brand new feeling, one that only comes from knowing you now belong.

Uncle Axel and Aunt Selma were very happy for us and they wanted to treat us to supper. Uncle Axel brought us to a Swedish restaurant at Kimball Stand. It was owned by Henning and Imogene Pearson, friends of Uncle Axel's. They served Swedish dishes and that was special. The Pearsons had arrived here about ten years earlier and they had bought this building which they told us was only a shed at the time. Being a good carpenter, he renovated and built on to make it appear like a little Swedish "*stuga*" (house). As one stepped through into the restaurant, one imagined walking into a Swedish kitchen with the warm fire burning in the fireplace. It was a lovely quaint restaurant. The menu of that day offered "*rotmos*" (mashed potatoes and rutabaga), fresh pork and peas and homemade rye bread. Dessert was a Raspberry Torte with whipped cream.

The time was about 6:00 PM and all of a sudden a man named Petrus Peterson arrived with his wife Alice. Uncle Axel introduced them to us and told them we had just become citizens. They both congratulated us and then they went to speak with Mr. Pearson. We were told that Mr. Peterson was a musician and came each Friday evening to sing and play for the customers. By now the restaurant had become packed and "Petrus" began singing in Swedish.

We all have experiences that will forever be pertinent in our lives. This was an unforgettable one from my youth. My parents joined "Scandia Lodge" located at Point Stockholm on Lake Chautauqua. These were all young Swedish families who found the need of joining into special Swedish celebrations much like any ethnic group away from their motherland.

As autumn approached, the young families began preparing the celebration of "*Varnamod Marknad*" (Harvest of Fall Bazaar). The weekend began with a presentation of an all Swedish-speaking play performed by some of the young Swedish immigrants of our area. This was usually preceded by an all-Swedish Smörgåsbord dinner. Then on Saturday morning Swedish singers would perform, sometimes with guest groups and musical groups. Even my grandparents would enjoy the music. Later in the day the Bazaar would begin, bringing into the building every imaginable craft item. Many of the men were very creative in woodworking which of course proved to be a most beneficial aspect to Jamestown's becoming one of our country's most important furniture centers as time went by. They also created the beginning of the Swedish Metal Manufacturing Empire in Jamestown.

It was good to have so many family members often coming to our house, if only to stop in to see Mor Mor and Mor Far. Always, of course, there was a little treat of baked goods and coffee. Mama found she needed to bake often as we never knew when one of our relatives would come to visit. It was a home where wonderful aromas of baked goods, etc. met a visitor along with a cheerful and happy greeting to all, coming from the heart. My Uncle Carl Dawson often came to see me and often would bring me candies or something that he thought I would like. He was a very kind man, and he was always loving when he spoke with his mother and father. Mama told me that he and Aunt Anna had had a girl about my age who had died of pneumonia and Uncle Carl could never get over it. Mama felt I reminded him of Margaret, and it made him happy to be here with me.

Mom and Piper

Maj-Britt and cousins in Sweden

HOW SWEDE IT IS

by Elizabeth (Beth) Richetti

As a language teacher, I always found it intriguing to consider that here in the U.S., a common question among friends and acquaintances is, "What's your nationality?" If you asked that question in France or Italy, or for that matter, in almost any other country, you would be met with a stare of incredulity. But here in this great melting pot that we call home, the answers to the question are myriad and always interesting. My answer is that I am *Swedish*.

Actually, my answer probably should be, "I'm a hybrid." While mathematically I think that Swedishness would be the larger slice of the genetic pie, a healthy mix of English, Scottish and Welsh makes up the remainder. But in our household, growing up, it was the Swede in us that won out, and that was celebrated in Old World traditions during the holidays. Perhaps that is because my grandfather was an immigrant who arrived here in Jamestown at the age of nine, giving us a real, live tie to the old country. Perhaps it is because there was Swedish on both sides of my mother's family. Or perhaps it was really the food.

Now, Swedish food is a tradition to consider. Some of the preparation techniques leave culinary savants scratching their heads. For instance, in order to make his fabulous pressed *sylta*[1], my grandfather put some meat and things into a bread pan, covered it with waxed paper, set a brick on top, and put it in the garage for about a month. We all ate it, loved it, and astonishingly, no one ever died from it. Christmastime root beer was homemade—I don't know *how* they did that—and tasted nothing like the sicky sweet concoction in the grocery stores today. Making Swedish *pepparkakor*[2] involved heating some ingredients on the stove and then shoving the pan into a snowbank for a quick cool-down (I *still* do that, just to show off for the grandchildren a bit). Emeril would envy this level of creativity.

But Swedish food had more than just nutritional uses. Sometimes when we told folks that we were Swedish, they would ask whether we could speak the language. "Of course," we would reply, and then rattle off something like the following: *"Var så god! Yule whinke! Bruna bönor! Vort limpa! Tack så mycket!"* It sounded good, they didn't know the difference, and everybody was happy. (I beg the indulgence of those who can spell Swedish words, but I bet there isn't anybody . . . .)

Swedish names are another business altogether. You could be somebody's son (Johnson, Larson), or you could be the son of a place (Öland's son—Erlandson). It was pretty likely that you could take most any one-syllable Swedish name part and successfully add it to another: Lund, Lind, Blom, Quist, Malm, Berg., etc. could be combined to make Bergquist, Lundberg, Lindblom, etc . . . . a very handy technique for creating names with variety.

But it wasn't just their names and their Old World traditions that these immigrants had in common. They came here to a country they didn't know, to where a language was spoken which they didn't know, to customs and people they didn't know, and to futures they could not predict. What stuff were they made of that gave them the courage to do this? When I consider that my grandfather never spoke English with an accent, I wonder how he did it . . . and then it occurs to me that while his generation had only rudimentary opportunities, the subsequent generations in my family became much better educated and had more prosperous lives than their forebears. It becomes obvious that the intelligence, drive and determination were certainly part of my ancestors' makeup, even if they didn't have much in the way of material gain to show for it. They knew that their children, and their children's children, would be the ones to benefit. What vision was theirs. And what a privilege to grow up Swedish.

[1]*Sylta.* A loaf of pressed spiced meat, cut into thin slices and often served with vinegar.

[2]*Pepparkakor.* Thin spice/molasses cookies, cut into shapes, typically made at Christmastime and, according to my brother the purist, frosted only in white icing.

QUEEN MARGARET I—
RULER OF ALL SCANDINAVIA

by Arland O. Fiske

"God be praised to all eternity that he laid this unexpected victory in the hands of a woman, put shackles on the feet of kings and handcuffs on their nobles." This is how a Danish chronicler expressed the feelings of many after the Battle of Asla, Sweden, in 1389, when Margaret became the supreme ruler of the Scandinavian lands. From Lake Ladoga in Finland to Greenland in the west, and from North Cape in the far north of Norway to the Eider River on the south, this emancipated woman ruled with shrewdness, charm, patience, self-confidence, religious faith and an aura of integrity.

Who was this woman of such ability and how did she attain her great power? Margaret was born in 1346, the daughter of Danish king Valdemar IV. It was not a good time. The "Black Death" had traveled across Europe when she was but a little girl. In 1349, it came to Denmark, Norway and Sweden, all in one year. Two-thirds of Norway's population, one-third of Denmark's and as many in Sweden died in swift order. It brought out the worst in people. Death was dealt to those accused of "poisoning" the wells. Jews were especially marked out for pogrom. Disease, starvation and poverty reduced the ability of the north lands to govern themselves. Many villages were decimated and the land reverted to forests and the wild animals. Death spread particularly among the clergy, as they were required to minister to the dying.

It was into this world of realism that Margaret was bargained off in marriage through a treaty between the kings of Norway and Denmark. At age 10, she was hustled off to Akershus, the fortress castle in the Oslo harbor. For six years she did not live with her husband, King Haakon VI, while he was busy leading armies and seeking fame. She was treated more as a helpless royal hostage in those early years, rather than as a Danish princess or the Queen of Norway.

Times were hard in the royal palace, too. She and her household were in danger of starvation, not to mention freezing to death in that old fortress. Margaret had to write to her husband begging for money. "I have to inform you, my dear lord, that I and my servants suffer dire need of food and drink, such that neither I nor they get the necessities." We don't know if she received the money or not. But Margaret had two things going for her. First, she had inherited her father's strong will and, second, her governess was the daughter of one of the most famous women in Swedish history, "St. Birgitta." Birgitta is still revered for her piety, courage and visions, which often had a political inference.

When Margaret was 17, she gave birth to a son, Olaf. He was only five when his grandfather, King Valdemar of Denmark, died. Olaf was elected king of Denmark, but Margaret served as regent. Just five years later in 1380, his father died. The boy king was recognized as Olaf IV of Norway and ruled with his mother as advisor. At this time Slesvig was added to Denmark and much of Sweden also fell in line. The young Olaf died in 1387 at just 17 years of age. With him, came the end of the male line of Norse kings which had begun with Harald Haarfagre ("Finehair") and included Olaf Trygvasson and Olaf Haraldsson (St. Olaf). The new ruling family traced its line to Gorm, the founder of the present royal Danish house.

Margaret knew how to handle the situation. She used her influence to have her sister's grandson, three-year-old Eric of Pomerania, elected king. He was also the nephew of Sweden's King Albert. Though Eric was crowned king of all Scandinavia in 1397 at age 13, Margaret remained the real ruler until her death in 1412.

The rule of this strong woman was agreed to by both the nobles and the bishops. In Denmark, she was called the "all-powerful lady and mistress and the regent of the whole Danish kingdom." The crowning event of Margaret's political skill was the Union of Kalmar signed on July 13, 1397, which bound the Scandinavian countries into one kingdom. It was written that they "should eternally have one king and not several so that the realms will never again be divided, if God wills."

How did this little girl, who was bargained off into a marriage designed as a part of a political treaty, become the mightiest ruler of the North Sea? There are many factors, including accidents of birth and death, pressure by the merchants of the Hanseatic League and other rivals destroying each other. But it was mostly Margaret herself, her personal charm and her belief that she was born to rule.

Margaret is a proud name in Scandinavia. Now I understand the confident look on the picture of my great-grandmother in Surnadal who bore that name. Long live Margaret I and Margrethe II, the present Queen of Denmark.

TWO DIFFERENT WORLDS MEET IN THE NEW WORLD

by Martha E. Lindner

On September 25, 1899, in Brooklyn, New York, two Swedish immigrants, Gustav Vincent Lindner and Ingeborg Siegfrida Birgitta Lennartson, were married. They were my grandparents, and this is their story.

My grandmother, known as Frida, was small and pretty, with abundant dark brown hair. She and her six brothers and sisters were raised on a farm in Tingsås, Småland, Sweden. The family farm was unable to support the large family, and in 1891, when she was 14 years old, she, her sister Karin (15), and her brother Ture (16), set sail for the New World in steerage class. The crossing was stormy, and as the frightened and seasick teenagers later told the story, at first they were afraid that they would die and then they were afraid they wouldn't! They finally alighted at Castle Clinton, the entering point for immigrants before Ellis Island was opened in 1892. They made their way to Brooklyn and found jobs in a yarn factory. Within the next ten years, Karin met and married another Swedish immigrant, John Lonngren, and Ture also married. Frida met Gustav, a young Swedish immigrant with a background very different from hers.

Gustaf was a young man of medium height with dark hair and a thick black mustache. He was the oldest of the 13 children of a Lutheran minister, Per Torkelson. Because of the large numbers of Swedes with identical last names, most of which ended with "son," the Swedish government requested that when possible, Swedish citizens choose new last names for themselves. Per renamed his family "Lindner" for the linden trees growing around his church. Gustav was supposed to follow his father into the Lutheran ministry, but he insisted on going into law instead. After receiving his law degree from Lund University, he was given a summer trip to the United States as a graduation gift. One day, as he was strolling on a Brooklyn street, he heard bells ringing and saw several street construction workers put down their tools and head into a nearby church. He was shocked; in Sweden at that time, men would not be welcome in church in their work clothes. He followed them inside, and after the service, stayed behind to look around the church. He encountered the pastor, and one conversation led to others. When he returned to Sweden at the end of the summer, he told his astounded family that he had converted to Roman Catholicism. He was promptly disinherited, and he returned to the United States.

There he met and married Frida. She had not completed the seventh grade, but he undertook to perfect her English and oversee a wide program of reading in literature, history, and philosophy. His Swedish law degree was of no use here, but he found a job at *The New York Herald* newspaper, eventually becoming head of the paper's research desk. He co-founded the Saint Ansgar's League, an organization of Swedish-Americans, which exists to this day.

Gustav and Frida had two sons: Lennart Ingve Gustav, my father, born in 1900; and John Vincent, born in 1908. I never knew my grandfather, who died in 1917 at the age of 47. After his death, my grandmother and her two sons moved to Jamestown, New York, where her sister Karin and her family lived. She died in Jamestown at the age of 79.

LIVING WITH AN IMMIGRANT FATHER AND MOTHER WHO WERE SWEDISH

by C. Philip Thorsell

My father and mother were born in Sweden. My father, Arvid John Thorsell, was born in Westergötland; my mother, Martha Alida Niord Thorsell, was born in Östergötland in 1892. My father and mother met in the United States and were married in Jamestown, New York.

Jamestown at that time was a town of about 35,000 people. It had four Swedish Lutheran churches and two Swedish Covenant churches, all of which had services in both English and Swedish. In the 1920s and 1930s, the clerks in the stores had to speak both English and Swedish. There were at least five Swedish bakeries in Jamestown.

Christmas seemed to be the biggest holiday event with its Christmas Eve smörgåsbord with various syltas, ham, pickled herring, and the ever-popular lutfisk which would turn the silverware black. My father would fix the lutfisk from scratch, cutting the rock-hard fish with a saw. He would soak the fish in lye for two weeks and then flush it out with running water for two weeks. The lutfisk was served with cream sauce and boiled potatoes. It was my least favorite food.

When I was young I remember being told that my grandfather Adolf Niord was killed in an automobile accident and my Aunt Alma Niord was injured. It was the first automobile death in Sweden.

One thing I thought about when I was writing this, and now that I am a grandfather and great-grandfather, is that myself and people whose parents were born in Sweden and came to this country never had the experience of knowing a grandmother and grandfather.

THE STAVE CHURCHES OF NORWAY

by Arland O. Fiske

There is nothing so Norwegian as a stave church, not even lutefisk. Once there were over 1,000; today, there are only about 30. They can be found as far north as the Folk Museum in Trondheim and as far south as Telemark. These churches were built between the 11th and 14th centuries, almost all before the "Black Death" which struck Norway in 1349.

These timbered structures were built around huge poles planted into the earth and made their appearance about the same time as Christianity entered Norway. The first ones rotted away, but later churches built on sills and beams have survived to this day.

The designs of the stave churches are both ingenious and beautiful. Timbers were selected for size and strength in the days before Norway's forests had been exploited. They are called "stave" churches because of the heavy corner posts and wall planks. When a tree was selected, the branches were trimmed off except for the very top. In this way the tree would die slowly and the lumber would cure. This is why some are still standing after 700-800 years.

The earliest stave church is in the Folk Museum in Oslo's Bygdoy Park. It was moved from Gol in Hallingdal about 100 years ago. Having fallen into disrepair, it is now in excellent condition. The paintings by the altar date from 1652. The largest stave church is called "Heddal" ("Hitterdal") and is located at Notodden in Telemark. It's a huge structure surrounded by a cemetery. It's in excellent condition, having been restored. Both crosses and serpent heads decorate the exterior. The early builders retained some of the images of the pagan past, while committed to the new religion.

One of the interesting features found in some stave churches is a little window near the altar. It was used to serve communion to people with leprosy. They were not allowed into the churches but were given the sacrament through this opening. Leprosy was a major health problem in Western Norway in the Middle Ages due to unsanitary conditions in the homes. In 1873, Dr. G. A. Hansen, a physician from Bergen, isolated the bacillus. Today Norway is free of the disease.

The oldest stave church which remains almost exactly as built is at Borgund in the Sogn region of Western Norway. Constructed about 1150, it is one of the best known of these churches and is often seen in pictures. It is the model for the "Chapel in the Hills" near Rapid City, SD, home of the Lutheran Vespers radio broadcast. Completed in 1969, it's built of fir and cedar and is visited by over 50,000 people each year.

The Hedalen church in Valdres boasts an interesting story of a lost hunter and a bear. During the Black Death, the entire population of some communities was wiped out or people just fled in fear. Years later, a hunter far from home, missed a bird with his arrow and it struck the church bell. After recovering from fright, he investigated and found the lost church and a bear asleep in front of the altar. A bearskin hanging in the church testifies to the tale.

One of the most impressive features of these churches is the wood carvings about the entrances. In some cases, the ceilings are built like the frame of a Viking ship. The origin of these buildings is rooted in mystery, but there is a beauty about them that describes the faith and piety of the people. One tradition tells that St. Olaf made a deal with a troll to build the first one. Whatever it was, they are magnificent structures and remind us of a different Norway than the one we know today.

> ***Editor's Note:*** There are also many stave churches in Sweden, and while visiting Sweden with my father in 1974, our relatives took us to a stave church. The door was unlocked, and we went in. After a bit, from outside an elderly man entered. We were not sure if he might have been the caretaker, the gardener, or a parishioner, but he greeted us warmly and proceeded to tell us about the church. When our relatives told him that I was married to a clergyman, he casually reached down under a pew and brought out a cardboard box. To our amazement, the cardboard box contained a beautiful, gleaming silver chalice and paten which he said were several hundred years old. He encouraged us to hold them, so we reverently examined and

admired them. When we were finished, the elderly gentleman carefully wrapped them in their tissue paper protection, put them back in the cardboard box, and returned the box to its resting place under the pew—and I suppose the door was left unlocked.

PRESERVING SOME OF THE "OLD COUNTRY" IN A NEW WORLD

by Dennis Shows

Immigration to America in the late nineteenth century through the early 1900's often resulted from the dream for a better life, with greater opportunities for working in factories. The growth of industry certainly offered the potential for more jobs for Europeans, especially in the northeastern United States. Folks willing to work hard, learn new skills (on the job), and/or apply the European work ethic in the construction trade quickly became wage earners and perhaps even union members in the new country. Sweden was often referred to as "back in the old country." Just as is the case today, immigrants from each country tended to be attracted to the location and lifestyle described by family members or friends who had encouraged or offered lodging in the "New World."

My maternal grandparents, Ellen and Gustav, were immigrants from different communities in Sweden, but appeared to have similar backgrounds. Grandmother was from Vimmerby, growing up in a traditional household of both parents and eight other siblings. My grandfather, however, was reared in Kalmar in foster homes and had only one older brother who came to America before he did. Neither of my grandparents had lived in coastal towns, so their family meals were selections from baked goods, potatoes and other homegrown vegetables or berries, and farm-bred animals for meat. With the exception of certain holiday specialties, seafood was not a usual part of the family menu.

Both grandparents reportedly had one or more siblings who had preceded their move to America. Ellen (17 years old) and Gus (19 years old) met in Warren, Pennsylvania, sometime after their arrival from Sweden. They had traveled to the United States alone. Ellis Island must have represented some uncomfortable memories for them, perhaps mostly culture shock as they made their way through the streets of New York City. If for no other reason, they spoke no English. Neither of them talked freely about that experience or the trip aboard ship from Sweden. When asked, they said that they didn't remember much about it.

I didn't have as many friendly chats or conversations with my grandfather about his childhood or his adult years, for he died while I was in my mid-teens. Realizing that the details of their "new life" in America might be of more interest to us descendants some day, I asked my grandmother many more questions over those next eight years she lived following his death.

While living with her sister, she was able to find employment as a nanny/maid for a wealthy family in New York City. The family also had a house in Washington, DC, with separate hired help for each floor. My grandmother was the upstairs maid, and a French maid was downstairs. Speaking no English, out of necessity somehow the two maids communicated and enjoyed each other's company. Finally, Ellen resigned her post with the family, moving when her sister left New York to Warren, Pennsylvania, where their brother lived.

Ellen's brother Hjalmar was living in Warren at the time that Ellen and her sister moved there. He had become friends with Gustaf and introduced him to Ellen. By this time various siblings of both of them were settled in cities such as Portland, Maine; Chicago, Illinois; and Los Angeles, California. Hjalmar, Ellen, and Gustav remained in Warren for the remainder of their lives, but Hjalmar (at 84 years old) was the only one who ever made a return visit to Sweden.

Ellen and Gustav had three daughters. Hjalmar, by that time already married himself, arranged for Gustaf to obtain work in the lumber industry of the Allegheny National Forest for a few years. Life was fairly simple for all of them, but they eventually were able to buy a house. Social life consisted of friends with whom they associated in their Lutheran Church and with whom they became acquainted at the logging camps where they worked and sometimes slept. Sometimes the wives would come on weekends to cook in the camps, so that picnics became a frequent entertainment for them. Some persons had learned to play mandolins, as the young Swedes sang Swedish songs and frolicked with their own spontaneous attempts at dancing. Mandolins were popular in the early 20th century in America, even on college campuses. I recently had my grandmother's mandolin, stored for many years in my attic, overhauled.

After World War I my grandfather was hired by the United Refining Company in Warren, which processed its own petroleum products, including a by-product much like wax. He took advantage of the company's offer to its employees to use a small island in the Allegheny River for those whose own land or properties were not conducive to gardening. For several years in Spring or Summer of the 1930s and '40s, he walked from his home several times a week, usually pulling a wagon full of tools or vegetables to/from the island. One of the favorites for planting was dandelions, exactly like the nuisance plants or weeds we struggle to kill in our lawns. It was explained to us that the island location for the garden was far better than plots used elsewhere (backyards, for example), because the island could never be favorite urination spots for dogs or cats to do their "business."

My grandmother was not the typical homemaker that we know today. Lasting until well into the afternoon, her preparation methods were lengthy as she reserved *every* Saturday morning for baking from scratch one or more of her special delicacies to go with the coffee she served guests: Swedish limpa rye bread, white bread, fruit pies, cardamom rolls or cookies. Filling the kitchen with the magnificent aroma to which we children had become accustomed, these items were far from the ordinary items that we grandchildren had observed in our friends' homes—cake-mix cakes, ready-made cookies, frozen pies, packaged rolls. In fact, when the screen door to the porch was open during summer, neighborhood children could not resist asking for samples when that aroma reached them. I always believed that, as much as she loved her role in the kitchen, part of the duties involved there were to have fresh snacks available to any visitor, family friend, or neighbor that stopped by. To do otherwise was neither being hospitable nor welcoming as a hostess for any visitors. Christmas and Thanksgiving family get-togethers were usually held at her home and included many of these baked items as part of desserts with coffee following the meals. When eating any meals at her house, children were always served first, almost as if they were so precious and worthy of such special treatment. My own mother, her daughter, and my aunt, her daughter, followed this tradition with their own children. It didn't appear, however, that the reason behind this was to coddle or spoil the children, for afterwards the adults could have their own peaceful and enjoyable dinner, once the children were satisfied. Besides, as an added effort by my grandmother to encourage the children's healthy appetites for a variety of foods, she often needed a little extra time to make faces or other decorations on prepared vegetables, using olives, shredded carrots, raisins, or other edibles. Mashed potatoes were always formed with a "well" in the middle, filled with gravy, and my grandmother said this was a bird's nest. The reason she gave for us to eat our carrots was that they were good for our eyes. She then justified her argument with the comment, "You've never seen a rabbit wearing glasses, have you?" Lastly, her "meat and potatoes" meals on dinner plates, no matter what the holiday, were served with a sprig of parsley or an orange slice at the edge of the plate. Eventually, with that special touch, we grandchildren learned to appreciate and to eat that bit of elegance that she had learned so many years earlier when working as a maid for the wealthy family in New York City.

In the last years of his life, my grandfather asked for space to have a garden at our home each year. He truly loved sharing with others the skills he had acquired through experience, for eventually he involved himself in the landscaping of our property, volunteering his talents just to stay busy. Once he passed on, my grandmother continued the baking, only on a smaller scale. She shared what she had with neighbors and family. My own father, her son-in-law, loved her as if she were his mother. He did construction work in Warren, and was invited to her house daily for lunch. She fixed him a full meal, beginning mid-morning, so that the tradition of serving and sharing would not be interrupted. I believe he enjoyed the attentiveness she demonstrated, as much as the quality of the food she prepared. If I could have left my school to join them, I would gladly have done so. To make up for missing lunch with them, I stopped many days on my walk home from school, only to get scolded for "snacking" so near the supper hour so that my appetite was not much at my own family's dinner table.

JACKSON'S DAIRY

by Chuck Jackson

It was an historic day for Jackson's Dairy—the fourth generation person had delivered milk for the nearly fifty-year-old dairy! Timothy Jackson, son of Charles and Susan (Andersen) Jackson, had spent time on the milk route running to houses with the dairy products. He had been preceded on that job by his father, his grandfather Kenneth and great-grandfather Charles E. Jackson. The dairy had been founded by his great-grandfather in the 1920s. Prior to that, Charles E. had also been involved in the Jamestown Ice Cream Company as early as 1909.

Many Scandinavian immigrants in the Jamestown area became involved in milk processing and formed their own dairies. They received the raw milk from the farmers who brought it in to town each day from the farms. The processing was done in many different plants, one of which was at 20 Woodlawn Avenue. Each of these plants pasteurized the milk, separated the cream, and delivered the products to homes each morning before breakfast. Later in the morning they would deliver to stores and factories. As technology increased, plants made available homogenized milk and products such as ice cream, cottage cheese, and butter. Most of the plants were of the size that produced between 1000 and 2000 quarts a day. Today's processing plants handle many thousands of quarts per day.

As New York State got involved with health regulations and requirements, many of these dairies combined with each other and eliminated the smaller dairies so that they could afford the newer equipment and larger plants, hence reducing costs. Even many of those had to give way to the larger corporations that presently run processing plants today.

Some of the other Scandinavian names that were involved in milk processing and delivery plants were Jacobson, Johnson, Nelson, Seiberg, Haglund, Swanson, Anderson, Gustafson, and Carlson.

Milk was bought each day from the farmers in their 40-quart cans. Today you see large semi-trailer tankers that pick up the milk from the farms. It was not uncommon in those days for the farmer to have 30-40 cows as a herd. In today's world, milk production farms have to have 700 to 800 cows to make it financially.

The picture below is of Charles Jackson, son of Kenneth, standing next to a Jackson's Dairy delivery truck.

Editor's Notes:
(1) On the corner of Cole and Forest Avenues, across from my grandparents' home at 342 Cole Avenue, was Root's Dairy. When I was very young, my Grandpa Tuline would take me for walks in the neighborhood, often stopping at Root's Dairy to say hello to the family members working there and perhaps purchase some milk or cream.
(2) Whenever my family went to visit my *Far Mor* and *Far Far* Hillman in West Newton, Pennsylvania, my mother always insisted that my dad stop at a store in the downtown area of West Newton to purchase *pasteurized* milk to take to my grandparents' home where they always had milk straight from the farm. Perhaps the fact that my mother had studied nursing had something to do with that.

Chuck Jackson—1940s

WHAT'S IN A NAME?

by Barbara Hillman Jones

Finding our Scandinavian ancestors can be a difficult and daunting task. As the saying goes, "Things are not always as they seem," and many of us have discovered that to be true when trying to fill in the blanks in our genealogy. Many Scandinavians changed their last name, and there were several reasons for this: originally, sons and daughters were named combining their father's first name with "son" or "dotter," but it proved to be confusing, as we well know when we try to trace our family. Sometime in the 1800s the government outlawed those practices and asked the populace to take a new last name. Some took names after other family members, some took names that reflected the name of their family farm, and some took names that simply appealed to them. When they emigrated to America, at their point of entry, they were asked to declare their name, and many of them chose a new one at that time. Some chose a name for the same reasons as their family in Scandinavia did. Sometimes the person writing the new name did not hear correctly or did not know how to spell it correctly, and often the names became scrambled.

My mother was Florence Esther Christine Tuline Hillman. She was the middle daughter of three, and all three daughters had three given names while my grandmother had only one. Her sisters were named Jennie Mildred Evelyn (she went by Evelyn) and Margaret Elsie Elizabeth. Was that a Swedish custom?

My *farfar* (father's father) was *Klaes Bertil Hellman*, born November 14, 1881, the eldest of eight children, who were all born on the family farm called *Altomtabro* located in Vänge (Brunna), Sweden. When *farfar* emigrated from Sweden to America around 1900, he changed his surname from *"Hellman"* to *"Hillman."* After pondering the reason for this, the only possibility we could think of is that perhaps as he learned English he realized *"hell"* may not have been a word he wanted to be part of his name.

His first name became the Americanized version of *Klaes,* and so he was now Clyde Hillman. He settled in West Newton, PA, south of Pittsburgh, and worked all the rest of his life in mining the soft coal in that area, a very dangerous occupation in those days.

My *farmor* (father's mother) was born Hilda Kallen in Sweden in 1875. She became Hilda Hillman after her marriage to my *farfar*. We always called them *farmor* and *farfar* as taught to my sister and me by our father. *Farmor* had a sister who settled in the Chicago, IL area who had a son named Wilbert. My dad and his cousin Wilbert were the best of friends, and when they were young single men, they took several automobile trips out West. In fact, Wilbert went with my parents on their honeymoon trip to Salt Lake City! Some of my *farmor's* relatives had settled there, and I suppose Wilbert wanted to visit them, also. A couple of mysteries—why did these particular Swedes move all the way to Utah when their relatives were in Pennsylvania and Illinois? And what prompted them to become Mormons, a most unlikely choice for these Swedes who had been born and raised Lutherans?

My father's cousin, whose name was also *Claes,* but spelled with a "C", sent me a picture of the home where my great-grandmother, Matilda Elisabet Classon Hellman, was born on September 30, 1851. The home is what is termed a *crofter's house* (farmhouse) named *"Bohus,"* located in Värsås, Skaraborg County.

My *morfar* (mother's father) was born Johan Albin Bertilson on May 24, 1880 in Varberg, Sweden and came to America in 1902, settling first in Kane, PA where he worked on a farm. He then moved to Dagus Mines where he worked in the coal mines. He met and married my grandmother on June 5, 1907. They had three daughters, and the family moved to Jamestown, NY on October 25, 1925, where they lived until the last one passed away in 2002. Grandpa had been a gardener and florist in Sweden, and that undoubtedly explains the beautiful flower gardens in his yard at 342 Cole Avenue in Jamestown. There were six brothers and sisters in the family, and at least three brothers in addition to my grandfather came to America. Sadly, one brother traveled to Canada and was never heard from again.

Why these brothers chose their particular name is a puzzle to me, and especially why none of them spelled it alike! Grandpa changed his name to *Tuline,* and so he became *John A. (Albin) Tuline*. His brother Einer who married and also lived in Jamestown spelled his name *Thulin.* Another brother, Otto, settled in Providence, RI, and spelled his last name *Thuline*. And . . . how did my grandfather get from *Bertilson* to *Tuline?* Apparently, it is to remain another family mystery.

My *mormor* (mother's mother) was born Esther Strandberg on May 18, 1886 to Paul Peter Strandberg, a carpenter, and Anna Christina Janson in Halland Län Sweden. There were ten children in her family. Grandma's mother died when Grandma was very young. One sibling died while a baby on Palm Sunday, 1895. At least one of the Strandberg children was adopted. Grandma emigrated in 1904 when she was 18 years old. Her father, then a widower, brought her and two other sisters to Dagus Mines, PA, where Grandma kept house for her father. She told us that when they arrived at Ellis Island, one of her sisters had the measles, and the authorities were not going to allow her to enter the country. However, after much weeping and pleading, the authorities who were kind and understanding, relented, and the sister was allowed to enter the country with the rest of the family. After two years, my great-grandfather returned to Sweden to marry my *mormor's* Sunday School teacher. Grandma was always happy about that because she loved her Sunday School teacher.

At least two other siblings came to America at another time, probably earlier. One was a brother, Otto, who settled in Cicero, IL. Otto must have thought *Strandberg* was too long a name because he shortened it to simply *Berg*. Grandma had two other sisters who lived in Jamestown—*Selma Potentia Strandberg* who married Ernest Emil Mattson and lived at 104 Hazeltine Avenue, and *Carrie Strandberg Lindquist* who lived on Foote Avenue. She had other relatives in Kane and Ridgeway, Pennsylvania, whom we visited from time to time. Some of her relatives owned and operated a restaurant in Kane for many years—as a little girl our family would occasionally drive to Kane to have a meal in the restaurant of *Sig* and *Teckla Strandberg*.

So, what's in a name? Whether it's *Hellman* or *Hillman*, *Bertilson* or *Tuline*, *Strandberg* or *Berg*, really doesn't matter. What's important is the person represented by those names and the memories those names bring back to us. Often we're left with more questions than answers, and thus we continue our quest to learn more about our ancestors, wishing we had been more diligent in our pursuit while there were still those family members living who could fill in the blanks for us.

ONE OF OUR SWEDISH MIRACLES

by Sandra Sandy

My husband, Don, had three grandparents who were emigrants from Sweden to the United States. He has spent a great deal of time doing genealogical research and managed to locate the different areas from which each one came. We have been fortunate enough to visit these areas and have contact with relatives. In some instances, it has been the first contact in many decades.

One year we were traveling in Sweden for a month with our young adult daughter, Amelia. It was great to see the country anew through her eyes and see her excitement. We had recently identified the area where one of the grandparents had lived. We visited the small village of Ulrika for the first time, driving on very narrow roads through the forest. We were delighted to find the church in the middle of the village. It had been built in 1725. The three of us went into the wooden church and were awed by its simple but elegant beauty. There was no one there, so we explored on our own, quietly browsing around, sitting in pews and examining the altar, happy with our discovery.

Amelia and I decided to walk about in the churchyard cemetery while Don further explored the church building. As we were strolling and reading gravestones, a young gentleman came up to Amelia and asked if we were Americans. He said Americans were usually the ones who wandered in the cemetery. He introduced himself as Christer, the sexton of the church. When Amelia explained why we were there he asked to go meet Don. A short time later Amelia came running to me saying I had better come into the church because her Daddy was crying. When I got inside, Don pointed out a list of names painted very prominently on one wall of the church. With tears in his eyes, he explained that Christer had shown him the name of the building supervisor when the church was built. It was Don's grandfather, seven times removed! And Christer turned out to be a distant cousin! What a miracle to be there, to make such a wonderful discovery and find relatives.

We have attended church there a couple of times in the past few years. We take communion with the only chalice the church has ever owned, the one that has been used since the church's beginning. We partook from the same cup the relatives before us had used. We have become great friends with Christer, his wife and daughter, and visit them whenever we can.

We always have a fantastic time when visiting Sweden, but this is a highlight we will always remember.

>**Editor's Note**: Sandra is the president of the Norden Women's Club, and I'm especially appreciative of her personal support and enthusiasm for this book.

Church at Ulrika

VISITING SWEDEN

by Jean Wistean Seastedt

My husband and I have been to Sweden nine times in the past thirty years. We had just returned from one of those trips when my husband Robert found a yellow faded paper in his desk that was addressed to my sister-in-law. It asked if anyone knew the whereabouts of several Jamestown people, and among them were my mother and father, Theodore and Anna Wistean. We wrote immediately and had a response back within ten days. We found in the records at Växjo Immigration Center that my grandmother, Augusta Johansdotter, had been born in 1856. We planned another trip to Sweden for the next summer.

Of my two cousins and their wives, Assar and Elvy Svensson and Bjorn and Lillimore Holmberg, only one spoke English. It was difficult at times but we managed to communicate, and it was wonderful. My cousins lived on the same road that my grandmother had lived and walked on.

Grandmother Augusta came over from Sweden alone in 1880 when she was 17 years old. She was expecting to be greeted by her sister who had arrived earlier, but much to her sorrow, her sister had died when grandma was enroute to us. As was the case for most Swedish girls, she got a job keeping house for one of the prominent families in Jamestown.

My mother's father, John Olson, a widower with two boys, fell madly in love with Augusta, and they were married in 1888. My mother, Anna Marie, was born in 1889 and two years later in 1891 my Uncle Carl was born. Her beloved husband John died of pneumonia before Carl was born. Such sadness and courage this poor woman had. They had a home at 42 Highland Avenue, and it was stated that she walked every week with my mother and uncle in the buggy to Lakeview Cemetery to visit her husband's grave. She eventually moved to Brocton and married her brother-in-law John Peterson, who was her deceased sister's husband.

Augusta drove a horse and buggy and a drunken man hit her with his car. The horse survived, but Grandma suffered a fractured hip. Hips were not able to be set back in those days, and so she was always bent over and pushed a chair in front of her to help her walk, just as people use walkers today.

Grandma lived with us from the time I was born in 1928 until her death in 1943. As a young child, I sat with her hours at a time, and how I wish she had taught me the Swedish language!

I remember my mother telling about the day Grandma died. It was war time, and Henderson and Lincoln Funeral Home made sure my mother turned in to them Grandma's sugar ration card and her shoe ration card!

While in Sweden, it was thrilling to sit in the same church Augusta worshipped in. All of my grandmother's family have died, but my grandfather's children's children are still running a large grist mill that has been operating for many years. The home of his sister Josephine is still standing, and relatives are still living there.

If only my mother, uncle, and grandmother could have known I visited all these places. Guess I'll have to wait until heaven to tell them.

Jean W. Seastedt

FINLAND—LAND OF SURPRISES

by Arland O. Fiske

Finland is little understood by the rest of the world, but five million Finns (Suomi) are very happy to live there. For over 700 years Finland was ruled by outside powers, first by Sweden and then by Russia. But all during that time, they had a sense of their own identity.

One word best describes the Finnish character—"sisu." It really cannot be translated but means "I may not win, but I will give my life gladly for what I believe." This is the spirit that enabled Finns to such patriotism in resisting Stalin's 1939-1940 invasion. It was also the "spirit" which gave them the determination to pay their war debts to the United States when other nations defaulted.

Until 1548, Finnish was only a spoken language, not written. Michael Agricola, the bishop of Turku who had studied under Martin Luther and Philip Melancthon, published their first alphabet book and translated the Bible. The old stories of Finland's past have been preserved in a special book called "Kalevala." Elias Lonnrot, a physician, went back to the ancient "runes" to put these together. They were taken from songs which were sung by people facing each other on opposite benches.

The Kalevala, published in 1835, came at the same time as the national spirit of Finland began to rise. The Russians had taken over the country in 1808 from Sweden. The Finns had gotten used to Swedish rule, but the oppressive spirit of the Czars was too much for them. Even though the Kalevala was pre-Christian, the Finnish spirit was aroused to pride and patriotism. They were ready for their freedom in 1917 when the Russian government fell.

The Finnish people have deep social concerns. Not only do they have social security and medical insurance for everyone, but the Finns were the first to give women the right to vote. Most women in Finland have careers outside the home, many of them in medicine, teaching, and government.

To help with the care of children, they employ "park aunties," who are professional baby-sitters. "ERA" [Equal Rights Amendment] is not an issue in any of the Scandinavian countries—it is taken for granted. It wasn't until about 200 years ago that a Finnish woman took her husband's name and she was not "subject" to him.

Finland is 99% literate and has a high priority for science and education. They have advanced far in the field of mental health. Social legislation, however, costs a lot of money and taxes are high. But the cost of having slums and an uneducated populace is even higher. A low crime rate is one of the benefits of this system. They have learned that survival and prosperity are not private pursuits, but rather goals for all the people. A socially responsible capitalism seems to be working for the Finns.

Finland's nearness to the Soviet Union presents problems. Officially neutral, anti-communism is strong, but its leaders avoid inflammatory political statements. Finland trades with both East and West.

One of Finland's foods is "Lipea Kala," called "lutefisk" in some countries. Not everybody likes it, of course, but its aroma covers the land each December. Some say this is what has made the Finns brave!

LEONARD EDWARD FAULK'S STORY

"written by himself"—1987*
Submitted by Leonard E. Faulk, Jr.

Leonard Edward Faulk (changed from Lennart Edvard Carl Falk upon arrival to USA) was born in Älvsjö (a suburb of Stockholm, Sweden) on February 20, 1916. He was the son of Henry C. Faulk who was born in Lundsbrunn, Sweden in 1881 and Anna Maria Johansson Faulk who was born in Lidköping, Sweden in 1885.

Farfar, farmor:

My father's parents were farmers in Lundsbrunn, Sweden. Lundsbrunn was a farming community located near the castle of Maria Dahl and perhaps less than an hour's drive from the beautiful lakeside village and resort of Lidköping—my mother's ancestral home.

Morfar, mormor:

Mother's parents were merchants in Lidköping where they imported cloth and dry goods for wholesale and retail sales. They owned an entire city block located at Stenportsgaten 47, located on Lake Vanern. A "sentimental journey," memories of my childhood in Älvsjö, Sweden is still very vivid even at age 71. Our family—mother, dad, Karin (Corrine), Gunnar, Herbert and I—lived very comfortably in an upstairs apartment over our grocery store and meat market. Burdette, our youngest brother, was the only one born in the United States of America. Our property consisted of several acres of land with an orchard. Besides the store and living quarters, there was a single family home and an apartment house. A short distance away lived mother's sister Elin (Mrs. Carl Lindgren). My aunt Elin and husband, Carl, had two children, Brita (now Mrs. Folke Mellvik) and Uno, who is my age. Uno seemed like a brother to me as we were always together. Brita is about two years younger. Although Brita lives in Alingsås, Sweden (near Gothenburg), she and Uno still own the lovely home in Älvsjö that their parents left them. It is my understanding that mother and her two sisters each inherited a total of 120,000 Swedish Crowns upon the death of their father, Anders Gustaf Johansson—a small fortune in Sweden in the 1900's. (Uno and Brita have no children). As a boy I remember Herb and myself riding with Dad on his bicycle to a nearby lake to hunt for crabs. I also remember riding with dad on his bicycle to town to have my tonsils removed at a doctor's office. Afterwards, he wheeled me home. I recall my class at school at the age of six. My favorite subject was cross country skiing! In the ensuing years I recall making a ski jump in front of our home along with several friends and oh, how high that hill was when we skied down it. But when I went back thirty-seven years later, the hill had all but shrunk out of sight!

USA—"Here Come the Faulks"

In June 1923 it was time to set sail for destiny. We had sold our home and were staying with the Lindgrens. I remember my uncle driving up the driveway, in a new Horsch touring car to drive us to the railway station to take the train to Gothenburg and then board the Liner Drottningholm. It was an exciting time for Dad as all of his brothers and sisters, except one, lived in the USA. But I still remember mother's anguish overhaving to leave her two sisters behind. As it turned out, she would never see them again in this world. She had made plans to go home to Sweden for Mid-summer in 1939 and had purchased many gifts to take to her relatives, but she died very suddenly on January 24, 1939.

The Ocean Journey

The journey across the ocean was very stormy, but I kept dreaming of a book that Gunnar had been reading while in Sweden. The cover depicted an Indian scalping a white man in the wilderness that we were migrating to which was called America. Most of the family had seasickness for the majority of the trip, except probably me. This gave me lots of time to explore. We came over on the tourist class, but I ate most of my meals in second or first class. Nobody knew whose boy I was because most of the other families were sick, also. One day I discovered a narrow ladder that led up to the top of the ship. Thinking that I could see America through the fog if I got up higher, I climbed the ladder and stood next to the Drottningholm's big smokestack (it only had one). Of course, I could see nothing from the top deck, because of the dense fog. But as I stood there, the fog horn went off with a tremendous sound and a jet of steam to warn other ships of an approaching boat. After this happened I could barely distinguish sound and, as it later turned out, both of my eardrums had been shattered at that instant. In school I had to sit in the first seat, not because I was in any way the teacher's pet (quite the opposite), but I just could not hear well. My dear wife will tell you I have poor hearing still, as the scar tissue still remains. After passing the Statue of Liberty (which I remember so well), we landed in New York.

A Place Like Sweden

From New York City we took a train for a town in western Pennsylvania coal country called Elbon and, yes, we also stayed in Weedville, Pennsylvania. My Dad had two sisters living in Weedville, the Andersons and the Bloomquists. My Dad's brother, Uncle Will, lived in Elbon and was superintendent of the Shawmut Mining Company. Dad had worked for Uncle Will many times before in Elbon as a young man before he married. Dad crossed the ocean a total of seven times—the last time going back to get a wife and start to raise a family. Dad's original plans were to travel on to the West Coast to Tacoma, Washington where his younger brother, Gust, lived and there stake his fortune. But Uncle Will had other ideas. He took us all to a place much the same as Sweden—Jamestown, New York. There he rented a cottage on Chautauqua Lake at Bemus Point and had Dad starting to look for work. The manufacturers all knew how ambitious and talented the Swedes were and hired Dad immediately to work at Watson Manufacturing Company.

Growing Up by the Boatlanding

Dad and Mother purchased a home on Fairmount Avenue which was near the boatlanding or outlet of Chautauqua Lake—a really tough kind of territory for a boy to grow up in. One day a friend and I found an old rowboat at the outlet and proceeded to launch it in the water. Out in the middle the boat began to sink. We called for help and luckily someone heard us and called the fire department rescue squad who got to us in the nick of time as neither one of us could swim at that time. Two of my best friends were Chief Halftown and Oliver Silverheels, both full-blooded Indians. Chief Halftown became very famous as a vaudeville singer and now tours the world as an exhibitionist bowler. Another friend was Joe Miller whose family emigrated from Poland—they had a much longer name which no one could pronounce. Joe and I swam together across Lake Chautauqua and back many times unescorted by any boats and not protected by life preservers. I'm so glad that kids are so much more sensible today! At age 15, I worked at Celoron Park operating the Merry-Go-Round and always riding the open air street cars.

A Pinto Named "Injun Chief"

Around 1930 the Kendall Club of the Jamestown Police Department decided to hold a fundraising circus and carnival. In order to sell lots of tickets, they purchased a colorful brown and white Indian pinto to be given away to the person selling the most tickets. They needed someone to feed and exercise the pinto. They screened applicants for this job on the lawn at Love School on 8th Street. I happened by just as one of the last applicants was dumped on the ground. I don't think the pinto had been ridden much, if at all. I asked them if I could try riding him and, of course, they had to know of my experience. I told them I had riding experience (riding my friend's fat pony called Jingles). Well, they said O.K. I didn't stay on the pinto more than 20 seconds. But I wasn't hurt and said I'd try again. This time the horse reared right up on his back legs and tried to throw me, but I stayed on. Well, I guess he knew we were going to become friends because I rode him around the school and got the job! We had many months of companionship and he only let me down a few times. He had a habit of thinking every road branching out to a farm was his home. As we were galloping along, all of a sudden he would make a quick move up a drive and dump me into a ditch! But I never broke any bones, just bruised my pride. I'll never forget you, "Injun Chief."

Driving for Mother

In the early 1930's Dad suffered a paralyzing stroke and was unable to work. Mother said she would rather starve than go on relief, so she got a job going from door to door selling dresses. She was very successful and later started selling ladies' foundation garments and doing the fittings and alterations herself as she was an excellent seamstress. We purchased our first car in 1931, a 1928 Buick sedan, from the Hause Garage and in 1932 bought a new V8 Ford so she could extend her territory. Mother's business again proved successful, but the driving became too much for her. At this time I decided to quit school in my junior year and drive for mother. Later, however, I went to night school for several years and received certificates of accomplishment from New York University in drafting, engineering and mathematics which would stand me in good stead in later years.

Work Years and Flying Adventures

During these years my work and interests have been many. At a very early age I not only got my driver's license and became interested in cars, but I also received my pilot's license. At the beginning of World War II, I was able to use the training I had had in night school as I began a job with American Aviation in their construction of a pilotless drone airplane to be used aboard aircraft carriers in the Pacific against the Japanese. The drones were to carry a huge bomb and to be guided to a target. Thereafter, I worked on the C46 Commando troop and carrier plane for Curtiss-Wright. At the war's end I went to work at Crescent Tool Company as a tool designer. I left Crescent in 1953 to go full time in the real estate business which I had been doing part-time since 1949. In 1957 another enterprise was started—Foreign Cars of Jamestown, Inc. We had franchises for cars such as the BMW, Volvo, Jaguar, MG, and Austin-Healey and handled many others such as Ferrari, Mercedes, and Rolls Royce. A really fun business! In 1968 I sold this business and built a new franchise in Warren with Volkswagen. Then, I added a Dodge franchise in a building next door.

During the early 1970's I formed another company with two partners. It was called Trans Air Executive Corp. We flew charter service as far as Texas. We had two full-time professional pilots to fly our Beechcraft

Queen Air and Beechcraft E Baron. We also had another plane for training and rental purposes. I was president of Trans-Air for the years it was in operation until the commuters started flying into our terminal in Bradford, Pennsylvania.

Cars and flying were always my most interesting hobbies. I can't relate many interesting happenings with cars, but I do remember a few flights that I would just as soon forget. As mentioned before, I started flying about the same time I started to drive a car. Never had too many exciting things happened up through 1940 except a forced landing and once, when I landed on Lake Chautauqua on the ice, I hit a soft spot and the ice underneath broke and I got a little wet! But with a little help we got the plane to solid ice and I took off without any damage to the plane. During the war years after Pearl Harbor, I worked at the airport for American Aviation and at the same time I belonged to the Civil Air Patrol in which I had been appointed operations officer. So many times, I was called upon to fly strategic materials, propellers, army personnel, etc. On one occasion civil defense officials called me late at night and asked me to fly the Mayor of Jamestown (Mayor Samuel Stroth) and Don Anderson, the head of Civil Defense, to Utica, NY for a meeting. It was wintertime and very bitter cold, but by 7 o'clock in the morning I had the plane all warmed up when my passengers came. We hadn't any difficulty until we reached a point beyond Penn Yann on the Finger Lakes south of Rochester, NY, when we started running into snow squalls. We were flying at 1000 feet and were not in any serious trouble until the engine started to miss. Now, of course, we couldn't get any power out of the engine and started a slow descent. At 200 feet it became obvious we would have to pick a spot in a snowy field and land. It was snowing so hard and the wind was blowing so hard that it was difficult to pick a good field, and I didn't. As I brought the plane into the wind at a fast speed I noticed ditches or crevices in the field and a sure crash with a solid line of trees ahead of me. Only one decision! Pull the nose of the plane over those high trees, shove the nose down and pull the stick back and pray. On the other side of those trees was a big ravine. The snow had been blown by winds up to 50 miles per hour and had left a huge snow-bank on the windward side of the ravine. So the plane just settled down in that snow bank and never moved an inch. No damage, no injuries—just three happy souls.

In a few minutes we could hear sirens coming at us, and sure enough, two state patrol cars were winding their way on the roads in the distance.

What we didn't know was there was an air-raid warning station on a hill not far away that reported a downed plane and we had people coming from everywhere. With some help we dug the plane out of the snow and got a mechanic from Canastota who found the carburetor heater not working and the fuel line frozen. In the meantime we had a visit from the state troopers having to walk up a long steep hill. They made out their reports and left to phone them in. But they said to me that the plane would have to be dismantled to get it out of there. I made no promises. I made arrangements for my two passengers to be taken by car to Utica and asked several husky fellows if they would push on the wing struts as I revved up the engine. As mentioned we were at the top of a fairly long steep hill with a row of trees and high tension wires at the bottom, but a good strong wind with lots of lift blowing. Well, I revved the engine as high as it would go and yelled at the fellows to start pushing and down the hill we went. I can still see the amazed look on the troopers' faces as I pulled the nose of the plane up just over the treetops and high tension wires. *The New York Times* reported the news at the time and called it a "miracle landing."

> * "Leonard Edward Faulk's Story" was written by Leonard in 1987 to be a part of the "Leonard E. and Doris E. Faulk: A Family History." The family history was prepared to celebrate Leonard and Doris's 50th Wedding Anniversary celebration. Doris Elizabeth Swan Faulk's parents, Hulda Elizabeth Gustafson Swan and Lawrence Warner Swan, were also Swedish. Her father was born in Sweden and celebrated his first birthday on the ship when his parents were coming to America. Leonard and Doris were members of the "Swedish" Zion Covenant Church of Jamestown, New York. Leonard died in 1998 and Doris in 2006. They had five children (James W. Faulk, M.D.; Priscilla M. Moore; Leonard E. Faulk, Jr., Ph.D.; Deborah E. Reed; and Dennis W. Faulk) and many grandchildren and great-grandchildren.
>
> —Leonard E. Faulk, Jr., August 2012

MY TRIP TO THE UNITED STATES

by Nels Nelson

as told to Yvonne McNallie

In May of 1926 my mother brought my sister, Allie, who would turn three in July, and me, John Nels Nelson, to America aboard the Gripsholm. I would turn five in July, the day before Allie's birthday.

We reached New York, and my first recollection was of two men in white approaching me and taking me away in a wheelchair. I cried and called for my mother, but the men continued to wheel me to a hospital where I was taken to a room with a big brass bed that seemed to me to be six feet tall. I cried and screamed and a Black nurse appeared—the first Black person I had ever seen!

I was in the hospital for fifteen days and during that time my mother and sister had to stay behind. I could see them through a fence which was a little comforting to me. Dad, who had resided in Jamestown, New York, since 1923 to earn enough money to send for his family, had been called. However, because he was not told what was wrong with me except that it was a contagious disease (which turned out to be measles), he decided that he'd better stay in Jamestown until we could travel there.

After the fifteen days I was considered fit to travel, and we came to Jamestown, where my father had an apartment on Willard Street. Since I was still only four years old and school was almost over, I didn't start until the new school year began in September. I spoke no English and apparently the teacher didn't know what to do with me, so she gave me the task of sewing an apron. I came home that day and said I didn't want to ever go back to school. Of course, that didn't work out, and I continued in school like everyone my age. It was easier after I learned to speak English, though I was never overly fond of school.

My first job was in 1939, and I remember receiving a total of $11.01 for a week's work. A penny per dollar was taken out of my pay for Social Security. That was an expenditure that certainly paid off for me!

When Allie grew up she became a school teacher, and I went into sales after I served in the Navy from 1942 to 1946. I married my wife Alberta, and we had two children, Steve and Debbie. We lived most of our married life on the west side of Jamestown and still have an apartment in the Schuyler Street Apartments on the edge of town.

I often think of how brave my mother was to leave her homeland with two children under the age of five and none of us able to speak the language of the country to which we were going. In a time when communications were slow and unreliable and the likelihood that immigrants might very well never return to see the land of their birth and their relatives and friends, it was a step of great courage and foresight. I am thankful that my parents were among those heroes of long ago.

Nels' mother and father,

Nels and his sister Allie

KNUT—THE DANE WHO RULED ENGLAND

by Arland O. Fiske

One day King Knut ("Canute," as the English call him), ordered his throne carried to the seashore when the tide was out. It was near Chichester on the south coast of England. Then the king took his place on the royal chair and commanded his officers and courtiers to stand at attention "before him."

As the tide rolled in, King Knut spoke to the rising waters: "You are within my jurisdiction, and the land on which I sit is mine; no one has ever resisted my command with impunity. I therefore command you not to rise over my land and not to presume to wet the clothes or limbs of your Lord." But the water kept rising and soon king, throne and royal attendants retreated to higher ground.

What kind of madness would possess a king to utter such a command? Had power crazed his mind? No such thing. Back on dry ground, King Knut addressed the people: "Be it known to all inhabitants of the world that the power of kings is empty and superficial, and that no one is worthy of the name 'king' except for Him whose will is obeyed by heaven, earth and sea in accordance with His eternal laws." Then he took off his crown of gold and never wore it again.

Who was this Knut? He was the great-grandson of Gorm, the founder of Denmark's royal family. It is the oldest monarchy in the world with its heirs also on the thrones of Norway and England today. It was Knut's grandfather, Harald "Bluetooth," who converted to Christianity and began a royal line of faith which has been unbroken for 1000 years. Knut's father, Svein, conquered England but died only five years later on February 3, 1014.

Knut became England's king on November 30, 1016. He brought peace to a torn nation and was a champion of justice and the rights of the people. The English still call him "Great," a title reserved for only a few rulers in the world's history. The only thing they held against him was that he was "Danish" and not "English," but they came to respect and love him dearly. His rule was firm and he promoted the church's mission. These were happy days for the ancient island.

King Knut, however, was no friend of Norway's King Olaf Haraldsson, later called the "saint." He drove Olaf into a Russian exile and declared himself king of Norway. At the Battle of Sticklestad on July 30, 1030, Olaf's army was crushed by the much larger force of Knut and Olaf died, though perhaps by Norwegian hands. Now Knut was "lord of the whole of Denmark, England, Norway, and also Scotland." He was undisputed ruler of a North Sea kingdom. He was a natural leader of men.

Like Emperor Charlemagne (d. 814) and many other great leaders, Knut's empire did not survive his death in 1035. Britain went back to native rulers. The end of Scandinavian dominance was at hand. His remains are buried in Winchester Cathedral. He was sort of a "saint" in their eyes.

The Danes had a long established kingdom in the north and east of Britain with Jorvik (York) as its headquarters. Its main political and commercial rival was Dublin, the Norwegian capital of Ireland. Recent archaeological diggings have shown that the ancient Vikings were first-class builders and effective community organizers. The Scandinavian part of Britain was called "Danelaw," the area where Danish laws prevailed. Even today the physical appearance of the people and their language betrays their Nordic past. The big difference between those earlier Vikings and Knut's reign was the civilizing influence of the Christian faith found in Gorm's descendants.

If you go to Denmark, you can visit the site where old King Gorm and his wife, Thyra, are buried. It's near Jelling, a few miles to the northwest of Vejle in Jutland where "Lego" blocks are made. The English still regard Knut, their Danish king, as worthy of London. And the Norwegians also owe a strange debt to Knut. After all, it was Knut's ambition for a North Sea empire that propelled Olaf Haraldsson into "sainthood."

However you may feel about Olaf the Saint, this story belongs to Knut. He was also a distant relative of Norway's King Olav I and Denmark's

Queen Margaret II. And there are thousands of others who also claim a share in this royal bloodline but who have no political inheritance. The Danish portion of my household quietly makes such a claim. Long live Kings Gorm and Knut in the Scandinavian tradition. And you too, if that's where your heart is.

FAMILY STORY

by Julie Lindblom Boozer

My paternal grandmother Ida Christina Fornander (1869-1956) was born in Frödinge Parish, near Vimmerby in the Kalmar region of Småland. She grew up on her grandfather's Alsta farm and set out alone for America at age 18 in September of 1887. Her passage was during the Great Migration of Scandinavians to America, which occurred from 1860 through the late 1800s and is called the "Steamship Era." Steam power shortened the journey to a matter of weeks rather than the months it had sometimes taken on old sailing ships. She followed the exact route that almost all Swedish emigrants took at that time. Her journey began at Gothenburg, where she boarded a ship for the two-day passage to Hull, England. From Hull, she took an overnight train across England to Liverpool harbor, where she boarded her ocean-going steamship to New York harbor. Bunks were stacked in the hold, sometimes eight-high. In the absence of plumbing or running water, body excretions were deposited in large slop pails that were hand-carried up a long ladder to the top deck and tossed overboard. The North Atlantic was known for tempestuous storms and towering waves, which in the absence of modern stabilizers, provided perfect conditions for frequent bouts of seasickness, so the odors of human habitation permeating the hold were dreadful. It is hard, if not impossible, for our modern minds to even imagine the stench of seasickness, vomiting and diarrhea that prevailed in those closed quarters. The weary immigrants longed for an occasional calm day when the captain would allow them topside for a breath of precious fresh air! My shy 18-year-old grandmother, traveling alone, hung her sheet at the side of her bunk to gain the only privacy available.

Arriving in New York, tired and weary from her tempestuous voyage, she was jostled through long lines and processed through chaotic Castle Garden, an old 1812 fort that had been converted to an immigration authority by the State of New York to screen for communicable disease. She boarded a westbound train in New York City arriving in Jamestown, New York, at the Erie Station on Second Street at midnight, where she was delighted to hear men speaking Swedish on the station platform. She grabbed her bag and disembarked alone. It was October and a cold rainy wind was blowing. She was approached by a gentleman who was seeking a seamstress to work in his wife's dressmaking business. Luckily, Ida Christina was a skilled seamstress and accepted his offer on the spot. She followed him home slopping through the deep muddy ruts along Second Street in the dark. They continued on foot across town and up Swede Hill to his house. She declared, "I took a chair by the door in case his intentions were not honorable." She breathed a sigh of relief when his wife, dressed in a long nightgown and sleeping cap, appeared and verified her need for a seamstress. Thus began Ida Christina's career in America as a dressmaker. Sometimes her work would take her to live with a family for a few weeks to sew clothes. One of those live-in assignments was with the Lind family in Scandia where she made dresses and clothing for family members.

Most of the time, however, she was living and working in the home of her employer on Swede Hill and attending the Swedish Mission Church in Jamestown, where she sang in the choir. As a choir member she noticed a handsome tenor, Karl Oskar Andesson-Nero Lindblom, who had recently emigrated from Frinnaryd Parish in the Jönköping region of Småland to escape serving in the King's Army. They married in 1892 and began their family on Linden Avenue. He was a butcher and eventually had neighborhood shops on the south side of Jamestown.

Their story exemplifies the role that churches played in Americanizing new immigrants. Not only were churches a source of spirituality, but played an important role in helping new immigrants to socialize and adjust to the mores and customs of a strange new land. You might say that I am who I am because a Swedish tenor once winked at a shy Swedish soprano in the choir loft of a Swedish Mission Church and harmony began!

REINDEER BOOTS

by Katie (Cathy) Peterson

One of the most memorable stories that my grandmother told me was when I was quite young, and then she told it to me again when she was about eighty years of age.

She had come to this country at the tender young age of six from Stockholm, having been sent to relatives here ahead of her mother. Her name was Britt Anna Lindquist, and I loved her dearly.

The story she told was how some children had made fun of the reindeer-hide boots she had worn when she came to this country. When she told me the same story in her later years, after all those years had passed, it was quite obvious to me that she was still hurt by the children's unkind remarks made so many years ago. I'm guessing that the boots were quite beautiful, although not common in Jamestown.

"Brita with Candles and Apples" by Carl Larsson
(Note the reindeer boots!)

LIKE COMPARING ORANGES TO ORANGES

by Celeste Nelson Kerns

My father, the late Arvid Nelson of Jamestown, New York, came to this country from Markaryd, Småland, Sweden in 1925 at the age of eighteen via Ellis Island. Among his early employment experiences was one in a kosher kitchen at Grossinger's, a resort in the Catskill Mountains of Eastern New York State.

While emptying crates of oranges into bins, he caught the attention of an irate supervisor, *"Whaat are you doing? Them are Flaaridahs!"* Unbeknownst to my dad, the oranges were supposed to be sorted according to variety; but to this "green" Swede, an orange was an orange. This incident became a family joke over the years with my dad asking, *"Are them Flaaridahs, Ma?"* whenever mom brought oranges home from the store.

Another story from my dad's early years in his adopted country was of a road trip he took with his friend, Hokan Johanson, who eventually settled in Michigan City, Indiana. One day the two young men were at a service station in a remote area of the Midwest. Getting out of the car and confident that they would not be understood by anyone within earshot, they began speaking in their native tongue about the decrepit condition of the ramshackle business establishment, while the attendant, and presumably the owner, went about servicing the car.

Imagine their chagrin when as they drove away, the gas station owner gave them a smile and a wave along with, *"Tack så mycket, pojkar. Komm igen."*

SNORRI STURLUSON: ICELAND'S "ROYAL STORYTELLER"

by Arland O. Fiske

Those of us who love the Scandinavian heritage owe a great debt to Snorri Sturluson, Iceland's most famous saga writer. A saga is a story, usually based on facts, which tends to grow a little as it is re-told. Who was Snorri and how did he become so famous?

Iceland is an unusual place. According to geologists, it is the newest country in the world. It was formed through a series of volcanic eruptions "only" 20 million years ago. Kathleen Schermann, who wrote a delightful book on Iceland, called it "Daughter of Fire." Its earliest name was "Thule," given by a French navigator in 330 BC. Roman coins minted between 270-305 AD have been found on the island, indicating that the Roman navy stationed in Britain had visited there.

The first known inhabitants of Iceland were Irish monks in search of solitude during the seventh century. It was, however, the Norwegians coming in large numbers during the late ninth century who built the colonies which still exist. Despite its closeness to the Arctic Circle, Iceland was a hospitable site for settlers. Its temperature was two degrees warmer then and 24 percent of its surface was covered by trees. There are very few trees in Iceland today.

The original Norwegian settlers were of very proud and capable stock. They left their native land because of the oppression of civil rights by King Harald Haarfagre. This caused the landowners to pack their belongings in their *"knorrs,"* a Viking cargo ship. In Iceland they laid the foundations for the world's oldest democracy.

The Sturlusons were latecomers among the chieftain families of the island. Snorri was born in 1178 as a minor chieftain named Sturla. His grandmother, however, had descended from Egil Skallagrimsson, the greatest skaldic poet of the land.

Though a gentle man himself, Snorri's life was turbulent. He was constantly involved in feuds, lawsuits, and politics. When Snorri was three, a famous judge, Jon Luftsson, became his "foster father." This was not unusual in those days. Jon's grandfather, Saemund the Learned, had studied in France and had founded a famous cultural center at Oddi in southern Iceland. He had written a history of the Norse kings in Latin. Jon's mother was an illegitimate daughter of King Magnus Bareleg of Norway. (The matter of irregular birth was not a social handicap among Vikings.) This placed Snorri into a position for social climbing.

When Snorri was only five, his father died and left him little inheritance. His foster father died when he was 19, leaving him an education. He gained his wealth and power by good business skills, family support and favorable marriages. At 21, Snorri married the daughter of a wealthy farmer. Three years later, the farmer died and Snorri became a rich chieftain. Then he contracted to take care of an elderly farmer with a large estate which became his. Among his wives and mistresses was the wealthiest widow in Iceland. He also married off his daughters to politically influential families.

In politics, Snorri advanced quickly. At 35, he was elected "Law-speaker," the highest office in the land. This required a thorough knowledge of legal matters. His education at Oddi was not wasted. Having succeeded so well in Iceland, Snorri next tried to establish his fame with the kings of Norway. In the style of the times, he wrote poetry to flatter the people from whom he wished favors. All went well for a while. It brought him gifts and titles. But absolutist kings give nothing for free. Each time Snorri received recognition, his political position in Iceland was compromised. The Icelanders had good memories. They knew that their freedom was safest when the Norse rulers were looking in other directions.

Finally, the very success which he had purchased through marriages and favors turned against him. Two of his sons-in-law, having feuded with Snorri about land, became agents of Norway's King Haakon. They were ordered by the king to either arrest Snorri and return him to Norway, or kill him if he resisted. They chose to murder him on his farm. He was 61 years old.

So why do we remember Snorri Sturluson? He has written the sagas of the Norse kings called "Heimskringla." It is our best source of information on the Viking age. His style is gripping, even in translation. Basic to his writing was the belief in the sainthood of King Olaf Haraldsson which has remained a central feature of Norwegian Christianity.

It is ironic that the Icelanders, themselves refugees from Norway, became the recorders of a major part of the Scandinavian heritage. What's more, the Icelanders are the only people in the world today who still speak a language similar to the "Old Norse" of the Viking days.

HOFSTEDTS OCH JONASSONS FRÅN ÖSTERGÖTLAND

by Newkirk L. Johnson

The following narrative of my family's journey from Sweden to America does not come from direct experience, as I am a third-generation Swedish-American born in 1969. Nor does it come handed down to me generation to generation, because even though he was 100 percent Swedish, my grandfather never spoke about his Swedish roots. (I look back on that fact now with some regret, especially because he passed away in 2008 so I can never again ask him about these things.) Rather, much of what follows stems from my own research over the last several years, including a pilgrimage to Vadstena, Östergötland, Sweden to dig through old demographic church records at the regional Landsarkivet. I have also relied on the memories, photographs, and documentation from older living family members for some facts and anecdotes. The further I explore my Swedish roots, the more interested in the subject I become.

My great-great-grandfather Johan Pettersson Hofstedt was the first in my Swedish family tree to emigrate to America, initially in 1869. Johan was born in 1837 in Sandby near Hov, Östergötland, about ten kilometers south of Vadstena along the northeast shore of scenic Lake Tåkern—which today, along with its surrounding shoreline, is a formally protected nature reserve providing some of the highest quality bird habitat in all of Northern Europe. Johan had four siblings, including his younger brother Anders Pettersson Hofstedt who with his wife Maria also emigrated, settling in Youngsville, Pennsylvania. Anders went by "Andrew" in America.

My great-great-grandmother Johanna Andersdotter was born on the Hesselby farm in Rogslösa, to the northwest of Tåkern, in 1836. This was less than ten kilometers from Sandby. She and Johan met at some point along the way and married in Hov in 1862. My great-grand-uncle Peter

Hofstedt was born to Johan and Johanna in Sweden in 1865, as was my great-grand-aunt Anna Hofstedt in 1873. It appears Johan made at least two trips to America and back by himself at first. Eventually, he secured a permanent residence in Stoneham southeast of Warren, Pennsylvania, and presumably saved enough money to pay for the rest of his family's passage to America. Johanna, Peter, and Anna joined Johan in Stoneham in 1875. My great grandmother Jennie Hofstedt was born to Johan and Johanna in Sheffield in 1876. The Hofstedts lived in a small house that still stands today on what's now State Route 6. Johan was called "John" in America, and Johanna sometimes went by "Hanna." The Hofstedt surname was sometimes anglicized to "Hofstead," but not always.

Another branch of my Swedish family tree did not arrive in the United States for more than a decade after Jennie was born, but as it happens they also hailed from Östergötland. My great-grandfather Fredrik Wilhelm Jonasson and his brother Axel Henrik Jonasson emigrated to America around 1890. In 1897 they jointly purchased a farm of nearly 70 acres on Morris Road near Sherman, New York for $1,725. Fredrik and Axel had grown up in Vånga, east of Vadstena by 55 kilometers, with many siblings. Their father and my great-great-grandfather Peter Anders Jonasson, was born at Vreta Kloster, about 20 kilometers west of Vånga, in 1843. Their mother and my great great grandmother Sofia Albertina Bergström was born in Götlunda, Örebro a little north of Östergötland in 1840. Records suggest the Jonasson family also later spent some time in Linköping, just south of Vreta Kloster, which was then and is still the largest city in Östergötland. Axel married Clara Palm from Norrköping, Östergötland, and together they had six children, all born in America. Upon arrival here, the Jonassons adopted the common "Johnson" spelling for their surname. Two of Axel and Clara Johnson's sons operated the family farm all the way up until 1972 when they were finally forced to sell. My father, aunt, and their cousins have great memories of frequently visiting and playing at this farm as children in the 1950s.

At some point Fredrik met Jennie Hofstedt, because he did not stay with Axel and Clara on the Morris Road farm for long. By 1900, he and Jennie were married, already had two children (one of whom died as a 13-day-old infant), and lived next door to Jennie's parents John and Johanna in Stoneham. Fredrik's occupation was listed in the 1910 U.S. Census as a motorman for the streetcar system. In fact, there was a large brick streetcar powerhouse constructed in Stoneham in 1906 on Fullerton Road on the other side of Dutchman Run. Three large Westinghouse generators operated there, one 500 horsepower and two generating 750 horsepower each. This structure still stands today, with faded "Fullerton Machine Co." lettering visible on its side. In 1920 Fredrik was a leather inspector with the Penn Tanning Company, and in 1930 he was a refinery laborer—perhaps at the United Refinery in Warren, which of course still operates today. My grandfather Ellsworth Johnson was the fifth child born to Jennie and Fredrik, in Stoneham in 1915. His siblings were Harold, Lillian, Violet, Fred Jr., and Charlotte.

John Hofstedt was listed in the 1900 Census as a tannery laborer, as was his son Peter. There was in fact a tannery in Stoneham during this time, which was fairly long-lived under various ownerships, located approximately where the old Crossett garage stands today on Route 6. The Stoneham tannery opened in 1867 and operated nearly continuously until it was shut down for good in 1912. Located just a few hundred yards down the road south of the Hofstedt and Johnson homes, this is likely the tannery at which John and Peter, and possibly later Fredrik, were employed. They would simply have had to walk five minutes down the road to get to work every morning.

Tanning, the process of turning animal hides into leather, was a very important industry in the region at the time, relying upon the surrounding natural resources of Penn's Woods to prosper—namely the ubiquitous ancient hemlock trees. The three primary ingredients needed for tanning are hides, water, and tannic acid. The bark of the hemlock trees supplied an abundance of tannic acid.

Stoneham had many Swedish immigrants working in the wood products industry in the late 19th and early 20th centuries. Walter Casler wrote of the area in *Tionesta Valley: Sheffield, Brookston, Loleta, Bear Creek, Cherry Grove* (1973) that "a large number of workmen were needed to cut timber, peel bark and run the mills and tanneries. Local help was scarce, and large numbers of men had to be imported from outside. Many people who came to Sheffield and the surrounding area were of Scandinavian descent, mostly from Sweden. They made excellent woodsmen and expert tannery workers—many of their descendents still reside in this area." According to former Allegheny National Forest historian Philip Ross, "the rise of the tanning industry in northwestern Pennsylvania coincides quite precisely with the completion of the Philadelphia and Erie Railroad across the Allegheny Plateau in 1864."

Before he died, my grandfather told me a number of stories about growing up in the house in Stoneham, the interior of which was austere with no carpeting, had bare wooden floors, and was sparsely furnished. Before the Johnsons had electricity and therefore refrigeration, they had blocks of ice delivered from Warren by horse and carriage, used gas lighting, and of course there were no electric washers or driers. They washed their laundry by hand, and hung it out to dry behind the house. Because the above mentioned Philadelphia and Erie Railroad ran directly past their house, this could be problematic—if they heard a train coming it was critical to quickly bring in the clean laundry; otherwise, it would be coated with soot from the passing train. When State Route 6 was constructed directly in front of their house in the 1920s, it dramatically changed the landscape in which my grandfather, his siblings, and their friends played, including destroying a tennis court they had constructed with their own hands. After Fredrik died in 1935, Jennie worked as a seamstress at home, and also took a job as a cleaning person at the old Mineral Well Restaurant & Motel less than a half-mile up Route 6 toward Warren, a job which she walked to and from until she began to lose her eyesight in the 1940s.

The railroad tracks were also the site of a terrible accident that dramatically affected my great grandparents, and was covered by all the local newspapers at the time. On Sunday, October 22, 1911, James Gass, a prominent doctor residing in Sheffield, and his wife and nine-year-old son were on their way to the Warren hospital in their 18 horsepower Hupmobile to check on some of Dr. Gass's patients. Where the railroad tracks cross Griff Hill Road directly behind the house, their car was struck by two pusher engines coupled together returning to Warren at 25 miles an hour. The impact threw the Hupmobile 15 feet through the air, turning it completely around. Dr. and Mrs. Gass were killed instantly, with gruesome injuries. Their son was not seriously hurt, but was thrown from the vehicle. The first people on the scene were Fredrik and Jennie Johnson. The October 23rd *Warren Evening Mirror* quoted Fredrik as stating "... I found the car in the ditch and Mrs. Gass was partially in it .... I looked at her but there was no sign of life and I saw she was dead. Dr. Gass was a little ways from her and he too lay still and made no move." The October 26th *Warren Mail* reported that Jennie was overcome: "Mrs. Fred Johnson ... who with her husband saw the accident and helped to carry the dead to her porch, collapsed a few minutes later and is under the care of a physician."

This event left an indelible mark on the Johnsons, and for years later the children and grandchildren were the recipients of stern warnings not to play on or near the railroad tracks.

For decades, large family reunions were customary. My father, aunt, and their cousins attended these events during the 1950s, one being held at the Tassel Club on Dutchman Run Road in Stoneham. At these reunions the adults would prepare a large pile of sawdust for the many children in attendance into which they tossed their pennies, nickels, and dimes. On the signal from an adult, the kids would jump into the heap and scramble for the coins, keeping whatever they could find. Sometimes an additional prize such as a toy was awarded to the child who collected the most money pawing through the sawdust.

Much earlier, a Tuesday, August 10, 1926 article in *The Warren Morning Mirror*, titled "Hofstead and Gustafson Clans Have Meeting: Mr. and Mrs. Johnson Entertain Many Members of Two Families at Annual Reunion at Their Home," reported that "nearly one hundred members of the Hofstedt-Gustafson clans gathered at the home of Mr. and Mrs. Fred Johnson at Stoneham, Saturday, for the annual meeting. The elaborate affair was preceded by a short prayer by Victor Gustafson of Falconer, N.Y. When all had fully enjoyed the dinner, the business meeting was called to order by the vice-president, Clarence Vestling, of Warren, in the absence of the president, Arvid Gustafson, of Frewsburg . . . ." Listed attendees at this reunion included Andrew and Maria Hofstedt of Youngsville, Peter and Lottie Hofstedt of Jamestown, Walter Vestling of Stoneham, Axel and Clara Johnson of Sherman, and many others. The last of these large Swedish family reunions was held in the early 1960s near Stedman, New York.

Fred Johnson, Jr. moved to Bradford, Pennsylvania in the 1920s at a young age and began working at the Davis Bakery on Mechanic Street. He became the bakery manager in 1928, and took ownership outright in 1932. When my grandfather Ellsworth Johnson graduated from Warren High that same year it was of course during the Great Depression, so he moved to Bradford to work with his older brother at the Davis Bakery because it was his best—perhaps only—option for a reliable source of income at the time. In 1948, Ellsworth with his wife Evelyn expanded the Davis Bakery operation by opening the Cake Shop at 145 Main Street (approximately where McDonalds is located today). Later, the Cake Shop moved a few doors down into the Hooker-Fulton building, where the movie theater is housed and where today the Bradford Area Chamber of Commerce is located. Everyone of a certain age in Bradford remembers the Swedish brothers Ellsworth and Fred Johnson and their Cake Shop and Davis Bakery, both of which operated until 1981. Though they both offered a wide variety of baked goods, two of their most popular specialties were always Swedish rye bread and Swedish kiffel cookies.

Discovering the Hofstedt/Johnson family plot in Oakland Cemetery in Warren in May of 2009 was a seminal moment for me personally. It is difficult to describe the "homecoming" feeling I experienced to touch those headstones, read the names engraved on them, and suddenly realize in a tangible way that I really am Swedish. The idea became far less abstract and academic in that moment. When I later visited Hov, Sandby, Tåkern, Vadstena, Vånga, and other Östergötland locales, it was not lost on me that I was to the best of my knowledge the first of the Hofstedt and Johnson American descendents to come full circle and return to these sites of our family's Swedish roots. Later still, I discovered just how deep our Scandinavian roots likely run. Through a DNA analysis recently performed by the National Geographic Society, it was shown that my paternal genetic haplogroup is "I1-M253"—strongly suggestive of a Viking background, and indeed likely Scandinavian going back perhaps 10,000 years or more. It's literally in our genes!

Hofstedt House Stoneham—1890

Per Jonasson   Menu from the Cake Shop

MY FAMILY STUGA

by Donald K. Sandy

For as long as I can remember, I have dreamed about visiting a family home (stuga) in Sweden. Three of my grandparents came over in the late 1800s, and as far as I knew, nobody had ever returned to visit a family homestead. I had no idea where these homes could be located or even if the buildings could still exist.

With the help of my grandparents' death records and some professional genealogists, without much effort, I was able to find the church parish in Sweden where the families lived just before they emigrated to the United States. Anyone who has looked at these parish records knows that they were the official records for Sweden at the time and recorded the comings and goings of people as they lived in the parish. They identify where people lived and the dates they were there.

While visiting Sweden, one of my goals was to visit these churches of my ancestors. The first church I visited was Stora Malm just outside Katrineholm in the province of Södermanland. With the help of relatives, it was discovered that the family farm had been torn down as part of the expansion of the city. The second church I visited was Vesta Broby just outside Helsingborg in the province of Skåne. Although I was able to find the address of the building where they lived, nobody has yet been able to locate the exact spot. Perhaps someday.

(As a side note, while doing research in the city hall land records, a local Swedish lady decided to help me since I was having difficulty reading the Swedish language. It turned out that after she had researched my family she found out we were related through a common ancestor seven generations back. A remarkable coincidence.)

The third church I visited was in Ulrika, not located near anyplace and in the province of Ostergötland. (My wife Sandra has written a story about our first visit to this church.) It turns out that Christer Andersson, the sexton, was quite informed about the area. (It was also discovered that I was related to him seven generations back. Another coincidence?) He noticed in the records that my family's home was named Brotorpet. You can imagine my shock when he stated, "I know where that house is located and it is still there. Would you like to see it?" I could not believe my ears. In one second a dream came true! He further indicated that we could visit the home right now. I was ready!

We drove a few miles away from the church and he then told me to turn down a road. That was fine. Shortly he indicated that we needed to turn down a path, not a road, into the forest. There on a small rise, he identified Brotorpet! There was even a sign by the house with the name on it. There was no question. What made this visit even more remarkable was that the house has not changed much since my ancestors left. There is still no electricity or running water. The house consists of two rooms—a kitchen and another room that was used for sleeping as well as activities of daily life. The kitchen still has a wood stove in the style of one hundred years ago. When I think of my ancestors living there for about three generations and at times raising at least five children, I marvel at the living arrangements. There was space for a small garden and a couple of outbuildings. Across the path are several large boulders that many of my ancestors must have climbed around as children. Our daughter scrambled up on the rocks and declared that her great-great-grandmother must have played on them, also.

Brotorpet was a home for my family, but it was owned by the area farm where my ancestors worked. It is now a summer cottage for a family that lives about 40 miles away. We have not yet been able to meet them or been able to step into the house. The current owners have indicated that we could sleep over in the house someday. My wife expresses some concern about the primitive conditions, but I trust that someday we will step into the house and really return to our roots. My ancestors left this home for the American dream. It was not long before they were able to purchase their own land in America which is perhaps the first land ever owned by this family line in the history of mankind.

When I visit Brotorpet, I cannot help but think that I have reconnected with my past. It has come full circle. During one visit, I played a few Swedish folk tunes on the accordion. I doubt that my ancestors ever thought that over one hundred years in the future, somebody would return and marvel about the family's home. Whenever we return to Sweden, I try to reserve time for a brief visit to my roots at Brotorpet.

> **Editor's Note**: Don Sandy has been the coordinator of the Scandinavian Folk Festival in Jamestown, New York for several years. He is also very active in many Scandinavian organizations, musical groups, and various other endeavors to promote the Scandinavian Heritage in the Jamestown area.

The Road to Brotorpet

Brotorpet

The Kitchen at Brotorpet

ÅLTOMTABRO

by Barbara Hillman Jones

Åltomtabro was the name given to the farm of my paternal great-grandparents, August and Matilda Hellman. The farm is located in Vänge (previously known as Brunna), Uppsala Municipality, in East Central Sweden. August and Matilda must have lived there for many years because all of their eight children were born on that farm in the late 1800s and early 1900s. The oldest was my grandfather who was born in 1881. After their parents died, one of the brothers, Magnus, took over the farm until he passed away in 1939.

When my dad took his first trip to Sweden in 1928 with his parents, they stayed with dad's grandparents on the family farm. He had heard the farm described by his father, and he had heard his father's account of how all of the eight children worked together, the girls with their mother cooking and baking and cleaning the red farmhouse, and the boys with their father in the fields and taking care of the animals that were kept on the farm. They did manage to find some time for fun, though.

While visiting us a few years ago, my father's cousin Sven told us a story of how the boys made a Fourth of July celebration for their 20-year-old American cousin during that 1928 trip. Having heard that the Americans set off firecrackers on the Fourth of July and having none, the boys made what they thought was a good substitute. They helped themselves to a stick of dynamite that their father probably would have used to remove tree stumps and inserted it into a crevice of a large rock in a field on the property. When the dynamite was lit and it went off, there was a much bigger explosion and a much greater noise then any of them could have imagined. In their eagerness to make their American cousin feel "at home" on the Fourth of July, they indeed created a huge celebration. When their father heard the explosion, he came running, terrified, then seeing that all the boys were safe, he got very angry with all of them. He was well aware of what could have happened but, thankfully, no one was hurt. When Sven told us this story, he laughed until the tears rolled down his face just reliving that experience—Sven had been one of those boys.

Dad always spoke of Åltomtabro with great affection as he remembered that trip and how much it meant to him to actually meet his father's family. He did not know that on our trip to Sweden together in 1974 that he would be privileged to visit that homestead once again. This time another cousin, Claes Hellman, and his wife Karin surprised us by taking us to the farm. Claes had been in touch with the current owners and explained to them that the farm had been owned by Claes's grandparents in the late 1800s and early 1900s. Their American cousin had visited the farm in 1928 and they wanted to surprise him with another visit forty-six years later. Claes asked if we could have a picnic on the grounds of the farm, and the present owners graciously consented for us to do that. So I was privileged to visit the farm of my great-grandparents. Not only were we able to enjoy a picnic there, but when we went to the house to thank them for their hospitality we were invited to take a tour of the house. Dad remembered clearly how it had looked in 1928 and, happily, he noticed that it was still much the same.

Unbeknown to us, Claes later asked the owners if he could have a branch of the huge birch tree that stood in a field near the house. Claes was a master woodworker who made all kinds of beautiful trays, cooking utensils, little figures, and decorative items for the home which he sold in his shop called *Praktisk Konst* (practical art). When he and his family visited us in 1976, he brought with him several items he had personally made for each of us from that birch branch. He carefully planned each one so as to get as many items from that piece of wood as he could. We have a kitchen fork and a letter opener, and with the very last tiny piece, he made a lovely rattle for my sister Karin's daughter Sara who was just a baby at that time.

I inherited a pair of brass candleholders that came from the old Hellman homestead, Åltomtabro, in Vänge, Sweden. When my father gave them to me, he told me they were at least 150 years old, so now they are close to 200 years old. Obviously, they had been handed down from generation to generation for a very long time. They occupy a prominent place on the mantle in our family room, and I often find myself looking at them, trying to imagine life at Åltomtabro so many years ago.

PANCAKES AND PEPPARKAKOR

by Norma Carlson Waggoner

My Swedish Dad had three sisters—Emy, Marie, and Hedwig, who settled in Chicago and raised their families there. They were excellent cooks and bakers. Being at Aunt Hedwig's house or when they came to Jamestown meant breakfasts of her Swedish pancakes served with orange wedges. Just the best breakfast ever! My sister Dee and I still eat a lot of oranges—maybe a taste acquired from those breakfasts. Oranges are still plentiful but Aunt Hedwig's Swedish pancakes are just a wonderful memory. Dee makes Swedish pancakes now. At her house we've had "international breakfast"—Swedish pancakes, Canadian bacon, and oranges or cantaloupe. Very good! She sent me a recipe for Swedish pancakes, and I really must try it soon.

Going to Aunt Emy's always found us sitting around their dining room table having coffee, milk and countless tasty baked goods. My favorite was Swedish *pepparkaka**, which is somewhat like a banana bread. After I was married, I wrote to Aunt Emy and asked for the recipe. She sent it to me, written in pencil on a thin strip of paper. I made it many times, especially at Christmas, and my family loved it. When my daughter Sue's youngest son Marc was in grade school, his class was doing a project on foods from their heritage. Sue called me for the *pepparkaka* recipe which they made and was a hit when Marc took it to school. My recipe is about fifty years old now and holds special memories of sitting around Aunt Emy's table.

*For those who are not Swedish, there is a difference between *pepparkaka* and *pepparkakor*—the first is a cake, and the second, thin ginger cookies.

Aunt Emy's recipes follow:

SWEDISH PEPPARKAKA (cake)

Sift together 2 cups of flour, 1-1/2 cup sugar, 1 teaspoon cinnamon, 2/3 teaspoon cloves, 1 teaspoon baking powder, ½ teaspoon salt. Stir in 1 cup of milk and 2 eggs. Last, add 1 teaspoon baking soda diluted on 1 tablespoon of water and ¼ pound melted, cooled butter. Blend well. Bake in greased loaf pan about 50 minutes in a 350 degree oven. Let stand in pan 15 minutes. Cool on rack.

PEPPARKAKOR (cookies)

¾ cup shortening, 1 cup sugar, ¼ cup Brer Rabbit molasses, 1 egg, 2 teaspoons baking soda, 2 cups flour, ½ teaspoon cloves, ½ teaspoon ginger, 1 teaspoon cinnamon, ½ teaspoon salt. Melt shortening. Cool. Add sugar and egg. Beat well. Sift flour, spices, soda, and salt, and add to first mixture. Form 1-inch balls, place on sheets, and press down with bottom of glass. Bake in 375-degree oven for 8-10 minutes.

AUGUST ERICKSON CAME TO BE AN AMERICAN!

by Harold & Dorothy (Bush) Erickson, Julie Erickson Nygaard, Lynette Erickson

After being raised in Jamestown, New York, it surprises us that we ended up living these last twenty years in California. Living here is different from living in Jamestown in the 1900's. But yet it probably was not a lot different from the multicultural atmosphere that August Erickson encountered when he came from Sweden in 1904.

August was a 20-year-old young man who left Sweden, his homeland, for a better life in America. Traveling with his good friend of the same age, John Soderquist, these young men knew that America offered them opportunities that they would not have if they continued to live in Sweden.

The same can be said for many immigrants that we encounter each day here in Northern California. These people see America as the land of opportunity for political freedom, financial gain and an improved lifestyle. But there is one significant difference between some of these immigrants and August Erickson. When we go a mall or a restaurant, we hear many conversations in languages that we don't understand. It might be Mandarin or Spanish or Farsi. At times we seldom hear English and we never hear Swedish except when we visit the Scandinavian Deli or Bakery—especially at holiday times.

When August went to a coffee shop or a store in Jamestown, he probably heard some English, but more likely many of the people around him were speaking Swedish. August was unhappy when people spoke to him in Swedish when non-Swedes were present. He admonished his family with the words, "I came to America to be an American and we speak primarily English." About 1912, he took the significant step to become a citizen of the U.S.A. with the assistance of Atelia (Tillie-his wife) Johnson's father.

August always encouraged his family to celebrate their Swedish heritage with traditional foods, Swedish holiday celebrations and customs and in upholding their regular Lutheran religious observances. Even today most of our family enjoys a good smörgåsbord, including korv, pickled herring, Swedish meatballs, rice pudding, and some of us even love lutfisk. He always saved several bundles of oats to hang in the trees over the winter for the birds in cold and snowy weather.

The attitude of adapting to his new environment and enjoying his new homeland served August well throughout his life. When he arrived in Jamestown, New York, he chose to board with the Bush Family whose native language was English. He taught himself to speak, read and write English. He started working at Watsons, a factory that manufactured windows and doors. However, his real dream was to buy and work a dairy farm. After his marriage to Tillie Johnson, they saved enough money to buy a house on Francis Street and in 1925 they bought a farm on the Wellman Road in Ashville.

August didn't know a lot about farming, but he read everything that he could get his hands on about farming and crops and especially flowers. He had the most beautiful flower garden of any farmer in Ashville and he tended it all himself! He also taught himself to play the piano and violin—unusual accomplishments for a man who only had a grade school education in Sweden.

As August's sons (Alvin, Julius, Stanley and Harold) grew, they learned more about the mechanics of farming than their dad knew. In fact, Harold (his youngest son) and his wife Dorothy Bush Erickson bought and worked the farm until 2003 after August died in 1955. But August loved his Guernsey and Jersey dairy cows and spent many happy hours in the barn milking them and singing to them. He always said that they were more content and gave more milk when he sang to them!

It was in the non-milking times in the barn that he demonstrated his desire to be a better American and English language proponent. He kept a dictionary in the barn so that he could look up words that he heard on the radio or read in a farming magazine. He wanted to be able to use those words when he spoke or wrote letters.

August Erickson treasured his Swedish heritage, but after he immigrated to the U.S.A. he was committed to becoming an American. He was not just a Swede, speaking only Swedish and associating only with other Swedes. He was a man who fully adopted, integrated into and loved his new country, the United States of America.

SWEDEN—ITS PEOPLE AND ROYALTY

by Arland O. Fiske

Sweden is the largest of the Scandinavian countries. Almost 8,500,000 people live in 173,630 square miles, a little larger than California. This northern country is warmed by the Gulf Stream in the Atlantic and is surprisingly mild. Sweden has almost 100,000 lakes and over half of it is covered with forests. Over 2,500,000 people live in three cities: Stockholm, Göteborg and Malmo. And they still eat *lutfisk* for Christmas.

A glacier covered northern Europe 15,000 years ago. About 9,000 years ago, fishermen and hunters began to settle in Sweden. Then about 2,500 years ago, another Ice Age began which lasted 400 years. The present inhabitants of Sweden, as well as Denmark and Norway, are a part of the Teutonic migration that came from Germany.

The center of power in early Sweden was the "Svea" tribe near Uppsala. The name "Sweden" is derived from them. Many historians also identify the "Goths" who spread over Europe to have originally migrated from Sweden.

Once the center of Viking activity, Swedish traders and soldiers of fortune traveled eastward into Russia and then southward to Constantinople. They established the first kingdom of Russia at Kiev and many became known as "Varangians," the Greek emperor's elite palace guard. The name "Rus," modern "Russia," originally meant Sweden.

In those Viking days, the worship of Odin, Thor and Frey struck terror in the hearts of the people with their great appetite for human sacrifice. It was the Christian missionaries from Germany and England who gave them new direction.

In 1397, Sweden was joined to Denmark and Norway in the Union of Kalmar. In 1523, the Vasa family came to power and created an independent

Sweden. They also established the Lutheran Reformation. The most famous of these Vasa kings was Gustav II Adolf (Gustavus Adolphus), known as the "Lion of the North." Swedish immigrants founded a college at St. Peter, Minnesota, after his name in 1862.

The Vasa family ran out of heirs in the early 1800s and made an agreement with Napoleon to invite his marshal, Jean Baptiste Jules Bernadotte, to become the crown prince. He accepted and took the name "Karl Johan." Then he switched sides over to the British for which he was rewarded by being given Norway. He was not Norway's choice of king, but did prove to be a good ruler for them.

The Bernadottes continue as the royal family of Sweden and are very popular both in Sweden and among Swedes in America. The present king, Carl XVI Gustaf, was given solid academic preparation for his ceremonial position. His wife, Silvia, is of German and Brazilian background. Crown Prince Harald of Norway is also a Bernadotte through his mother, the late Crown Princess Martha.

Sweden has had peace since 1814 and this contributes towards its great progress in science, statesmanship, and for its leadership in Christian humanitarianism. This is also why so much of Sweden's magnificent architecture of the past remains for us to see when we visit Stockholm. In 1976, Sweden elected a non-socialist Prime Minister and continues its cautious neutralist policies. In a world of so much conflict, there is much we can learn from the Swedes.

1976 ROYAL VISIT

by Carol Lind Kindberg

Early 1976 was a busy time in the Swedish community of Jamestown as plans were being finalized for the visit of King Carl XVI Gustaf. Gunnard Kindberg, a traffic officer of the Jamestown Police Department was part of security for the visit. The Swedish government has certain requirements which involved a trip to the home of the Swedish Ambassador in New York City as well as planning Jamestown security.

It was a cold, rainy day when he came, needing to land in Bradford because visibility in Jamestown was too low. People stood along the roads from Bradford to Chandler's Valley to Jamestown, waving small Swedish flags to welcome him. Lunch was served in the City Hall lobby to approximately 100 people with the program on the plaza in the rain. Because of the rain, the king suggested dessert be served so the program could begin. A very memorable day for all involved directly as well as those who waited patiently just to see him.

104 HAZELTINE AVENUE

by Gordon Henry Mattson

I checked Google Earth today, and the little white house at 104 Hazeltine Avenue is still standing. All my memories of Jamestown emanate from and around that cozy little dwelling.

My grandmother, Selma Potentia Strandberg, came to America in 1899; my grandfather, Ernest Emil Mattson, in 1902. They met and were married in Byrndale, Pennsylvania. Ernest was employed as a coal miner with the Dagus Mining Company. Their three children were born there—my father, Carl Henry, in 1905, and twins, Sigfred B. and Sigrid E. in 1915.

Working in the mines in those days was pure hell, so my grandfather deciding that he must never "owe his soul to the company store," left his wife and children and went to Alaska in search of gold, the result being that in 1926 he was able to buy the little Hazeltine Avenue home.

The future looked bright for the family. Ernest got a good job with the Art Metal Furniture Company, but then tragedy struck. The twins Sigfred and Sigrid both received two-wheeled bicycles for their 11th birthday. Sigrid rode hers into the street and was struck and killed by a car.

A family plot of five graves and a large MATTSON headstone were purchased.

My father left Jamestown for Detroit, met and married my mother, Esther Neubert. I was born in 1938 and my sister Carol Ann in 1946.

At least once every year my Dad would get homesick and we would journey to Jamestown. For me, a kid growing up during the Second World War, getting there was always an adventure. We went by train, by bus, by lake steamer, by car, and by airplane. There were always lots of uniformed service personnel on board. The most memorable ride was on a Greyhound bus packed with folks standing in the aisle. Word quickly spread throughout the bus that the "Harmonica Rascals" were sitting in the back of the bus. The passengers pleaded, and the "Rascals" played all the way from Detroit to Buffalo.

The ride on the old Jamestown Westfield trolley along Lake Chautauqua was like an amusement park thrill ride, rocking and bumping along so high up and so close to the edge, I had to hold on tight and hold my breath, as well.

I remember Grandma's kitchen always smelling like a bakery and Grandpa's little enclosed front porch smelling like an ashtray. I remember picking wild strawberries with Grandma in the field across the street. I remember wondering why she carried a garden hoe while we were picking and learning why when she beheaded a rattlesnake with it. I remember walking to the Guernsey Dairy with her to buy the fresh whipping cream that would cover the berries. I remember being awakened one night by what sounded like gunfire down in the cellar and finding out that Grandpa had put yeast in Grandma's homemade root beer and the bottles exploded. I remember climbing to the very top of the backyard apple tree to get the season's last apple. I remember biting into it and finding half a worm.

My Uncle Sigfred and his wife Svea were my heroes. They never had any children of their own. Sig was a pilot and scared the pants off of me a time or two in the old open cockpit biplane he used to rent. Svea worked at Billings Bakery. A sweet treat was a sure thing when visiting her at work. They always rented a cottage on Lake Chautauqua for the summer. I found a lot of fossils and drowned a mess of worms there. They were both charter members of the Skyline Archery Club. Sig was employed by the city as a gardener, and the Mattson plot at the Lakeview Cemetery was always well cared for.

I remember the amusement rides at Celeron Park, I remember Allen Park swimming pool and pony rides, I remember family reunions up on Swede Hill, and I remember picnicking in Allegheny State Park.

I remember Ernest and Selma's 50th wedding anniversary in 1954.

My wife Carole and I were married in 1958. We have three children—Cheryl, Gordon, Jr., and Jillian. Visits to Jamestown became less frequent. There was one, however, that was indeed memorable because it was pure luck, not proper planning, that placed us in the Jamestown City Hall Plaza Square in 1976 when King Carl Gustaf of Sweden was there. Looking back on that day, I am amazed at how little security there was.

I remember my Grandfather's funeral and how moving the hymn "Abide With Me" was as sung by a lady from the Salvation Army.

After his passing, a decision to sell the little Hazeltine house was made. It was agreed that my Grandmother Selma would stay six months in Jamestown with Sig and Svea and six months in Detroit with my parents which she did until her passing in 1972.

Sigfred's wife Svea passed away suddenly June 25, 1989, and Sig was devastated. Svea was buried in the Mattson plot in Lakeview Cemetery.

Svea's sisters Ruby and Dorothy were a comfort to Sig as were his fishing buddies and the McDonald's morning coffee club. When the Lucille Ball Museum opened, we brought our granddaughter Erin Dirmeyer who knows every episode of "I Love Lucy" word for word to Jamestown to visit Sig. On another trip, the Roger Tory Peterson Museum and the Kinzu Dam were introduced to my grandson Connor Henry by Uncle Sig.

In 2003, someone sold Sig's boat. He had a bad fall in the basement of his apartment and the owner was going to raise his rent, so in 2004, Sig came to live in Florida with Carole and me. He was able to fish from the pier at the neighborhood park. He was able to get to and from the park on a blue and yellow "Swedish" tricycle. He was adopted by a neighborhood cat, and he enjoyed playing cribbage at the Elks Club. Things were going well, but then "Jean" paid us a visit. Sig knocked on our bedroom door and said, "Gord, I've got a water bed," and I said, "No, you don't," and Sig said, "The hell I don't—you come and see!" And sure enough the hurricane had taken the entire roof off of Sig's bedroom. We were without power, and the cleanup took days. FEMA blue-tarped the roof, but Sig contracted pneumonia, and by advance directive passed away in hospice care January 29, 2005. The last date was carved on the Mattson plot headstone, and its faithful caretaker was gone.

Ernest Emil Mattson, my grandfather, had eight siblings: Hilda Augusta, Emma Christina, Oskar, Carl Kenrik, Ivar, Bror Fritz, Elmer Hugo, and Gustaf Einar. All but the last two came to Amerca. Ernest never met the two that stayed in Sweden. In 2012 with help provided by the Swedish Council of America and Marie Louise Bratt of "Bridge to Sweden," I was able to locate three children of the two who stayed behind. Elmer Hugo's son Bo Mattson and Gustaf Einar's daughters Lena Satterstrom and Christine Friman. I was also able to locate the dwelling in which Elmer Hugo and Gustaf Einar were born. It was called *"Schweitzerhuset."* It was moved three times because of road construction and now sits beside a children's museum called *Krreativum* and has been converted into living quarters for the museum's docents.

Armed with this information, my son and I went to Sweden where we met our relatives. We were photographed at the ancestral home at the same time King Carl XVI Gustaf's daughter Victoria was being married. We were amazed that there was more interest among the local Stockholm Swedes in the World Cup Soccer Games than in the wedding!

> **Editor's Note:** The author's grandmother Selma Strandberg Mattson was a sister of my own grandmother, Esther Strandberg Tuline. I also remember very well the little house at 104 Hazeltine Avenue where we often gathered as a family for a meal. I always wondered how we could get so many people in that little house! As a child, the "breakfast nook" in their kitchen fascinated me, and I loved sitting there. The author's Uncle Sig and Aunt Svea were very special to me, also, and while in high school I would walk over town to my part-time job at Geer-Dunn's. I almost always stopped at Billing's Bakery to see Svea, and I would never leave without receiving a cookie and a hug from her. Sig and Svea rented the second-floor apartment at 55 Charles Street, the house owned by my Aunt Evelyn and Uncle Bill Carlson for many years; the Carlsons resided in the first-floor apartment. Sig always took care of the yard and planted the flowers around the house. Aunt Evelyn and Svea were the best of friends, and after they retired, they loved going "to town" almost every day. After Gordon's grandparents passed away, Sig and Svea were always included in the Tuline family gatherings.

The little house at 104 Hazeltine Avenue

Twins, Sigfred & Sigrid Mattson

Ernest & Selma Mattson's wedding

THE SCANDINAVIAN "OSCARS" AND THE "FRENCH CONNECTION"

by Arland O. Fiske

Everyone knows that an "Oscar" is an award for outstanding acting in the movies. Long before there was a Hollywood, two "Oscars" were kings of Sweden: Oscar I (1844-1859) and Oscar II (1872-1907). Actually the Oscars of Sweden were not Swedes at all, but French. The stage for this change in Scandinavian politics came through the wars of Napoleon.

Denmark and Norway had shared the same rulers since Queen Margaret I in 1380, when the last "Norwegian" king of Norway died. The arrangement seemed everlasting. This was made clear to me when I visited Surnadel, a community about 75 miles southwest of Trondheim. King Christian V (1670-1699) traveled from Copenhagen to that Norwegian valley in the summer of 1685. The king presented a plaque to the people which now hangs in the Mo Church. As an American whose family left there in 1892, I was surprised at the importance still attached to that "ancient" event. The point was that both Denmark and Norway seemed to believe that they would stay together forever.

The political destiny of my ancestral valley, however, was to change radically by new events taking place on the continent of Europe. Napoleon was on the march to conquer the world. Except for a bad winter in Russia, he might have succeeded. Napoleon ordered his marshal, Jean Baptiste Jules Bernodotte, to occupy Denmark if the Danes would not declare war on England. King Frederick VI (1808-1839) was immediately confronted with an English counter-threat. After weighing his unhappy choices, the Danish king cast his lot with Napoleon. He concluded that Denmark had

117

more to fear from the French armies than from the English navy. On April 12, 1801, Lord Nelson directed the British bombardment of Copenhagen. The Danish navy was destroyed and its merchant ships were taken to England as prizes of war. The Danes were never compensated. It also meant that Norway was cut off from Denmark and suffered severely from a blockade.

Another surprise took place. Sweden's royal house of Vasa had run out of heirs. In searching about for new royalty, they elected Marshal Bernadotte as crown prince, to the pleasure of Napoleon. The French emperor privately disliked and feared the marshal and this was an opportunity to send him to Sweden. It could also provide him with an ally against England and Russia. Once in Sweden, Bernadotte switched sides. He joined the enemies of Napoleon. His reward was Norway. At the Treaty of Kiel, signed on January 14, 1814, Denmark gave up Norway to Sweden under threat from the "superpowers." It was to be Sweden's compensation for its loss of Finland to Russia just a few years before. The French marshal was secretly wishing for Napoleon's defeat and hoped that he would become the new king of France. He had accepted the Swedish offer with some private reservations. When that time came, however, the French chose their new king from the House of Bourbon.

Bernadotte chose the name of Karl XIV Johan. English historians call him Charles John. The main street in Oslo leading from the palace to the parliament building is called "Karl Johansgate." He never did learn to speak Swedish, much less Norwegian. His son, Oscar I, and his grandson, Oscar II, also served as kings of both Sweden and Norway. The Bernadottes are the royal family of Sweden today and Carl XVI Gustaf is dearly loved as a true Swede.

History ought to be read like a detective novel or a mystery story. One of the mysteries to me has been why so many Norwegian families named their sons "Oscar." After all, Norway had been forced into accepting a Swedish ruler by military threat. Besides, I'd heard some things as a young boy that Swedes and Norwegians were supposed to be "cool" toward each other. Why then did so many Norse immigrant families name their sons after King Oscar who lived in Stockholm?

I think I have found the answer. Oscar II was king of Norway from 1872 to 1905, when he resigned the Norwegian throne. He lived two more years as the king of Sweden. That was the main emigrant period from Norway to America. He was a popular king in Norway and had been called the "Norwegian prince." Immigrant families honored King Oscar by naming their sons after him.

There may be another reason, too. In my community, almost every family had a son named "Oscar." I learned that a great many of these immigrants were from Trondelag, the area around Trondheim (it was called "Trondhjem" until 1930). D. K. Derry, an English historian who lives in Oslo, has pointed out that the early migration into Trondelag had come by way of Sweden and there has always been a pro-Swedish sentiment in that part of Norway.

So one of the great mysteries of my childhood is solved. I now know why my father was named "Oscar." If he ever knew the reason, he never told me. And I suspect that he lived his whole life quite unaware of the "French connection."

SWEDISH MEMORIES

by Sharon Lofgren Garrison

My grandfather Rudolf Lofgren, the oldest of ten children, came from Kösta, Sweden. He told me that when he was eight years old, he started working in the glass factory in Kösta by sweeping the floors. Also at eight years old, he had his tonsils removed without the benefit of anesthesia or numbing. His mother was with him, and on the way home she said, "Rudolf, why don't you sit on my lap?" He said, "No, mama, the boys will make fun of me."

My grandfather Lofgren came to America with two of his brothers, and they all went to Corning, New York where they worked as glass-blowers in the glass factory there. On their voyage to America, one of the brothers, Thor, met a girl from Norway whose destination was Chicago. When Thor made enough money, he went to Chicago, married this girl, and started a neon-sign factory in Franklin Park, Illinois. In one of the buildings in his factory he employed only handicapped people. I believe it was one of the first because he was honored by the White House and received an annual dinner invitation from the President for many years.

I was fortunate to have my grandparents so long. They celebrated 72 years of marriage and lived to be 95 and 97 years of age.

My mother was Swedish as well as my father. They both spoke Swedish, especially if they didn't want my sister and me to know what they were saying. I had a wonderful childhood, and we observed many of the Swedish traditions. My grandmother Lofgren had three sisters, all married, but they had no children, so my sister and I were the only young people, and at Christmastime we were spoiled—but only in the Swedish way, conservatively!

These wonderful aunts made the most amazing food, Swedish of course. Christmas Eve was a feast. It seemed as if it must have taken three days to prepare. After eating the lutfisk with cream sauce, korv, sylta, sill, chicken, meatballs, lingonberries, vegetables, cheese, breads, pickled beets, for dessert we had boiled rice in cream sauce with cold milk if you wanted it, cinnamon on the top, and an almond in the bowl. Our tradition was that whoever got the almond would be the next one to marry. It always seemed to end up with the old uncles who, of course, were already married. Oh well, there was always next year!

After this Swedish Christmas Eve feast, we went home and participated in our neighborhood bonfire and carol sing, another tradition. Christmas morning (very early—I think around 6:30 AM) we went to our church, the Swedish Lutheran Church, for Julotta service. I felt very proud that my mother knew and sang all the songs in Swedish. I learned a few lines. The service was beautiful in candlelight and seemed to be the way to begin Christmas Day.

Very good friends of mine, Ann and Axel Lager (both of Swedish descent), were like grandparents to my children. When King Carl XVI Gustaf first visited Jamestown in 1976, my friends took my son who was around five years old with them to the airport to see the king depart. It was raining and all the dignitaries, including the king, were wearing black raincoats. My son asked, "Where is the king?" My friends pointed him out and my son asked, "Why isn't he wearing his crown?" My friend explained that he only wears his crown on very special occasions. My son thought for a moment and then said, "Yeah, like Thanksgiving."

I have another story which happened during my trip to Stockholm, Sweden. I visited all my many aunts, uncles and cousins and stayed about a month before I departed for Germany where I would live for two years. The relatives I stayed with took me to the Strand Hotel, a very fancy hotel, for dinner and a goodbye celebration. Before dinner, I had a Swedish drink (they are very strong), and during the meal wine was served. After dinner, we moved to the dance floor. I felt very outgoing, and as I was showing one relative the Twist that was popular in the United States at that time, the relative said to me, "There is the Crown Prince Bertil." Not really thinking about what I was doing, I danced over to him and tapped him on the shoulder. He turned to me and bowed, and I made a quick curtsy. I'm sure my relatives wanted to be invisible! Of course, we all know Swedes—they wouldn't have said a word.

J. HENRY CARLSON

by Tanya Bilicki

My father, J. Henry Carlson, was born in Jamestown June 12, 1912. Henry was born into a family of former merchants. His father, C. S. Carlson, was born in Västergötland, Sweden, in June 1883 and came to America in 1903. He ran a restaurant in Sheffield, Pennsylvania, before coming to Jamestown in 1909. On November 30, 1910, he married Edith Erickson from Dalarna, Sweden.

C. S. Carlson first worked in Oscar Linbloom's meat market, then ran his own business at East Second and Cross Streets and was a partner of Hilding Rockman (Mardell Hanson's father) at two Foote Avenue stores. Eventually, Grandpa started his own meat market in the old City Public Market in Brooklyn Square, where many immigrants wanting to be successful merchants opened their own businesses. Grandpa's stall was distinguished from other meat stalls by being known as *"Baptist Carlson."* He was a pillar of the Swedish Baptist Church and was pleased when son Henry married Viola Edstam, daughter of Pastor Edstam.

The Public Market in Brooklyn Square closed in 1965 at which time Henry and Viola opened Viking Foods on West Third Street featuring Swedish specialties. They ran the store until 1977, when they both retired from the business.

After they retired, the Swedish Christmas tradition of making korv was carried on in the basement of their home. The twenty-foot "korv table," along with grinders and sausage equipment, were brought from the store and Henry and Viola, with family members, Gladys and Lyle Peterson, daughter Tanya, and son-in-law Richard Stawiarski, continued the tradition for many years.

Tanya sent the following articles from the Jamestown Post-Journal carrying news from "Fifty Years Ago" (**1946**):

"For the first time in modern local history, every meat market in Jamestown will close for a full week beginning next Monday, because of the acute shortage, members of the Retail Butchers' Association announced." *(Post-Journal, 9-19-96)*

"Jamestown meat markets will reopen on an individual basis, ending the ten-day period in which all meat markets were closed, J. Henry Carlson, president of the Jamestown Meat Dealers' Association, announced." *(Post-Journal, 10-2-96)*

J. Henry and C. S. Carlson at their meat stand at City Market

1934 **CITY PUBLIC MARKET**

CARLSON'S MEAT MARKET
Stalls 11 and 12   City Market

Quality Plus Prices Have Built Our Business

TEL. 64-151   FREE DELIVERY

S. WREN CLOVER

Butter, Eggs and Cheese
Wholesale and Retail

City Public Market   Phone 64982
Jamestown, N. Y.

WM. S. JONES CO.

Wholesale and Retail
TEA and COFFEE
NUTS AND NUT PRODUCTS

City Public Market   Jamestown, N. Y.
PHONE 6-898

John A. Swanson

Full Line of Fresh and Smoked Meats and all Fresh Dressed Poultry

CITY PUBLIC MARKET
Stall No. 1   Phone 52-132   Stall No. 1
Jamestown, N. Y.

Advertising for City Market—1934

"PRILLAR-GURI": THE COUNTRY GIRL WHO SAVED NORWAY

by Arland O. Fiske

Perhaps you have seen a picture of a Norwegian girl playing a long horn called a "lur." If so, it was likely meant to be "Prillar-Gurl." It's a story that inspires courage and partriotism. The year was 1612. There was war between the Joint kingdom of Denmark-Norway and Sweden. In those days, there were often disputes between the Scandinavian powers that led to military conflicts.

The political decisions for the joint kingdom were made in Copenhagen. King Christian IV was the leader of a kingdom joined by the "Union of Kalmar" in 1397, when Margaret I was queen. In this war, the Swedish king had recruited mercenaries from Holland and Scotland to come to his aid.

It has happened only a few times in history that the "savior" of a nation has been a woman, and hardly ever a girl of 17. Guri was an exception. She played a key role in defending the land. For over 350 years, the story of "Prillar-Guri" had been told, but no book could be found on it. In 1968, Arthur Stavig went to Norway to look for the complete story. After a painstaking search, he discovered it was being serialized in the *Romsdal Budstikke*, a daily newspaper. He took the story back to America and together with Marvel Arseth DeSordi translated it into English. Now the whole world can read about this heroine of old Norway.

Guri was an orphan and had been reared by foster parents in Romsdalen, near Molde. She had been a sickly girl and for this reason was taken to an old stave church up in the File Mountains (Filefjell) for prayers of healing. St. Thomas Church was the place for pilgrims to visit on Annunciation Day (March 25). Many of them left their crutches behind as they journeyed home. Whether it was the prayers, the long hike in the mountain air or a combination of both, we do not know, but Guri became radiantly healthy. She was getting ready for her wedding to Kjell, just as soon as he returned from the war. Little did they suspect that their lives would be tragically changed by an event already in progress of which they were innocent. Invading mercenaries would pass directly through their valley.

The Scots might have traveled through to Sweden with little incident, as did the Dutch through Trondheim, if their leader, Colonel George Sinclair, had not decided on a campaign of terror to conquer Norway first. Sinclair was a soldier with a charisma for leadership but whose ambition would not hesitate to employ the vilest treachery. His army, with two notable exceptions, was a band of cut-throats, recruited from the lowest dregs of society in western Europe. Their arrival on August 10 began a 16-day reign of terror which has not been forgotten. Every farm building was burned to the ground, children and old people murdered and maidens were ravished. They looted and feasted on whatever food and liquor they could find. To make it even more frightful, Sinclair had a huge bloodhound named "Ralf" that was able to sniff out people and farms at a great distance.

Because of the war with Sweden, there were only old men with crude weapons to defend the valley which led to Gudbrandsdal, Kjell's home. Beyond that lay the unguarded heartland of central Norway. It was Guri who carried the warning about the unsuspecting Sinclair and his dog. He had seen her and had resolved to make her his prize of war. She traveled without regard to pain and danger of the wild animals in the mountains. With every breath, she prayed, "Lord Jesus, lead me to warn the people and to save Kjell's family from this terrible enemy." When she arrived at the end of her journey, she didn't look much like a bride. But the people had been warned and now worked feverishly to build an ambush at a narrow pass near Kringen, upstream from Lesje and Dovre.

In the strangest of happenings, Mary Sinclair was also hurrying through the mountains, trying to stop her husband. Carrying her newborn son, she wept bitter tears at her husband's deeds.

An avalanche of rocks was constructed to greet the invaders. Just beyond a bend on a narrow pass, a barricade was built. Across the river in plain sight of the enemy stood Guri. She was dressed in her bridal clothes, her wedding with Kjell having just been completed, as he had unexpectedly returned from the war. Guri played her lur as a signal to the defenders that the hated enemy was approaching.

A musket shot from the bushes mortally wounded Sinclair. Then the rocks began to roll. Almost all of the 800 invaders perished. Of the survivors, only 16 escaped massacre by the angry farmers.

The victory for Norway brought a tragic end to Guri's dreams. In the aftermath of the melee, Kjell tried to save Sinclair's son from harm. The child's mother, overcome with grief and fearing for her son, misunderstood Kjell's intentions and stabbed him to death. Guri's marriage lasted only hours, but she is remembered for what took place at Kringen that day, August 26, 1612. "Prillar-Guri" will live forever as a national hero in Norway's long struggle for freedom.

IT'S A SMALL WORLD AFTER ALL

by Sandra Sandy

Although I had only one ancestor who emigrated from Sweden, we were able to find out quite a bit of information about him. His name was Claus Olsson, the father of my paternal grandmother. He came from a small town called Gillberga in the province of Värmland. Although there are no longer any relatives to visit there, we wanted to see the area and the church.

The church was located a little distance from the town. We parked and walked around the church and were able to go inside that lovely building. It is always exciting to know you are walking where your forefathers have walked. The church sits up on a hill with a wonderful view of the countryside. One wall dates back to the 11th century. There are several large Viking burial mounds around the church.

The caretaker of the church came in and greeted us. We chatted with him for a few minutes and he mentioned that the pastor was from New York State. She was in Gilleberga on a two-year assignment. She was in her office in a detached building, and he offered to call her. We were strolling in the graveyard when she walked up. Her name was Lotta Cohen. She is an ordained LCA [Lutheran Church in America] pastor, schooled in the United States, but of Swedish birth. Pastor Cohen served some churches in a synod in upstate New York. When we mentioned that we are members of First Lutheran Church in Jamestown, she said that is one of the churches that sponsored her for her years in seminary. What a small world!

As we were walking and talking, she mentioned that there is an elderly gentleman in the congregation who may have some historical information about the area, and past residents. She offered to phone him. I spoke a little with him. He couldn't share much information, and there was a language problem. He was, however, able to indicate that one area farm, named Luserud, was likely the Olsson property long ago. He indicated the buildings are all gone but directed us to the area. We left the church, with many thanks to Pastor Cohen.

We drove past the area but there was nothing remarkable to see—just the knowledge that this was the right area. We are always amazed at how friendly and helpful the Swedish people are when you are searching for information from the past. And I will always be grateful for the opportunity given to me.

Orebro Church

I WISH I HAD ASKED QUESTIONS SOONER

by Lamae Ahlgren McCullor

I title my story *"I Wish I Had Asked Questions Sooner"* because I have lost so much family history by not asking family members to tell their stories before they passed. Though I do have many memories of my own and stories I have been told by my parents, I find, now that I am trying to create my families' genealogy, there is so much more I need to know. Ask your questions now—the tales of our Scandinavian ancestors are leaving us, never to be told again.

I am a 3rd and 4th generation child of Swedish immigrants. I would like to share a little of their stories about coming to the United States and starting a new life and families in the United States.

On my mother's side, my grandfather's family (Adolphson/Borkman) settled in Chandler's Valley, Pennsylvania, an early local settlement of Swedish immigrants. Information I have tells me these great-grandparents came to the United States around 1882, arriving through Philadelphia. As was the case of many of the early settlers, the men were listed as farmers and farm laborers on the early census records. The young women who worked outside the home were employed as housekeepers for other residents in the valley. The family attended both the Hessel Valley Church, where my grandfather was confirmed, and the Mission Church in Chandler's Valley, where a few are buried in the church cemetery. Some of this family remained in the Chandler's Valley area. My Grandpa Borkman moved to Jamestown and then to Busti, New York, just over the New York border. My grandfather was born in the United States and married a Frederickson from Jamestown who was also born here. My great-great grandparents Frederickson with their daughter, my great grandmother, and her other siblings came to the United States about 1887. The Fredericksons attended the First Lutheran

Church in Jamestown. When my great-great-grandfather Frederickson passed away, he was one of the oldest members of the church and a member of the Hultgren Sick Benefit Society. My great-great-grandfather Frederickson was listed as a quarryman at the Allen Street Stone Quarry. My Grandpa Borkman was an auto mechanic, working on cars dating back to the Ford Model A's and T's. My Grandma Borkman was a homemaker after her marriage but did work in the woolen mills in Jamestown early in her life.

Unfortunately, I never met my Grandma Borkman as she passed before I was born and my grandfather passed away when I was fairly young, also. I do remember fun times with Grandpa though, especially when he would take me for a ride in what I thought was an old car—not sure if it was or not. We usually stopped at a candy shop on Third Street near the bridge during these trips and I would get to pick out some candy. Grandpa had a real sweet tooth, and even at a young age I sensed Grandpa stopped here often as the gentleman behind the counter seemed to know him.

On my father's side, both my grandparents, Ahlgren/Holmquist, came to the United States in 1903, in their late teens. They did not know each other in Sweden; they met in Jamestown and were married here. Both of them came through Ellis Island and both had family members already settled in Jamestown, NY. My grandfather came with his mother and a sister; his father had passed away in Sweden. When they arrived in NYC, my grandfather and his sister each had $5 and their mother had $25. They also had train tickets to my grandfather's brother, John, in Jamestown with whom they stayed on Derby Street. My grandmother came with her sister and also arrived at Ellis Island in 1903. She and her sister each had $5 and train tickets to take them to their brother, Carl, in Jamestown. My grandparents owned a small farm at the city line on Forest Avenue. My grandfather was a carpenter and worked for a period of time at Dahlstrom's in Jamestown. My grandmother was predominantly a homemaker but also did domestic work for other families and worked in the woolen mills in Jamestown. They had a small farm at the city line on Forest Avenue. The farm provided them with food for their family and extra to sell to the public. There were often flowers and produce for sale in front of their home. I have been told that people often bought Sweet Pea flowers for corsages and Gladiolas for cemetery and home use from them. They also had regular customers for eggs and berry fruits which Grandma would walk to deliver throughout the Forest Avenue neighborhoods. She was also a weaver, making rag rugs for the families and selling some, too. They became members of the Swedish Salvation Army early on with a strong dedication to the church throughout their lives.

It was fun to visit grandma and grandpa. We often had to go up into the field to find grandpa tending his garden. I loved to see the chickens and what a treat when I was allowed to mow with grandpa's reel mower and feed the chickens the grass clippings. Grandma sometimes would let me help roll rags into balls, which she had previously cut into strips and sewn together for her rug weaving. I soon learned there was an art to making the ball evenly round. I don't think we ever left their home without something to take with us, perhaps some cardamom *"bullar"* (buns or rolls), eggs, berries, or a rag rug. We also almost always had coffee, which was never just coffee; there was always plenty of food to go with the coffee.

With a strong Swedish heritage, Swedish foods and traditions have been important in my life. I remember grandma making *saft* (juice) from her berries. What a treat it was to have a cold glass in the summer at her home! *Kräm* was another treat that was made from her own berries too. My grandma made the best cardamom rolls. *Pepparkakor* were always on the table at Christmas time, and grandma would be disgusted if she hadn't rolled the dough thin enough . . . "they are too 'tick'," she would say, but they tasted great to us. I try to carry on at least a few of the food traditions during the holiday season always making sill, korv, and pepparkakor every year; it just isn't Christmas without them.

DAD'S FLAG

by Barbara Hillman Jones

My dad was twenty years old when he went to Sweden with his parents in 1928. They were going to visit their relatives whom my dad had never met and whom his parents had not seen in many years since they left their homeland to make a new life in America. I'm sure my dad was very excited about meeting his grandparents, aunts and uncles, cousins, and other relatives, and I'm certain that his parents were looking forward to the visit with great anticipation. Perhaps when they left Sweden, they felt as so many immigrants did—very likely they would never see each other again.

My father's paternal grandparents lived on a farm called Åltomtobro, located in Vänge, Uppsala, Sweden. When they arrived, dad and his parents were happily surprised that their relatives had raised the American flag on the tall flagpole in the yard near the farmhouse as a welcome to them. Flying the American flag along with the Swedish flag was for dad's relatives the best welcome they could give their American relatives who had come back home. When they visited other relatives in other locations, they received the same kind of welcome.

My dad never forgot that trip and meeting his relatives in Sweden. Dad had learned to speak Swedish impeccably while he was growing up, and he spoke Swedish extremely well for all of his life. He would talk about things that happened during that visit, and they were often told with tears in his eyes.

Dad never forgot the welcome shown to them by their family on that trip by flying the American flag, and when he and my mother had their own home, he adopted the same custom. Every time they had Swedish visitors, the Swedish flag flew in their yard to welcome them. But the nicest thing was that after my sister Karin and I moved away, whenever we went home for a visit dad had the American flag flying for us. When we arrived, the first thing we saw was the flag in their yard in anticipation of our visit, and it flew until we had to go back to our individual homes. When we drove up their street and saw the flag flying, we knew all was well.

In 1974, I went to Sweden with my dad. He was sixty-six years old at that time, and it had been forty-six years since his first visit. We visited all the relatives who were still living, and everywhere we went, the American flag was flying to welcome us.

My husband David and I went to Scandinavia in 1991, and while we were in Stockholm, my father's cousin Sven picked us up and took us to his home to have lunch with him and his family. On the coffee table in the living room was a small American flag—upside-down! While Sven was out of the room at one point, David quietly untied the little flag from its pole, turned it around, and tied it back up. Sven never knew that it had been flying upside-down.

I remember those experiences with great appreciation and love for those people who honored us in such a delightful way.

SWEDISH COVENANT HOSPITAL, CHICAGO, ILLINOIS

by Karin Hillman Oeffling

My family lived in Jamestown, New York. I grew up with a happy Swedish heritage that we all enjoyed. We attended Zion Covenant Church, another part of our Swedish memories. Those dear old Swedes not only taught me about Jesus, but they showed me Jesus; and I committed my life to following Him at an early age. Swedish Sunday School teachers, Swedish hymns, Swedish foods and traditions were my life. I even studied the Swedish language in high school taught by Mrs. Esther Erickson. Swedish was offered every other year with Italian in between.

I wanted to serve Jesus whom I had come to love, and I felt I could do this best by becoming a nurse. The Covenant denomination had a college, seminary, and hospital in the Swedish neighborhoods at Foster and California Avenues on the north side of Chicago. Swedish Covenant Hospital had a three-year diploma program in nursing, and I applied for entry during my junior year of high school. It scares me speechless that I never applied anywhere else, but by the grace of God, I was accepted.

Swedish Covenant Hospital serves a large area of North Chicago. Even in the 1960s, faces were no longer mostly Swedish but included many people of different races and ethnic backgrounds. Today this impressive and up-to-the-minute facility covers many blocks and includes a huge cardiac center. I am very pleased to have been part of the last class of nurses graduated from Swedish Covenant Hospital School of Nursing in 1969 and proud of the role my hospital has taken in the community.

I loved the three years that I spent at Swedish Covenant Hospital as a student nurse, and I received a thorough and practical education. Young and a bit overwhelmed when I came, Miss Delores Johnson who was the Director of the new nursing program at North Park College, and from

Jamestown and Zion Covenant Church, invited me for supper one Sunday evening. She served Swedish cardamom coffee bread, Swedish rice pudding, cold meat and cheese. Just like home! I knew I belonged.

God has given me awesome experiences in nursing that began in Chicago. Not only have I been able to use my skills here in the US, but also in short-term medical missions in Peru, The Middle East, Kenya and Uganda. The Christian care and compassion that I saw modeled at Swedish Covenant Hospital had a profound influence on me. The effects of the vision, sacrifice, faithfulness, and hard work of those early Swedish founders of the hospital have benefitted the neighborhood and the world. To God be the glory!

ON MY SWEDISH HERITAGE

by Gladys Carlson Peterson

Excerpted from her presentation
to the American Swedish Heritage Foundation—February 1, 2002
(transcribed from a recording on U-Tube)

My Mom, Edith Erickson

My mother came to the New World in 1902. She said goodbye to all her family in her small village, not knowing if she would ever see them again or the land which she loved. She never did get to go back to Sweden. She always wanted to go back, but her dream never came true. Working as a chambermaid, she had saved money to take that trip back to see her family, but the bank in which she had her money went bankrupt and she had to give up her idea.

Poor economic conditions were the reason many left Sweden. My mother came from the province of Dalarna where the Dala horses were made. Children started school at age 7 and went for about 6-8 years, so that would make them about 14-15 when they quit school. After that, they had to go to work. My mom took care of an evangelist's children, and when he was going to America he asked if my mom would like to come along and take care of their children. Her family thought that would be a wonderful opportunity as America was known as the land of opportunity and freedom. So she applied for her "leaving papers" and in Swedish they contain the names of her parents, her birth date, and the place where she was born. It also says that she was vaccinated but "*not* confirmed in the Swedish church". You see, in Sweden the Lutheran church was the state church and you were baptized, confirmed, married and buried in that church. But my mom's parents were Baptists and not Lutherans, and the Baptists were a very small minority in Sweden at that time. My cousin Cornelia tells of having fights with other kids in the neighborhood because they were Baptists. Her papers also stated that she was a good citizen and eligible for marriage and that she was moving to the United States in North America.

When they came to Jamestown, New York, the evangelist said they couldn't afford her and that she would have to find another job, so she worked as a chambermaid for many wealthy families, including the Kents and the Fields. These families were good to her, teaching her the language and how to cook. She made 75 cents a week, but that included her room, board and her uniform.

During the period of great immigration, the 1860s through the 1920s, thousands of people came to Jamestown. It is estimated that at one time the population of Jamestown was 42,000, 22,000 of them were of Swedish origin. When the Swedes came to Jamestown by train, the Swedes from the churches would meet them and help them find a place to live and work and get them acclimated to life in America. This way they also got them into their churches which was my mom's life the whole time she lived. Their social life was their church, and that is where they met their future spouse and had so much fun with the other young people who spoke their language.

That is how my mom came to America, searching for a better life, and I think she thought it would help her family financially to support one less child.

My Dad, Carl S. Carlson

My dad was the youngest of six children. His brothers and sisters had come here before his arrival. He was 20 and also came in 1902, possibly to escape the draft as all Swedes at 19 had to serve in the Army. He possibly also came for religious freedom. He too became a born-again Christian through an evangelist he had heard in his area of Västergötland, Sweden. He also became a Baptist which was not a popular thing with his family who were members of the Mission Church. Then too, he had heard of the good life in America. Both my mom and dad came through Boston and not Ellis Island. Dad was born in 1883, the son of Carl Johnson, and when a boy was born in Sweden, he took his father's first name and added "son," so he was "Carl's son."

On my mother's passage contract, it says that the steamer line left Göteborg, went to England, and then after two to three weeks, it arrived in Boston. Then she went by train to Worcester. The cost was 146 kronor which was approximately $25 at that time. Dad took the train to New York City and from there to Austin, Pennsylvania. When he arrived on the train with the windows open to get air, he bit into some fruit that he had, and the juice went all over him. He thought it tasted terrible, and so he sailed the whole bag out of the window of the train! He had bitten into tomatoes, and he'd never seen them before.

Why did so many people go to Austin from Sweden? In Sweden the big industry was lumbering, and many Swedes worked in the woods, with the timber, lumber, and the sawmill in Austin. In nearby Sheffield, Pennsylvania he had an accident which caused his arm to be sawed off. He spent many months in the Warren Hospital where they tried a new process of screwing his arm together with many screws. That arm was always shorter than the other, and he had many abscesses from the screws which kept working themselves out. He had always wanted to go back to Sweden and had been saving his money for that reason, but with the accident and the hospital bills, it took all of his money. You see, there was no workmen's compensation in those days. So for a short time, he ran a restaurant in Sheffield. He never knew how to cook, but he served the lumbermen in the area. From there he went to Jamestown where started in the meat business. He became a citizen in Austin in 1911 disavowing his allegiance to Sweden and their king.

He had learned the meat business in Sweden and when we were over there to visit the home where he was born, we saw the slaughterhouse and we saw the land that was not conducive to farming. Naturally, I cried the whole time I was in Sweden because I was visiting the land my parents had told me about and the home where they were born.

After my mom's dad died, my *mormor* wrote my mom and told her that her dad had died and that things were hard in Sweden, wondering what they could work out. It was during World War I, and the letter with the black border meant that it was a death letter. Well, in 1919 after the war, my *mormor*, age 65, came with her two daughters and one son came. They stayed with us until the children found an apartment, and my grandmother stayed with us. She couldn't speak English, so we children had to learn Swedish in order to communicate with her.

At an early age, I learned the Swedish bedtime prayer:

Gud som haver barnen kär, se till mig som liten är.
Translation: God who makes the dear children, look after me who am little.

And He certainly has done that and continues to it. And then, of course, before meals we said the Swedish grace:

I Jesu namn till bords vi gå, Välsigna Gud den mat vi få.
Translation: In Jesus' name to the table we go, God bless the food we receive.

Yes, I know you all know that!

The older we get the more we appreciate our heritage and look back at our roots. My parents came to America because people in Sweden dreamed of the good life here where there was opportunity for work and freedom to worship and make a living. They found each other here in Jamestown at the Swedish Baptist Church, and I'm glad they did. They established a Christian home, learned the language quickly, and worked hard, thus enjoying the ideal place to live.

Letter—Death Notice

JEAN SIBELIUS AND THE MUSIC OF FINLAND

by Arland O. Fiske

There are few nations whose people I admire so much as Finland. There are few Finns so dearly loved by their countrymen as Jean Sibelius (1865-1957). His portrait of later years depicts a solid executive jaw with drawn cheeks and eyes focused on the future with determination.

Finland has produced many outstanding musicians. Among those who have become well known outside their country are: Erik Tullinberg (1761-1814), the first known Finnish composer; Selim Palmgren (1878-1951), called the "Finnish Chopin"; and Joonas Kokkonen (1921-1996), a leading authority in Finnish music.

But Sibelius is by common consent the greatest of them all. His "Finlandia" has been playing in my soul since childhood. The hymn, "Thee God, We Praise," is sung to this music, producing an expression of strength and reverence. The music for "Finlandia" was written when Sibelius was in his early thirties. The Russian rulers of Finland sensed its patriotic effect and forbade its performance.

Artists with the ability of Sibelius are not without their eccentric side. To make sure that his studio would have silence while he composed, he built a large "dollhouse" for his five daughters at a safe distance from his residence. This is in contrast to Edvard Grieg who built a "composing cottage" at a distance from his house in Bergen. Still, he was warm-hearted to his family and townsmen. Guests were served wines of rare vintage. As a young man, he fell in love with Vienna and the waltzes of Strauss.

Sibelius imitated no other musicians. His work flowed out of the loneliness and lofty aspirations of his own soul. The violin was his first love. He would stand in the bow of a boat and play to the birds and waves, reproducing the sounds of the wind and rustling branches. The Finnish epic myths, "Kalevala," influenced his musical expressions of patriotism. A magnificent concert hall has been erected in Helsinki in honor of Sibelius where over 200 concerts a year are held.

Finland passed from Swedish to Russian rule in 1809. Not until December 6, 1917, did Finland gain independence. During the Winter War of 1939-1940, Sibelius, then 74, refused to go into an air-raid shelter. Instead, he angrily charged out into the cold with an old hunting rifle and fired away at the Russian bombers.

Finns are a proud and patriotic people. It's true that they are often criticized for being careful not to publicly offend the Kremlin. But no nation has been so conscientious about repaying its war debts to the United States. In the secret conferences of World War II between the Allied leaders, Churchill and Roosevelt refused to allow Stalin to reclaim Finland as Russian territory.

Music continues to inspire love for native land in the hearts of the Finns. This little nation boasts over 60 music institutes and 11 symphony orchestras. Over 60,000 people attend the annual folk music festival in Kaustinen, a city of only 3,400. The world needs more people like the Finns. So if you are Finnish, you have reason to be proud.

SCHOOL DAZE

by Carol Lind Kindberg

In the late 1920s, my in-laws immigrated from Halland, Sweden. Thore and Svea Kindberg were married in 1931 in Jamestown where they lived on Wescott Street. Their eldest son, Gunnard (my husband), started kindergarten at Willard Street School on Swede Hill. Only Swedish was spoken at home. As he came home after his first day at school, he told his mother, "They talk funny!" Soon he was a part of the "funny talking" crowd. He never lost his ability to communicate in the "Mother Tongue."

THE EMIGRATION OF ANDERS AND ANNA LARSON AND THE REUNITING OF THEIR DESCENDENTS 141 YEARS LATER

by Denise Nichols

The emigration of my family from Sweden began in 1869, when my great-great grandfather, Anders Johan Larson, who was 32, took his wife Anna, who was 37, and left Småland, Sweden to emigrate to North America. Anders left behind his parents, Lars and Lena Abrahamsson, and his older brother, Gustav. Anders and Anna were so poor that the Lutheran church assisted them financially for the journey by giving them "poor relief."

Anders and Anna, whose last name was changed to Lawson, brought with them their four children, Johannes, age 11; Emelie Christine, age 7; Augusta Elise, age 4; and Claes, age 2. Sadly, Augusta Elise and Claes did not survive the journey and died in 1869.

Once they arrived in North America, Anders and Anna and their two children first settled in Falconer, New York where two more children were born. Fredrick, who was later to become my great-grandfather, was born in 1870 and the youngest, Selma, was born in 1872.

After 18 years in Falconer, Anders and Anna and their family moved to Willard Street in Jamestown. In addition to their homestead on Willard Street, they were able to purchase extra property on Willard Street Extension, which Anders farmed. Many years later, Ander's grandson remembered him telling that as he drove his horse and wagon up Willard Street, he would pick up the horse droppings that he found on Willard

Street to take to his farm land to use as fertilizer. This caused him to be referred to by his neighbors as "that crazy Swede."

Frederick remained in the Jamestown area, and in 1900, when he was 30 years old, he married Jennie Farm, whose parents owned a store in Jamestown. Frederick and Jennie had four children: Richard in 1901, Harold in 1904, Helen in 1909, and Marguerite in 1913 (who was later to become my grandmother).

In 1927, when Jennie was only 49 years old, she died of Spinal Meningitis, leaving behind her husband and her sons, who were 26 and 23, and her daughters, who were 18 and 14.

Frederick, who was 57 at the time of Jennie's death, lived 6 more years, during which time he traveled to Sweden for the first time in his life to meet his ancestors, who were still living in Småland.

At the age of 63, Frederick suffered a heart attack while cutting wood in the forest. His son Harold, who was 29 at the time, had been with him cutting wood until Harold had gone up to the house for dinner. When his dad did not arrive at the house shortly after as expected, Harold returned to the woods where he found that his dad had died. Harold carried his dad back to the house. After Frederick's death, correspondence between the family left in Sweden and the family in North America ceased.

In 1933, Frederick and Jennie's daughter Marguerite married Gilbert Thompson. Gilbert came from a family who had emigrated from Denmark. His parents, Peter and Johanna, along with Peter's siblings, had left Denmark in 1908 while Johanna was pregnant with Gilbert. The Thompsons had originally settled in Minnesota, where they had four more sons and a daughter born before moving to the Falconer area to settle. The older Thompson children had started school without being able to speak even a word of English.

Gilbert and Marguerite had two sons, Ronald born in 1935 and Kenneth (my dad) in 1937. Kenneth married Jeane Casler in 1963 and they had two children, Eric in 1964 and Denise (myself) in 1968. Ronald also had two sons, Daniel and Curtis.

The two brothers' families continued Swedish traditions at Christmas as the two families got together when the children were growing up and even today with grandchildren. Christmas dinners have always included herring and meat, barley and potato korv. Kenneth and Jeane have often made their own korv, using old Swedish recipes.

To stay connected with their Scandinavian roots, Kenneth and Jeane and Denise and her husband, Benjamin Steven, whose grandfather also was an emigrant from Sweden, attend the Scandinavian Culture study days in Jamestown and have learned some of the traditional Swedish arts. Kenneth has learned the art of chip carving and Jeane and Denise do Swedish weaving and Huck toweling.

In 2010, 141 years after Anders left his brother Gustav behind in Sweden and 77 years since the last correspondence between the two families, Gustav's great-grandchildren, Gillis Claeson and Berith Arvidson and their spouses, who were still living in Småland, Sweden decided to contact the great-grandchildren of Anders. Kenneth and Jeane received a letter from Gillis and his wife Dagny and Berith and her husband, Olof. The two families have now shared pictures back and forth and have been able to compare how life has turned out for the descendents of Gustav, who chose to remain in Sweden and how it has turned out for the descendents of Anders, who chose to emigrate to North America. The two families are now planning a reunion in Sweden in the near future.

Anders and Anna Larson

SOREN KIERKEGAARD—A DANE WHOSE IDEAS OUTLIVED HIM

by Arland O. Fiske

Danes are supposed to be of two varieties, happy ones and gloomy ones. That is, of course, an oversimplification. I know many who are serious about life and yet delightful company. Soren Kierkegaard (1813-1855) was called the "melancholy Dane." He has left a permanent mark on the world for being the "father of existentialism," a philosophy that struggles to find meaning to life.

Soren's father was a dominating influence in the home. As a little boy, he had lived in western Jutland, the same area from which my wife's family (Kirkegaard) originates. He had herded sheep alone in the open land, summer and winter, in all kinds of weather. This can be lonely. One day, he became so depressed that he stood on a sand dune and cursed God for his unhappy existence.

When Soren's father was 12, he moved with his family to Copenhagen. He grew up to become a wealthy merchant. At age 40, haunted by his past, he transferred his business to a relative and devoted all his time to his family. He must have been a hardy man as he lived to be 82. Soren was born when his father was 56.

Like his father, Soren had a brilliant mind and a melancholy spirit. He anguished over the meaning of life. He also inherited a vivid imagination. His father would take his hand and they would walk around the table imagining that they were in a forest or going past a bakery on a crowded street, with all the noises and smells of the city.

A stern brand of Christianity was taught in the Kierkegaard home. Sin and holiness were seen as "black and white," with no shades of gray. When he entered the University, Soren rebelled against the religion of his home. This caused a break with his father, though they were later reconciled.

At age 28, a traumatic event occurred in Soren's life. He was engaged to marry Regine Olsen. But he brooded over his unworthiness of her so much that he broke the engagement, despite Regine's contrary feelings. His condition has been described as "manic-depressive phychosis." He went from highest exultation to deepest depression. From the writings of Martin Luther, he learned how to face his suffering.

He had a running battle with the State Church. Though he graduated from seminary, he was never ordained. His attack was not on the Christian faith but against "rationalism" in the church, which made reason rather than Scripture the authority for faith. God was always a serious encounter for him. He saw truth as "dialectic"; that is, in opposite pairs. If God was holy, then Soren was sinful. His method of thinking has influenced both Christian and atheistic existentialism. He was a prolific writer. Among his best known books are "Fear and Trembling," "Either/Or," and "Edifying Discourses."

While I do not claim to be a "Kierkegaardian" (except by marriage), there is much of value that I have learned from this famous Danish religious thinker. He remains one of Denmark's greatest influences on the world. He was a Dane whose ideas outlived him.

NOBODY SPEAKS SWEDISH TO ME ANYMORE

by Yvonne Thorstenson McNallie

What I miss most (after my Mom and Dad and beloved Godfather, Albin Peterson), is hearing the Swedish language.

My Dad, John Thorstenson, came to America from Sweden via Canada. This was in the early 1920s and Dad was only about 20 when he came to Jamestown. Although there was a big Swedish community, it was difficult to find work without speaking English and as many immigrants did, he went to night school to learn the language of his newly adopted country. He always spoke with a Swedish accent but even when he spoke Swedish, he often threw in a few English words.

My Mom, Alice Swanson, was born in this country to immigrants from Sweden and spoke only Swedish until she went to kindergarten. I'm sure that Swedish was always spoken in their home, but my mother was the only one of the five siblings who spoke Swedish. In fact, her Swedish was purer than Dad's. Years later, when we had relatives from Sweden or when they visited Dad's home country, there was always laughing and teasing about which one was the born Swede.

I remember being among friends and relatives and hearing the Swedish. I learned to understand almost everything said but unfortunately never learned to speak Swedish. Before I visited Sweden in 1996, I took Swedish from Jeff Kroon at Jamestown Community College (in fact, I took it twice, once with my friend Joan Shevory and once with Svea Hjalmarson, who just wanted to polish up a little) but didn't seem to be able to work up the nerve to actually speak it. I'm not a particularly shy person, but somehow I was reticent about speaking a language that wasn't my first language, and I got by listening to Swedish and answering in English, while my relatives pretty much did the same thing in reverse. It worked, but I wish I had tried harder.

When I was a kid most of Jamestown was either Swedish or Italian, and it was customary to hear both languages spoken on the streets and in the stores. I imagine that almost anyone in Jamestown could speak at least a few words of Swedish. I thought little of having parents that spoke a second language, and I'm sure most of my peers felt the same way. I remember an incident in grade school at Charles Street School when a man of Albanian descent came to the office and could not make himself understood a girl in my class, Martha Vangel, was called to the office to translate for the man. That was not an unusual occurrence, although Albanian was not a common language in Jamestown at that time.

Back in those days parents did not hire babysitters to go out for an evening, at least not in my parents' circle, and I went with them when they visited friends and relatives. What fun it was to listen to their laughter and hear the Swedish language from friends of theirs like Gunnar Ahlstedt, Emil and Irene Seaburg, Carl and Mary Johnson, Carl and Ingrid Hogland, my aunt and uncle Thorsten and Greta, and of course, my Godfather, who remained a bachelor all his life but who spent much of his time with my family. There was always coffee and some of the wonderful pastries that Swedes make so well. I loved those evenings.

Mom and Dad belonged to the Skone Club, and that was fun, too. We always had treats and could run around in the large facility located in the Nordic Temple on the corner of Second and Prendergast Streets.

Dad developed dementia in his last few years and remarkably spoke Swedish less than he had before, but sometimes surprising us, as when he spoke a mild Swedish exclamation while coming out of anesthesia after surgery for a broken hip. Mom and I looked at each other and grinned . . . Dad remembered his Swedish!

After Dad died, Mom spoke Swedish less and less because there was no one left to talk to except very occasionally. She kept a clear mind and a remarkable memory, and I know that she hadn't forgotten anything; but the need wasn't there.

Now it is sometimes weeks or months at a time before I hear the language that was such a big part of my life. Thankfully, my cousin, Pete Thorstenson, speaks Swedish well and keeps it a little fresh in my mind. But if anyone speaks Swedish to me, I love to listen!

Mom & Dad, c.1932 or 1933

Thorsten and John, taken in Canada to send to family in Sweden

THE HAGLUND/NELSON EXPERIENCE IN JAMESTOWN

by Margaret Mae Haglund Lynch

Both sides of my family came from Sweden, including my Dad, Paul Thorwald Haglund who was two years old when he came here from Stockholm (born in Gävle 1/1/1904). They came to Jamestown and my grandfather, Paul J. Haglund, worked in a factory there. The family grew, adding sons Henry and Floyd and daughter Evelyn, and then my grandmother, Marguerite M. Westergren Haglund, died of pneumonia from knocking down icicles a couple weeks after their youngest son John was born in 1914. After his wife's death, my grandfather sent for his old girlfriend, Elin Persson, in Sweden to marry him and take care of the children. Another son, Ernie, was born to Paul and Elin.

Henry Haglund was pastor of three churches in the Jamestown area in the 1940s and 1950s. John Haglund was proprietor of Jensen/Haglund Memorial Works. John's son, Gerald Haglund, is chaplain of the Heritage Homes, and we felt good leaving my mother for the winter when he was there.

My mother's mother, Augusta Bartolina Hanson, was born December 24, 1875 in Skogaby, Sweden. She was the youngest of four children. Her mother died two weeks later. She emigrated to the United States at the age of 23. Her future husband Carl Nelson was from the neighboring community of Årnabärga. Between Skogaby and Årnabärga was a pond where they met ice skating.

She arrived in the US on May 4, 1899 aboard the ship Aurania, accompanied by Carl's two sisters, Emma and Jennie. Augusta continued on to the Midwest where she found work as a domestic servant in Des Moines, Iowa, working in a large house for 50 cents to a dollar per week while learning English from her employers. She had to kill a chicken every week for Sunday dinner. This was a task that she didn't like (but it was a useful skill for her in later years on the farm).

Carl August Nelson was born May 2, 1874 in Årnabärga, Sweden, and he and his brother Andrew emigrated to America. Carl did a lot of traveling in the Midwest, working in such places as Minneapolis, Red Wing, Minnesota and Eau Claire, Wisconsin.

On July 31, 1902, Carl and Augusta were married in Curtis, Wisconsin. There they claimed homestead land, built a house and barn and began farming. They had Christian neighbors and held church services in homes.

Three boys were born to the Nelsons in Curtis, Nils Hjälmar on April 16, 1903, Albert Emanuel (of Nelson & Butts Florists) on Feb. 1, 1906, and Joseph Daniel on April 2, 1908.

In 1912, they left Wisconsin to return to Sweden. On the way to New York they got off the train in Jamestown to say goodbye to Carl's two sisters in Busti. Emma had married Victor Pearson and Jennie had married Axel Anderson. The sisters convinced him to stay in Busti, saying that he wouldn't be able to earn a living in Sweden. So they bought the Pilling farm on Lawson Road in Busti, down the road from Victor and Emma Pearson, whose son Edwin later owned Pearson's Market. On July 30, 1913, Augusta gave birth to a daughter, Esther Marie, my mother.

One day Carl had gone into Jamestown and started walking home late. Augusta was concerned about him and sent the boys to meet him with a horse and wagon. They brought Esther along for the ride. When Esther lost her stocking cap along the way, Albert went back to look for it in the darkness. He picked up a dark object, but it turned out to be horse manure!

One day Al and Joe walked to Sugar Grove to get a birthday gift for Esther. They bought a little wagon and started on the way home with it. When they came to a long steep hill (Shaw's Hill), they decided to ride the wagon down the hill. The wagon broke under the weight of the two boys and Carl had to repair the wagon before Esther could get her birthday gift.

On April 20, 1916, tragedy struck the family. With a storm threatening, the whole family was in the barn. The barn was struck by lightning and the whole family was knocked unconscious. When they awoke, they discovered that Hjälmar was dead and his cow and calf were also killed. In their grief, the next year, they sold the farm and moved into Jamestown where Carl found a job working for the city.

Joe begged his parents to buy another farm, and in 1920, the family bought a farm and moved back to Busti. This farm was on Southwestern Drive, about 4 or 5 miles from Jamestown. There was no electricity. They washed in a basin and took baths in a washtub. There were few cars in those days, and the family didn't have one. For church and other activities they walked to Jamestown. Augusta made 80 pounds of butter each week that they sold and delivered. In 1929, they sold the farm and moved to 448 South Main Street in Jamestown. Esther, who was then 16 years old, says "this was one of the happiest days of my life."

In 1948, my Dad flew to Sweden with my Grandmother Nelson to visit their relatives, hers in southern Sweden, and then my Dad went to Gävle to visit his family. This was the first and only time they both went back. My grandmother lived with us after my grandfather died and we spoke some Swedish then, besides going to the Salvation Army for classes with Barbara Hillman. The word I'll always remember is *"järnvägstationen."*

We always had smörgåsbord at my Haglund grandparents' house on Christmas Eve, and my grandfather would read the Christmas story from the Bible in Swedish. We still continue the tradition with smörgåsbord at Christmas, but modified it a little. We love to wake up to the smell of cardamom bread which my husband Jim does quite often in the bread machine. Swedish bakeries are disappearing.

We belonged to First Covenant Church of Jamestown, where Swedish was spoken in Sunday school until I was in confirmation class.

My Grandmother Nelson lived to be 100 years old, and in April 1976, the King of Sweden passed through Jamestown visiting all of the Swedish-born centenarians, but she passed away in March 1976 and went to see "her" King. We saw King Carl Gustaf when he visited the American Swedish Museum in Philadelphia. A friend was quite involved there, and our kids were in the Lucia programs for quite a few years, with Becky being a Lucia queen in 1977, the year before we moved to California.

In 1985, Jim and I visited Sweden, celebrating our 25th anniversary. We flew into Frankfurt, Germany, where we rented a car and drove up to and through Sweden for a month, visiting relatives in the South and North of Sweden, having a wonderful time. Becky flew into Stockholm and joined us for two weeks at the end. Jim and I took some Swedish language classes before we went to Sweden.

I worked at a Scandinavian import store for a friend, Christ'l Nilsson, and had the first pick when new merchandise came in. One of my special things was collecting "tomtes" (Swedish elves), and I enjoy decorating with them every Christmas, along with other things. Christ'l gave me a mug with "101% Swedish" on it, and she says I'm more Swedish than the Swedes.

Becky led our grandchildren in singing "Tryggare kan ingen vara" ["Children of the Heavenly Father"] at our 50th anniversary celebration. We always ended our North Park choir concert singing that in Swedish. Becky and I both attended North Park.

Now retired, we are living in a retirement community in Cameron Park, near Sacramento. Our daughter, Becky, and her family are 10 miles away and our son, Dan, and his family are 20 miles away. We are happy being near family.

> **Editor's Note**: Margaret Mae and I are life-long friends. In fact, our mothers met on a street corner in Jamestown before either was married, and they became instant friends. After they married, the two couples remained friends for the rest of their lives. When Margaret Mae and I were growing up, we often played together, either at her house or mine. It seemed that each time I was coming down with some childhood disease (and I got *all* of them), Margaret Mae was with me—but fortunately, she never caught any of them!

Lucia Fest at American Swedish Museum in Philadelphia, 1977
Daughter Becky as Lucia

Lucia Fest 1977—Son Dan opening program with Swedish horn

Nelson brothers at school in Curtis, Wisconsin—1911

ERIK THE RED

by Arland O. Fiske

Ancient Iceland lacked the natural resources to build a society of culture. It had no forests, no metals and was not known for music. But Iceland excelled in literature and law. Its creativity was expressed in words. The long dark winters gave plenty of time to write. The need to kill off most of their cattle provided adequate calf skins for vellum on which to record their stories. The coming of Christianity in 1000 AD gave them the Latin alphabet and a writing style.

It's fortunate that Icelandic people have had such literary production. Without their gift to the world, we might not have known about one of the most exciting chapters in human history, the story of Erik the Red and the Norsemen's discovery of America.

Erik was born in Norway. While yet an infant, his father, Thorvald, was exiled for murder and set sail for Iceland. When Erik grew up, he also got into a brawl and with his sword revenged the killing of two of his slaves (probably Irish). Iceland, being a land of law and order, banned him for three years.

To save his life, Erik sailed off into the unknown seas to the west until he came to a vast icecap (715,000 square miles) which turned out to be Greenland. He explored until he found some grassy areas on the southwest coast. When the three years of exile were up, Erik returned to Iceland, a hero for his discovery. He told them that this new land to the west should be called "Greenland," knowing it to be a lie. But the sagas quoted him as saying, "Men will be more readily persuaded to go there if the land has an attractive name." He became a success in real estate!

After one winter in Iceland, Erik gathered 25 ships, crowded with 1,000 people and domestic animals, and sailed to Greenland. Fourteen ships survived the journey. It was 995, the year that Olaf Tryggvason became king of Norway.

That same year, a young sailor named Bjarni traveled from Norway to Iceland with a ship full of goods for trading. Upon arrival, he learned that his father, Herjulf, had left for Greenland with Erik. Determined to see his father, he sailed westward in search of the new land. Everything went wrong. Calm and fog set in. Then the north winds blew. When land appeared, it was not Greenland but the coast of North America, perhaps Cape Cod.

Bjarni did not allow the crew to go ashore, but kept on sailing past what may have been Nova Scotia and Newfoundland. Finally, he reached Greenland and was reunited with his father. They lived there for many years.

Erik was proud of his red hair and beard. It was the same color as Thor's, his hero-god. He also shared his pagan god's values. His three sons, Leif, Thorstein and Thorvald, held a lot of promise. His one daughter, Freydis, was illegitimate. Leif was the most adventuresome of the sons and sailed off to Norway. While there, he fell under the spell (and the power) of King Olaf Tryggvason in Trondheim, who had him instructed in the Christian faith and baptized. Leif really didn't have much choice. Olaf was a determined evangelist. But it was an opportunity for him to get ahead.

When it was time to return to his family, the king said, "You are to go to Greenland on a mission for me, to preach Christianity there." Leif was more than a little alarmed to face his Thor-worshipping father with such news. He told the king that it would be a hard task. But the king replied that he had not seen a man better fitted for the job, saying "You will bring it good luck!" That's how he got the name "Leif the Lucky." The king also held several hostages and sent "protection" to insure the success of the mission.

Leif's mother, Thjodhild, became a quick convert and had a church built near her house, under the rule of a priest sent by the king. His brothers also accepted the new faith, but Erik remained a staunch pagan. To him, the new religion threatened the very foundation of Viking society. Thjodhild, his wife, refused to live with him again. That was his penalty for "unbelief." It may also have been her revenge for Erik's illegitimate daughter.

Leif was burning with curiosity about the new land which had been sighted by Bjarni Hjerulfson. He bought Bjarni's large ship and assembled a crew of 35. Leif begged his father to lead the expedition. Erik, however, pleaded that he was too old, but was finally persuaded. On the way to the ship, his horse stumbled and Erik fell off, claiming that his foot was injured. Turning to Leif, he said, "You, my son, and I may no longer travel together." He was talking both about voyages and religion. Erik remained a loyal pagan to the end. This meant he couldn't be buried with his family in the consecrated ground of the church cemetery.

Erik had some admirable qualities and some not so good. But there is no doubt that he was a brave man and a good colonizer. The communities he established lasted about 400 years. Then they disappeared during the "Little Ice Age" of the 15th century, but without his courage and adventurous spirit, "Vinland" may never have been discovered and Columbus may not have taken his journey westward in 1492. It's recorded that Columbus spent time in Iceland gathering information about Vinland before sailing off to the "New World" which has become a home for so many of us.

HOMEMADE SWEDISH ROOT BEER

by Gregory Jones

Growing up on East Virginia Boulevard in Jamestown, New York as a young male of Swedish heritage, I fondly remember the tradition of my mother and sisters making Swedish food (korv, Swedish cookies, sill, sylta, etc). If you tried to sneak a cookie before Christmas, you might get your hand slapped as they were "special" for Christmas. Of course, after Christmas the desire for those Swedish cookies faded, which always resulted in many a "save that for Christmas" cookie going stale!

My job every year was to make homemade root beer which I believe we called *dricka*. This involved bottles and caps, root beer mix and dry yeast to give it the fizz. Bottle it up, cap it and let it "brew" in the attic until it was ready. Sometimes all worked out just fine, but on many occasions, late in the evening you would hear—"pop-pop-pop"—oops, Greg must have gotten the formula wrong again! This always pleased my mother to no end and began Greg's Swedish Christmas tradition—washing partially aged, sticky root beer off the attic walls which at that time was my bedroom. What fun!!!!!

A LETTER FROM AMERICA IN 1850

by Erik Johan Pettersson
Article printed in *Östgöta Correspondenten,* December 28, 1850*

Submitted by Julie Lindblom Boozer

This is the story of a young farmhand named E. J. Petterson, who set out from Tjärstad parish for America.

Sugar Grove, September 22, 1850

I wish to let you know how I fared on my journey to America. I must thank God for good health for the present and hope even that these lines may find you with good health as well.

On May 19, Pentecost Sunday, at 8:00 in the morning, we sailed from Göteborg with favorable wind. In the afternoon we saw Jutland. On the 23rd, we saw Scotland, and on the 24th (we saw) the Shetland Islands, after which we entered upon the high sea. On June 2, late in the evening, a violent storm caused waves to wash over the deck. On the 6th, we saw hundreds of large fish which are called dolphins. There was such a violent storm on the 14th that the high mast was destroyed and this caused much (extra) work for three days. On the 15th, we saw four whales. On the 17th, the weather turned quite cold. Seasoned seafarers believed we were in the path of the North Sea wind or the cold stream which comes down from the Arctic Ocean. Thereafter, we saw both whales and other large fish every day. We also saw birds, both large and small, which we never see on land.

On the 21st, the year-and-a-half-old daughter of Gustaf Larsson from Västra Ryd parish slept away. She was wrapped in fine linen and then placed in a coarse sailcloth wherein was placed old (pieces of) iron so that (the body) would sink to the bottom. The Captain conducted the burial service. Before the remains were lowered into the sea, Chorale (Psalm) No. 493 was read and the second verse of the Chorale No. 452 was sung.

We began to see sea grass on June 30th along with logs and pieces of timber floating on the water—all, which to our great joy, gave promise that we were near land. On the morning of July 2, about 2:00, we could see Boston's lighted lighthouse which burns every night on the heights to light the way for the seafarer.

Three or four hours later, the pilot came on board. We were able to see the expansive and beflowered city of Boston. Even the doctor came aboard to examine us so that no foreign illness would be brought into the country. After that, the sail was again raised and our pilot brought the ship to the shore at 8:00 in the morning.

Who was more mindful of Thanksgiving to Almighty God for good health and a safe journey over the dangerous depths than we? None of us have been ill during the journey, only a little seasick the first days since we weren't used to the roll of the sea.

That day we went sightseeing throughout Boston until nine in the evening when Jöns Hugner of Tornvik and I went with a Swedish man to Boston's theater (museum) where we found all kinds of animals (taxidermy) to be found on our earth. The animals were encased in large cupboards with glass doors. It was a building of three floors with a stairway in the middle of each floor. Animals lined the walls on both sides. Each floor seemed to be totally filled with them. After this viewing, a concert took place at the other end of the building. In the company of the same man, we even saw Boston's park, the likes of which I doubt I'll ever see again during my lifetime. It cost me a Swedish Riksdaler. (Note: Riksdaler was the currency in Sweden from 1664 to 1874. A Riksdaler would be equivalent to a Krona today.)

The other day, in the afternoon, we bought tickets costing nine dollars or 36 Swedish Riksdaler so that we could first reach Albany by steamboat, and then on to Buffalo via canal boat, then on to Chicago by steamboat. There were some who only purchased tickets for Buffalo which cost five dollars. Between Boston and Albany it took 16 hours—50 Swedish miles and even so, we had a waiting period of four hours. There were 38 other boats lined up behind the steamboat. We then set out by canal boat drawn by horses for Buffalo. It took 13 days. The (Erie) canal was out of commission, so we had a layover of four days.

When we arrived in Buffalo, we learned that cholera was rampant in Illinois and especially in Chicago. I then decided not to travel there but decided to accompany a lady who was on the same boat as I, whose husband had settled in Jamestown a year earlier. She wrote to him from Buffalo so that he would come there to meet her since she had no money for travel. He was a tanner by trade.

We were about 16 persons who set out with them and traveled and 48 (actually 71) English miles from Buffalo. The other countrymen from Tjärstad plus the remaining passengers continued on to Chicago. We have heard nothing since (their departure).

When we arrived in Jamestown, we spent a day-and-a-half in a Swedish household which had been established about a year previously. Soon thereafter, we traveled to a small town (across the border in Pennsylvania) called Sugar Grove. We arrived at twilight and immediately met three Swedes who had been there for four years. They spoke to us in English. We hadn't been there 15 minutes before we had a job. We were five farmhands who had traveled the nine miles from Jamestown to Sugar Grove.

I resided with an American for eight days. Then I contacted a Swedish fellow to talk to my overseer for my earnings. My friend asked him what he would pay me per month, and he replied that he would pay 14 dollars or 56 Swedish Riksdaler.

I worked for this man 33 days and received 71 Swedish Riksdaler. The food here is very good. In fact, I have not seen any table as nicely set in the house of a Swedish country squire as I have here every day. The overseer wanted me to work for him during the winter and he was willing to pay me 10 dollars per month. But some of my fellow Swedes wanted to travel down to New Orleans because they had heard that one could earn 3 to 4 dollars a day down there. That city is about 400 Swedish miles from here. I followed along.

I would also like to describe the surrounding nature here. There are numerous high hills and deep valleys, hardly any stones so one can till the soil wherever one chooses. The soil is like that in Sweden—rich, dark soil over clay bottom. (I understand) the soil is much better in Illinois.

However, not much wooded area as here where the forests provide (the owner) with considerable money.

I implore you, dear parents, that you never think about a journey here. Older persons who have cultivated land affording good harvests at home would be truly stupid to set forth on such a long journey. If they would purchase wooded areas and cultivate land, they would fare no better than at home.

Young folks, such as domestic maids and farmhands, could do no better than to make the journey to this land. For Swedish maids, who would come here would find things are quite different for they would never have to work outside the house. They would attend to the rooms inside and appear like the finest lady every day. Whether they would reside in the cities or out in the country makes no difference. The exact earning, figuring in Swedish currency, would be four Swedish Riksdaler a week.

>*This was translated from Swedish by Gerald Heglund, and first printed in English in Nordstjernan 1992 May 14.

>The writer, *Erik Johan Pettersson*, has been identified in Nils William Olsson's and Erik Wiken's *Swedish Passenger Arrivals in the United States* (1995), as person #3798. He was born in 1829 June 20 in Boda, Tjärstad, son of Peter Andersson and his wife Eva Lotta Persdotter. After some time in Sugar Grove, Pennsylvania, he later settled in Oneida, Knox County, Illinois, as a watchmaker and jeweler.

KARIN'S SWEDISH PICNICS

by Barbara Hillman Jones

Dad was a wonderful correspondent all of his life, delighting in writing to and receiving letters from his cousins, whether in Sweden or America. When Dad and I went to Sweden in 1974, we visited *all* the relatives, both his and my mother's, but we stayed primarily with his cousins Sven and Claes and their families. They most likely had become the closest to my dad, probably because they were the ones who corresponded most frequently.

Since my father was born in America, the cousins met for the first time in 1928 when dad's family returned to Sweden for a visit. It would be forty-six years until he would see them again. The time that we spent with each of them and their families quickly showed me why they had become so close and such good friends, even though an entire ocean separated them.

Claes had contracted polio and while in rehabilitation, he met a lovely lady named Karin who was also recuperating from polio. They fell in love, married and had a cute, happy, blond, blue-eyed boy whom they named Anders. Claes was very gifted in the art of woodworking and he made trays, kitchen utensils, and decorative items out of wood. He opened a combination shop and store within walking distance of their home which he called *Praktisk Konst* (meaning *"practical art"*). He went into partnership with another handicapped man named Hasse who was very talented in the art of painting the objects that Claes fashioned. Together, they built a good business, and soon busloads of people came to purchase items from their store.

Karin had an absolutely delightful custom. Every morning and every afternoon in good weather she packed a wicker basket and carried it to *Praktisk Konst* where a picnic table stood in the yard in front of the shop. The first time dad and I made that trip with her, we were very curious about what she was doing, but as she unpacked her basket, we could not help but smile. Out of the basket came first a linen tablecloth, then fine china plates and cups and saucers, real silverware, cloth napkins, china creamer and sugar bowl, and then several kinds of goodies fresh from her kitchen. I was astonished at the care with which she had selected the ingredients for that picnic and how carefully she set her table. On cue, Claes came out to join us, and if there were no customers, Hasse rolled his wheelchair out, also. We enjoyed coffee poured into those china cups and saucers and the coffee bread and other delicious treats served on china plates with cloth napkins.

Later in our visit, we drove to a historic site which I know we enjoyed, but now, many years later, I don't remember anything about that historic site. However, my memory of the picnic that Karin had again packed for us remains very clear as if it were yesterday. This time, there was no picnic table. Karin laid her linen tablecloth and cloth napkins on the ground, and we all sat down in the grass, treated to a delicious lunch served on lovely china plates and coffee that had been poured into beautiful china cups and saucers.

This was not something Karin did to impress her American visitors. It was her habit, whether or not guests were present. She did it regularly for Claes and Hasse twice each day because she delighted in making a pause in their busy day an enjoyable one for them. In the time we spent with Claes and Karin, I learned a valuable lesson from Karin's Swedish picnics——whatever we do, no matter how small, need not be mundane or commonplace. If we choose, we can carry out every task with grace and style, and that makes a world of difference.

MY GRANDPARENTS

by Karin Carlson Flynn

I had two sets of grandparents born in Sweden. My mother's parents were Aaron Sandberg and Ada Carlson. They were born in Alingsås, in the province of Västergötland, Aaron in 1868 and Ada in 1866. Ada was a candy-maker in Sweden and Aaron was a meat man. They were engaged to be married in Sweden but wanted to be married in America. They arrived in the USA in 1891 and were married in Jamestown in 1892. They made their home in Austin, PA until 1911, leaving before the great flood. Aaron was a mill man and they had a boardinghouse in Austin for workers in the tannery. When they moved to Jamestown, Aaron was an associate with Frank Holm in the Sandberg-Holm Meat Market at 152 Baker Street. They lived on Palmer Street and had two daughters, Esther Sandberg and Elsie Sandberg Carlson, my mother.

My father's parents were Marie and Samuel Carlson. Marie was born on her parents' farm at Sörfors, Umeå, Vesterbotten lan, Sweden in 1860. There had been dry years in northern Europe in 1867 and 1868 and salesmen were selling tickets to the USA for less than fifty dollars. Her brothers Johannes and Pehr came to the USA where Pehr settled in Warren PA and Johannes, who simplified his name to John, bought forty acres on the Priest Hollow Road in Scandia, PA in 1879, part of which later became Sam and Marie's farm. John did not marry. He built a log cabin on the land. Either from work in the tannery or something else, he was not in good health. Marie was a marriageable 26 when she came over in May of 1886, probably both to take care of John and to find a better life in America. At the time she came over, her father had died, her mother Christina, brother Olaf, brother Erik and his wife Kristina, and the first 7 or 8 of their children were living in the home—quite a crowd! She met

Sam in Scandia who was living with his cousin Mrs. Sampson. They built a home on part of her brother's property where they raised seven children, my dad Levi Carlson being one. They sold the farm in 1925 and moved to Jamestown where Sam died two years later at age 68. Marie died July 27, 1940 at the age of 80.

LATENT SCANDINAVIANITY

by Jay T. Stratton

(This is an expansion of an article that originally appeared in *Idunna* magazine, autumn 2010.)

Over the centuries Sweden has suffered through many catastrophes. The Black Death in the 1300s was so devastating that Sweden lost one-third of its population and some provinces resorted to human sacrifice in a vain attempt to appease the gods and stop the disease. Other centuries brought famines, peasant revolts and wars. The latter part of the 19th century saw another sort of catastrophe just as great which doesn't get the same sort of play in the history books. We may even try to glorify it with our American perspective.

Between 1850 and 1915 Sweden lost one-third of its population mostly through migration to America. Other sources may claim that it was only one-fourth or one-fifth. [The reduction through emigration equaled a loss of the population. Some sources suggest a change, depending upon the years in which the calculations were made.] The fact remains that we Swedish-Americans are the result of vast and somewhat unfortunate demographic changes that swept across Scandinavia in the 19th century. Why did we leave?

The first settlement of New Sweden was established along the Delaware River in 1638. Our "Mayflower" was the *"Kalmar Nyckel"* but this was a small commercial venture. It was soon overtaken and absorbed by the Dutch and then the English.

Most of the Swedes who came to America arrived in the 1800s and settled further west. The largest enclaves were in Minnesota and the adjacent Dakotas, Iowa and around Chicago. My own family was part of a smaller group that settled in Chautauqua County, New York and nearby areas of northwestern Pennsylvania. This Swedish enclave is centered on Jamestown,

NY. In the north it runs along the Lake Erie shore approximately from Fredonia, NY west to Ashtabula, OH and as far south as Warren, PA.

Supposedly the first Swedes travelled west along the Erie Canal to Buffalo around 1850 but they had no money for the steamboat passage along the Great Lakes to the Swedish enclaves further west. They decided to walk. The people were pretty tired by the time they got to Chautauqua County. The beautiful lakes, forests and rolling hills reminded them of home so much that they decided to stay. Their first jobs were in farming, of course, but before long there were furniture factories and forestry jobs to employ the thousands who emigrated later.

So what constitutes a Swedish enclave? Some of them were towns or regions where 100% of the people were Swedish immigrants, but usually the Swedes settled in pre-existing towns alongside other Americans. "The enclave" was any area that had a significant Swedish population above and beyond the 1% contribution which Swedes made to the American population in general.

Jamestown, NY was a sleepy little Anglo town in 1850. By 1900 it was a bustling little city whose population was over half Swedish. There were Swedish churches, factories, bakeries, newspapers and fraternal organizations. When my mother's Anglo-American cousins complained that the "dumb Swedes" were taking over "their" town, she horrified them by pointing out that we too were half Swedish. About 20% of Jamestown's population is still of Swedish extraction today. At some point a critical mass was reached which allowed our stories and something of our culture to survive in these enclaves, while a lone one-percenter outside the enclave quickly assimilated into American life and forgot about the old country.

So there are a lot of names ending in "-son" in my hometown of Westfield, NY. These names are the so-called patronymics. The old Viking naming practice was to use as a last name the father's first name to which was appended "-son" or "-dotter." The wife kept her own name until relatively recent times. This meant that people in the same family could have different last names. For instance my last name would be Davidson but my sister would be Davidsdotter and my mother would be Ardensdotter. As the population grew, this caused a great deal of confusion and difficulties with record keeping. I have a John Johnson in my family tree. Don't you have one, too? Today these naming practices persist only in Iceland.

In the 1800s the Swedish government encouraged people to take on new last names. The old practices were forbidden. You could end up with a "frozen patronymic"——you stayed a Johnson, for instance, no matter what your father's first name had been. Many other Swedes took on "decorative" last names. These last names were taken from nature or from the names of their farms, parishes or towns. Sometimes "-kvist" or "-qvist" was added at the end, meaning "twig" of that family tree. Some examples of "decorative" last names are Ek (oak tree), Söderström (southern stream), Söderberg (southern mountain), Lindström (stream-lined with linden trees), Stålberg (steel mountain), and so on.

In addition to this Swedish government-sponsored name change program, the immigrants often had their names anglicized so as to appear more mainstream American. In some cases this was done by the family itself but more usually it was a spur of the moment arbitrary decision by immigration officials instead. That is how Jon Jonsson and Johan Johansson could both turn into John Johnson or even John Jones! These names looked more American. Nilsson became Nelson, and so on. The special vowels of Swedish (å, ö, and ä) might be rendered by an ordinary "a" or "o" or changed to some other letter so that the English pronunciation of the name would be closer to the Swedish original.

So why did we come to America? There were several reasons. Poverty and famine is probably reason number one, especially in the 1860s. Another reason was that Sweden had a stratified social system which prevented people from moving or changing jobs without the permission of the church and of the local lord. Another was the draft, military conscription that took young men for the king's army where many died from poor conditions even though there were no more wars. There was also the issue of religious freedom. In Sweden the state (and only) church was Lutheran, while in 19th century America various Swedish born-again sects and the Swedenborgian church were flourishing. Sometimes people emigrated together as a family unit, but the vast majority of the immigrants were young people striking out on their own.

I am a "pure half-breed Swede," born and raised in Westfield, NY near the edge of the enclave. By this I mean that both of my parents were also half-breed Swedes. Four of my eight great-grandparents came from four different areas of Sweden. Three came over as single young people; only one came over with his parents and siblings. I will tell what I know of their individual stories later.

During World War I a wave of jingoism and xenophobia swept across the U.S. Speaking a Germanic language in the street might be enough to get you beaten up. Freedom of speech did not extend to choice of language! The extensive bilingual Swedish-English school systems from grade schools to colleges were shut down. They reopened in a few days with mostly the same students and teachers but all the books were now in English. It was not a good time to be seen as different from mainstream America in any way. Anything "ethnic" was icky, no matter the ethnicity.

My parents were never given a chance to learn much of anything about being Swedish. When Mother asked her grandmother how to say words in Swedish, she would claim that she had forgotten. Father grew up ashamed of his Swedish grandmother with her lilting accent and her strict old-country ways. So we were not raised on lutfisk and lingonberries. Being Swedish was something that you didn't talk about, sort of like sex, until the children were old enough to understand.

Mother brought it up first. We were living down South in the 1960s. "Black Power" bumper stickers had appeared and were causing much commentary in the white community.

"We ought to have one that says 'Swedish Power'!" said Mother.

"What's Swedish?" we asked.

It was time for the talk. It wasn't our fault; it was something our great-grandparents had done. It was OK, of course, but everybody didn't need to know about it. She broke the news to us that we were half Swedish.

"Half?" said Father. "That's too much! I'm half Swedish so the kids would be a quarter." He had never known that his wife was also half Swedish.

"That's too much!" he repeated.

Even in the 1960s the stereotype of Sweden was hardly flattering. Everybody knew that Sweden had been neutral in World War II. Didn't that mean that they weren't our friends? They dared to criticize the U.S. for the debacle in Vietnam. Diplomatic relations had been downgraded. Canada had thousands of American draft resistors but Sweden had a few hundred, more than enough to make President Nixon's "enemy list." We heard that it was an overly permissive place with high taxes, nudity and porn films. Buxom blondes were waiting to grab you at the sauna or massage parlor. Sweden had been lost to the dirty hippies, or so we were led to believe.

From *Farmor*, my father's mother, Elvira Victoria Johnson Stratton (1898-1985), I learned that my great-grandpa had emigrated to avoid the draft. As I approached draft age myself, I found this fact to be *very* interesting. I bought books and began to study the language just in case I might need to emigrate too! I took more Swedish classes later on in college and discovered to my complete amazement that Grandma (that's what we called her, not Farmor) could still speak Swedish perfectly. Being able to converse with her in Swedish for the last seven years of her life was very special for me and of course for her, too.

Dear dour great-aunt Florence Johnson Kazmaier could also speak Swedish. She bragged that as a child she had English school from Monday to Friday, Swedish School on Saturday at their Grace Lutheran Church in Erie, PA and of course Sunday School. School every day of the week? I certainly did not envy her for that!

I developed a theory of "latent Scandinavianity" to explain how you can grow up where every-other somebody is Swedish-American but no one ever talks about it. You may find yourself having certain Scandinavian characteristics, such as:

- a goofy or quirky sense of humor
- love of fishing, hunting and gathering wild foods
- appreciation for farm traditions, eating with the seasons, fresh milk and cheese, preferring to buy from farmers or U-picks and so forth
- having (or wanting to have) a *sommarstuga*, that unimproved woodland cabin or hunting camp where special family events can take place
- social egalitarianism, neutrality or pacifism
- a special attitude toward berries, even if they are straw—or blackberries instead of lingon or cloudberries
- the tradition of opening Yule presents on December 24th instead of Christmas morning
- veneration of the *Amerikakistan*, the junky old steamer trunk into which great-grandma packed her life and enough rye crisps and cheese to survive the ocean passage
- special foods. Even though we lost out on lutfisk and lingon, still we maintained a love of red currants, beet greens, rhubarb, celery root, horseradish, dill pickles and other odd things. And of course there were Swedish meatballs!
- celebrating *Midsommar*, the summer solstice, as a major holiday

- Scandinavian house décor, be it Swedish modern or un-modern

The list goes on and on. Do you recognize any of these? What characteristics would you add to the list? If you want to bring out your latent Scandinavianity, here are some ways to begin:

Talk to the elders in your family. Find out what towns or provinces your ancestors came from in Sweden. Collect any stories you can about the emigration or life in Sweden. Look at any old documents. Be aware, however, that some of the stories you hear can be very fanciful.

Nobody wants to tell the kids "We were dirt poor, lived in a hovel and ate tree bark." Yet if it hadn't been for that tree bark, I am sure that I would not be here today. It is a lot more interesting to claim that Grandma was "an illegitimate princess hidden in the countryside who had to flee for her life to avoid a Stockholm court intrigue." Another grandma was driven out of town as a witch after she had prophetic dreams about a terrible accident which came true. Swedes do know how to tell tall tales! This is how they survived those long winters in Hartfield, NY back before the television was invented.

If your family has the Swedish farm traditions, learn them. Who still grows Swedish brown beans *(bruna bönor)* or *Blanka* white currants? Can you make your own horseradish? How often do you eat dill? Can you eat crayfish without going Cajun? Swedish cuisine is not overly fancy—it's just good old farm-fresh food.

My father did not know what a *tomten* was, but he did tell us fascinating stories about a mischievous but protective spirit of the household and barn.

What is your attitude toward "No Trespassing" signs? In Sweden there is no such thing. Anyone can cross your farm or fish your stream or pick your wild berries, unless you have specifically posted that you are intending to use them for yourself. Any visitor will just have to pick them further away from your house and signs.

The draft ended along with the Vietnam War, so I never fled back to Sweden. Grandma died at the age of eighty-eight. Of course a vacation in Sweden is great fun, but I continue to seek out my Swedish heritage here at home as well. If you mine your latent Scandinavianity as I have mined mine, you will find a rich treasure trove indeed!

Johan August Bäckman (July 6, 1834—June 7, 1889)
Caroline Christina Nilsson
(December 4, 1839—November 29, 1921)

Johan August Bäckman was born July 6, 1834 in Hässleby, Sweden near Jönköping. Nothing is known of his life in the old country except that he emigrated on May 11, 1869 (at the height of the famine) to Hartfield, NY. He was 35. His wife and four children followed him to America the following year. Five more children were born in America. His name was anglicized to John Augustus Beckman. He must have been known as "Gus" in English because an 1881 map shows his farm at the corner of Plank and Prospect Station Roads as belonging to "G. Beckman." It was a smaller parcel right on the intercontinental divide adjacent to "Hartfield Swamp," as we know it, now called "Elm Flats Wetlands." He built a simple wood frame house there sometime before his death in 1889. We do not know about his employment but evidently he had carpentry and farming skills.

Here is the obituary from the *Westfield Republican* newspaper of June 12, 1889. Newspapers of that day did not publish obituaries as informative as those of today, so this accident report served as both news and obituary:

"A very serious accident occurred in this place on Thursday evening of last week. As Augustas Beckman, a Swede living on the old Plank Road, was on his way home from town his horse became frightened and he was thrown out in front of Cleveland Fitch's on Spring Street, striking on his head and face and bruising them frightfully. When he was picked up by Mr. Fitch he was unconscious. He was taken into a neighbor's house nearby, and everything that medical skill could do was done for him, yet without avail. He died at 12 o'clock on the following day. The funeral was held on Saturday and the remains were taken to Hartfield for interment."

My grandfather Arden Beckman never got to know his grandfather but he told me this story and more. The accident happened in front of 88 Spring Street in Westfield, just one block from where I have lived for most of my life. This made the story extra poignant for me. What the newspaper did not mention was that this accident was really a horse and buggy DWI!

My grandpa was perversely proud that his grandpa was something of a rogue and an infamous town drunk. An article on the same page of the newspaper mentions the WCTU convention in Mayville "showing with what ardor the women of Chautauqua are working for the emancipation of mankind from the bondage of the demon drink." John August Beckman had been conducting his "business" in town that day, most of which consisted of getting seriously drunk. As he rounded the corner of Third Street at a high rate of speed, he lost control of his wagon and fell out on his head. He is buried in Mayville Cemetery.

Comments made by my grandfather's cousins at family reunions in the 1970s suggest that great-great-grandpa was something of a drunken tyrant and that his family was not overly saddened by his passing. These cousins did not share my Grandpa's admiration for the rogue he never knew. John August Beckman only got to enjoy 20 years of life in America before his ignominious end. Still his life shows some accomplishments. He saved his family from the famine, transported them across the ocean and left them with a tidy house and farm.

The house was demolished around 2005 after staying empty for years. Today there is just a cluster of more modern barns on this corner.

His wife Caroline Christina Nilsson (Nelson) came from a farm called Näs in a parish named Rumskulla in the district of Kalmar, Sweden. Family tradition says she was a candymaker and a witch. Actually she was gifted with "second sight" and saw in her dreams a horrible accident that came to pass and resulted in loss of life. It was the ignorant Swedish peasant folk who accused her of being a witch and of having caused the accident. Of course Great-great-grandma had told her dream in an attempt to avert this misfortune, but the peasants did not see things that way. They shunned her and "ran her out of town on a rail," to use the English expression my cousin used in recounting this story.

In reality she was a kind and resourceful woman who saved her family from all kinds of disaster. The wives of drunks have to be! Her children were Christine Lindal (1859-1922), Charles Beckman (1862-1944), Albertena Currey (1865-1924), John William Backman (1867-1942), Fred Beckman (1870-1948), Frank Beckman (1873-1967), Josephine Betts (1875-1957), George Beckman (1881-1953) and Ellen Putnam (1881-1953). Most of these people lived in Westfield, NY but George lived in Cleveland, OH, Charles and Frank in Dunkirk, NY and Christine in Dewittville, NY.

Poor Christine married a drunk, as is so often the case with children of alcoholics, and moved out west to take advantage of the "free land" in the Dust Bowl. They lived in a sod house. Drought hit. The crops didn't come in. The husband took to drinking hard. Caroline received a letter from her daughter saying that things were bad, Christine and her baby were starving not in Sweden but in Kansas! She hitched her horse to the wagon and drove to Kansas alone to rescue her daughter and granddaughter. This happened around 1900 and the trip must have taken months! She loaded her daughter and the baby and all their things into the wagon and drove back to Chautauqua County leaving the drunk to his whiskey bottle. This story gives us an idea of her fierce determination.

(This baby was Jewel Parker who for many years ran Parker's Greenhouse on Meadows Road in Dewittville just across from the cemetery. Beckman family reunions took place here in the 1930s and 1940s.)

In her later years Caroline Beckman had a Concord grape vineyard on Bird Street in Westfield just adjacent to her son's and daughter's farms. She picked the grapes into "pony baskets" (the ones with a fancy handle) and drove them to the Westfield train station for shipment to Buffalo and sale.

Some people suggest that Caroline Beckman was illiterate because she signed her last will and testament in 1920 with an "X". She died in 1921 just shy of age 82. Perhaps she had been born too early to take advantage of Sweden's compulsory child education reforms of the 1840s, in which case her accomplishments in life are all the more extraordinary, or perhaps she was too feeble and shaky by this point to do a good job on her signature and let the "X" suffice.

John William Backman
(December 28, 1867-January 21, 1942)

John William Backman left Sweden as a toddler and grew up in Hartfield, NY. He must have understood Swedish as a child but he did not speak it. His parents used the name "Beckman." The spelling change was probably the result of an immigration official's trying to preserve the Swedish pronunciation with this new American spelling.

There are two conflicting stories as to why John William reverted to the old spelling, minus the umlaut. Bäckman is a decorative last name meaning "man of the stream." In one version John William was a traditionalist who demanded the original spelling. In the other version, he was so annoyed when the postman repeatedly left in his box mail intended for a relative who lived on the same street that he began to spell his name differently. He was also known as "Grandpa Jack" or "JW."

In his younger days John William worked at the milk factory in Mayville and was part owner of an ice house on Lakeview Street. This "ice house" was more like a tunnel excavated into the hill by the railroad tracks which happened to have a building-like façade. Here the ice blocks lay packed in hay and lasted all summer long. Chautauqua Lake ice was famous in these days before electrical refrigeration. I still have some of my great-grandfather's ice tools. Money could be made in the ice business but not by the seasonal laborers who actually harvested the ice. The work was exhausting and many workers died of pneumonia.

In 1889 John William Backman married Linda Anderson. They had four sons who lived into adulthood (Earle, Walter, Arden and Elmer Clarence, also known as "Uncle Pete") and one (William) who did not. The family relocated to Westfield, NY and John William established the Backman Construction Company. He and his three sons built dozens of houses in the area, especially those on Wells St., Kent St. and Backman Avenue in Westfield. My grandfather Arden would have worked with them too except that he shot off his arm at age 15 in a hunting accident and could not work as a carpenter. He went on to found Beckman Realty and sold some of those houses.

John William built more than just houses. He built the Grange block and the old 1924 firehall in Westfield, the beach house in Lake Erie State Park, a commercial building at the red light in North East, PA (My grandpa Arden claimed that this was his "masterpiece.") and much more. He built "Backman's Rink" on Elm Street in Westfield and ran it as a popular skating rink and dance hall. It wasn't profitable enough to suit him so he sold it to the village. They erected the enormous pillars in front and renamed it "Eason Hall." It is still in service as our town hall. Backman Avenue is of course named for him, as he built over half of the houses on the street in the 1910s and 1920s. One of the five street signs uses the spelling "Beckman." It seems very odd to outsiders that the village would purposefully misspell the name of one of its streets but we know that this is an appreciative nod to present day family members, as if to say "we know that this street is named for one of your ancestors."

"Man of the stream" is an appropriate name for John William, as he loved fishing. His cottage was the first to be built on Hartfield Bay right where Hartfield Creek (Big Inlet) goes into Lake Chautauqua. My mother's greatest excitement on a lazy summer day was to take the rowboat as far upstream as she could to the bridge, then wait for the frightening clatter of the trolley passing overhead. The Beckmans were conservationists before their time. They raised and stocked fish in area streams and planted wild rice in Hartfield Bay to attract more ducks way back in the 1920s.

John William may have been the first to complain about the high taxes on Chautauqua Lake real estate! He sold out in the 1930s and built another cottage on the cliffs overlooking Lake Erie where the land was not so highly assessed. Together with Otto Schultz of Westfield, he built Forest Park, a cottage owners' association community just west of Barcelona. "Peacock's Grove," an immense forested tract, was just then being subdivided and Route 5 was being completed along Lake Erie.

Backman Construction was not always a successful business. Sometimes great-grandfather would lose money on a project. He would go into a blue funk and not eat or talk to anyone for hours or days. He'd sit at his desk cursing himself and others, going through his account books and trying to figure where he'd gone wrong and how much he had lost. My great-uncle Earle was the "designated hugger." This meant that he alone dared to enter the inner sanctum, be affectionate, talk about how much the family needed him and so forth, until John William emerged from his blue funk and came to the dinner table.

(Earle was the eldest Beckman boy and the only one whom John William could afford to send to college. He was trained as an architect. There was a little bit of resentment about this. Earle left Westfield in 1939 to move to the Washington, DC area and help to build the Pentagon. The other Beckman boys stayed in Westfield and did just fine for themselves without college degrees.)

John William Backman died in 1942, nine years before I was born. I never knew him but seem to know so much about him, even though I never did any research on the subject. I merely listened to the stories. He was an avid vegetable and flower gardener. Celery root was his favorite vegetable and I still have a division from his yellow rose bush. He was also partial to pickled green seckel pears. I have some of his furniture, ice tools, carpentry tools and a very useful sickle for chopping down weeds. There were over a dozen small wooden planes that were divided among family members after his death. No one would use such tools today; you would buy the pieces ready-made. These planes were used to sculpt the decorative moldings around the windows, doors and ceilings of the houses on Backman Avenue.

Linda Maria Andersdotter (June 17, 1867-1940)

Linda Maria Andersdotter was born June 17, 1867 and lived on a farm named Boka in the village of Hällestad in Östergötland (eastern Goth land). Her parents were Anders Pehrsson (born 1835) and Emilia Andersdotter. Her siblings were Emilia, Anders, Carl Gustaf, Hedda Carolina and Elin Elisabeth. She left Sweden alone in 1887 at age 19 and emigrated to Swede Road in Brocton, NY. Her anglicized name is Linda Marie Anderson (Backman). I still have her *Amerikakistan*, the old steamer trunk with "L. Anderson" stencilled at one end. It would appear that her Americanization began before she had even left, as evidenced by this name change.

Linda had no money for her ticket. There were at this time many "recruiting companies" that would sponsor immigrants, that is to say find you a place to go and buy you a ticket. A farmer or factory owner could pay a fee to this recruiter and receive, a few months later, a willing worker whose wages (the cost of the ticket) for a year or two had already been paid. We do not know if Linda used a recruiting company or cultivated her own sponsor in the Swedish-American community, but she arrived in Brocton, NY as an indentured servant in 1887. She spoke little English but learned rapidly, was already literate and certainly knew how to milk a cow, stock hay and gut a chicken. Everybody did back in those days, except for the rich.

Swede Road meanders northeast across the Lake Erie plain through vineyards, hayfields, farms and forests from the edge of Brocton down to the lake. The land is perhaps not as good as other lands in the area which were settled earlier. An 1881 map shows a string of small farms, 10, 20 or 30 acres with Swedish or probably Swedish names: Peterson, Berg, Gabrielson, Lawson (probably Larson), Clavin, Tilwell, Spellman . . . . One hundred years ago Swede Road was crawling with Swedes but today few are left, if any, and many of the farms have been abandoned.

The farm family and Linda became good friends, as would not be expected had there been a perceived difference of social class. She returned to visit them often. I imagine her pride arriving in a motorcar to show off her four sons and prosperous husband! When my mother had her country rides in the 1930s, Grandpa Arden would always stop to visit. When it came our turn for country rides in the 1970s, of course we went out to Swede Road even though the NY State Thruway had turned it into a dead end, but Mother could not remember the family's name, nor which farm it was. We just know that we came from Swede Road in Brocton.

How many other Swedish-Americans come from Swede Road? Chautauqua County has another Swede Road over by Harmony and there used to be a third one in Busti, but its name has been changed.

Linda lived with her husband briefly in Hartfield, Mayville and West Virginia before settling down in Westfield, about 10 miles from Swede Road. The family built houses but did not have a house of their own at first. John William arranged for them to live in houses under construction while he completed the interiors. As soon as they were finished, the house was sold. In the early years she raised the boys in a perpetual construction site! At last John William built a house specifically for them, 8 Wells St. in Westfield.

Linda Anderson is the alleged illegitimate princess whose life was threatened by royalists trying to conceal the king's indiscretions, or so the story goes. I can imagine mother and daughter-in-law engaging in some sort of contest, bursting out in laughter as witch and princess compete for the most outrageous and entertaining story. I vote for witch! I have the vaguest memory of cousin Albertina telling a version of this princess story at a family reunion in Bell Creek gulf in the 1970s at Caroline Cowan's camp. Why would Albertina have been telling Sweden stories about a shirt-tail relative? Perhaps she did so because it made for such a good story, or perhaps some story-teller on my side of the family confused great with great-great grandma. Of course there's no reason why Caroline Beckman could not have made up two origin stories.

Linda Anderson was not a person to look back, except perhaps to Swede Road. She had no contact with her Swedish family and she never spoke of them. Her sister emigrated to nearby Mayville. They lived 6 miles apart for many years but never saw each other to remember the good old days. We assume that the good old days were not that good. She never spoke Swedish around the children, as the times demanded. In fact she refused to speak Swedish when asked to do so by her grandchildren. "I don't remember," she lied. She did have one old lady friend in town who was also from Hällestad. They had not known each other in Sweden but they knew the same places and perhaps some of the same people. Whenever they got together for coffee, it wasn't English they were speaking. These were the only tidbits of Swedish that my mother ever got to hear as a child.

As John William and Linda grew older, my grandfather Arden moved his family from Backman Avenue to 8 Wells St. My mother got to live in this special house. I too had the pleasure of living there for several summers as a teenager. There was an upstairs "sun porch" that stretched the length of the south side of the house, perfect for starting plants in spring or for drying the laundry. There was a little library room tucked in along the stairs with built-in book shelves and a "larder" or "pantry" (We used both words for this room.) alongside the kitchen and the basement door.

Linda ran her house just as if it were some self-sufficient Swedish farm. There was a huge vegetable garden, prune tree, pear tree, strawberry patch. She raised chickens and turkeys but this small village lot did not have enough room for a milk cow.

My mother Muriel Beckman (Stratton) described her grandmother's kitchen like some little ethnic shop of horrors! If you looked down into the soup kettle at a boil, you would see chicken heads and claws circulating in the broth along with the vegetables. If you dared to go into the cellar, you would see a bathtub with half a dead pig floating in brine. A small girl might awaken late at night and go to the bathroom only to find the tub filled with live, swimming bullheads (catfish). My Uncle Jack is still traumatized 70 years later by his memories of being forced to kill a turkey. Jack and his little brother Ned tried to behead the turkey with their eyes closed so as not to see the horrors, but of course the bird got away.

Linda had a tin drier, a very thin sort of metal box that covered all four burners of her modern gas stove. A small hole to one side let you put an inch or so of water into it. This may seem counterintuitive for a drier, but the minimal steam did not interfere with the drying process. The water distributed the heat evenly and protected the tin drier from melting through. Mother's job as a child was to turn the fruit or vegetables to make sure that they dried evenly. Linda inspected them before putting them up in jars and tins on the shelves as food for the winter. There were dried prunes, pears, apples, sweet corn, beans and a lot more. There were jams, jellies and conserves made from quince, red currant, wild black cherry and other fruits still common today. Perhaps you had to buy milk and butter and flour from time to time, but food was something that came from the home, not something from stores. Money was only used to buy the things that you could not make for yourself.

Perhaps on her infrequent trips to Jamestown or Erie, Linda could purchase lingon or pickled herring or some other Swedish specialties, but this was a rare luxury reserved for the adults. Due to her disadvantaged childhood, Linda may never have tasted vort limpa or saffron rolls or cardamom buns or the Christmas cookies that seem to define the Swedish identity today. She knew more about salt pork, head cheese, organ meats and wild-gathered foods.

The boys grew up and married Americans. That's how we half-breed Swedes got here! The new Beckman women had different ideas about food and money. The wild mushrooms might be poison. The wild leeks (ramps) were far too pungent to cook in the house. They refused to clean the fish or even to let wild game be cooked on their kitchen stoves. The menfolk reacted and "Swedish stink parties" were born.

Swedish stink parties were only allowed to occur in basements or the garage. Only menfolk were invited. The smells which gave the parties their name were from trout, bullheads, perch, muskies, venison, duck, pheasant, woodcock, wild leeks and unfamiliar wild greens, as well as the beer and cigars which inevitably accompanied them. That's what guys did back before there was football on TV.

John Lars Johnson (April 24, 1865—September 14, 1922) Hilma Rundqvist (May 24, 1868—July 9, 1940)

Frederika Olsdotter was born August 20, 1836 in the Norra Ryr parish of Munkedal, now called Lane-Ryr parish. She married Nils Rundqvist in Munkedal and had 3 children. Johan, the eldest born in 1864, never left Sweden. Gustaf, born in 1865, emigrated to Erie, PA in 1885. My great-grandmother Hilma Rundqvist followed him in 1888. They had lived in a house named Möe on a farm named Sandnäs in Foss parish of Bohuslän province, but all great-grandma ever said was that she was from Munkedal.

Old-fashioned rural addresses in Sweden are the names of a house and the name of a farm, not the name of a street and a number. Thor's hammer had a name; great-grandma's farm had a name. Do Swedes have a tendency to give names out to everything? Maybe this is why my family has a tendency to come up with names for cars, bicycles, cabins, articles of clothing and household appliances.

Gustaf and later Hilma came to Erie because their uncle August Olson (1853-1911) was already established there. Gustaf roamed further to the Dakotas and did return to visit Sweden once around 1910, the only person in our family ever to return to Sweden until my vacation in 1982. Hilma met John Lars Johnson in Erie, married him and settled down there. He was from the countryside near Uddevalla, a small city just a short distance from Munkedal.

Hilma never knew her father because he died before she was one year old. She did speak very fondly of Munkedal, her family, the ocean, the fish runs, the harvesting of lingonberries in the woods. Life was hard for a widow's children and coming to America was just the thing to do. Everyone was doing it. She never mentioned any particular reason for emigrating.

I liked how Farmor said it: "Monkey-doll." It sounded like a child's plaything. As a teenager I was thrilled to know the name of a town in Europe where we had come from, my first such discovery. Later I learned about Jönköping from Grandpa Arden's old maid cousins who had preserved one document from Sweden, an answer to a genealogical inquiry by mail in the 1940s. It was my first attempt to translate Swedish. All the rest I have mentioned, the names of other towns, farms and houses, comes from the lady at the Fenton Historical Society. She looked it up on the computer at the Scandinavian Festival in Gerry, NY this year (2012). All she needed was my great-grandparents' birthdays. I had my answers in minutes. It felt like cheating. It is nice to know, of course, but I prefer the stories I learned from my old relatives, even if some of them are lies.

The computer had nothing to say about John Lars Johnson. His emigration was not in the records and there were too many John Johnsons to track him down otherwise. This was no surprise, said the historical society lady, as soon as I mentioned that he had been a draft dodger. Young men were not allowed to leave Sweden until after they had completed their military service. Perhaps he snuck out of Sweden and emigrated to the U.S. from some other country. More likely he came with a false name and false papers. These were readily available in Denmark, for a fee. This must be why, of all my Swedish relatives, only the naturalization (citizenship) papers of John Lars Johnson have survived.

John and Hilma made their living running a Swedish-American grocery store at 832 Parade St. in Erie from the 1890s until about 1920. They attended Grace Lutheran Church and made sure that their older children attended the Saturday Swedish School there to learn how to read and write the language that they spoke at home. Their first child, Wictor R. Johnson, died as a baby in 1892. Arthur R. Johnson was born in 1893, then Florence Gertrude in 1895, Elvira Victoria in 1898, Walter R. in 1901 and Herbert R. in 1903. Notice that the girls got middle names but the boys got only the letter "R." It stood for "Rundqvist," of course, but the parents did not want to burden their boys with such a foreign-sounding middle name, so they kept it secret.

Arthur and Florence did attend the Swedish Saturday School, then the parents began to ease up. My grandma was the middle child, Elvira, but she preferred to be called "Vera." She was not forced to attend Swedish School but she spoke it just as well as her older siblings and could read and write it almost as well too. At this time the family still spoke Swedish at home. The young ones, Walter and Herbert, changed all that. They spoke English at home all the time and got away with it now that their parents had learned to speak English very well.

Great-uncle Walter could understand Swedish pretty well but he only spoke it one word at a time, surrounded by lots of English. I remember him saying at Thanksgiving dinner at Grandma's, "Want to pass me a *gaffel* over here? That's how we used to say it at home because we're *svenska*." These were the only two words of Swedish that I learned as a child. I got this strange idea that the Johnsons talked like this all the time, saying "*gaffel*" instead of "fork" and "*svenska*" instead of "Swedish." Perhaps they used a few other different words too, and that's all it was. I was totally amazed in my early 20s to discover that Grandma knew *every* Swedish word, or almost.

Of all my relatives, only John Lars Johnson seemed conflicted about his decision to leave Sweden and only John Lars Johnson made special efforts to preserve Swedish identity in his children. Farmor could list his arguments one by one. Sweden had long before renounced war as an instrument of foreign policy, yet still John Lars was afraid that he might die if he were forced to join the army. The food was not just bad; it was actually rotten and you could easily get sick from it. The barracks were virtually unheated. The clothing was so poorly made that it couldn't keep you warm in the first place and it soon ripped or fell apart. If you didn't die from pneumonia, you could die from the quack doctors that tried to treat you for it. The boots were so ill-fitting that your feet soon had sores all over them. With the poor hygiene that was so prevalent in the barracks, these sores could easily turn into gangrene. You could have your leg amputated and perhaps end up just as dead as if there had been a real war going on.

After 25 years of being a grocer on Parade Street, John Lars grew tired of having a store. He sold out and bought a farm in North East, PA. He was killed on September 14, 1922 by the tree that he was chopping down.

Had he lived, I'll bet that my father would have learned a lot more and had a more positive feeling about being Swedish-American. To this day I am still somewhat superstitious when it comes to chopping down trees and will not do it.

Farmor had married David Earron Stratton in 1921 and moved to Westfield, NY. He was a farmer but didn't yet have a farm. Back then it was a popular thing to have a Swedish maid, even a pregnant one. Swedes were clean and their food was just like American. Grandma lived and worked in the red brick mansion at 145 S. Portage St. and at another household on Sherman Road near Hardscrabble, but this house has burned down. David lived at home with his parents. They saw each other after work. This went on for several years, even after my father David Stratton was born in 1922. Note that my father had no middle name, but he could use the initial "E" if he wanted to. This time it wasn't to hide an "ethnic" name; it was because Grandma believed that "Earron" had to be spelled "Aaron" and Grandpa Stratton refused. This was their first major argument. The "E" was a compromise but in typical stubborn Swedish fashion, Grandma got her way and no misspellings were placed on the birth certificate. After a couple of years they had enough money to buy the farm at the corner of Bliss and Allen Roads. Then Grandma got to enjoy for many years the peaceful farm lifestyle that her father, John Lars Johnson, had missed out on.

Hilma Johnson in her store, Erie, PA—1915

John Lars Johnson, c.1900

Rundqvist Reunion, North East, PA—1920

DISCOVERING THE "VASA SHIP"

by Arland O. Fiske

One of the most interesting Scandinavian sites to visit is the Vasa Ship Museum in Stockholm. The "Vasa" was built in the days of Sweden's King Gustavus II Adolphus (1611-1632), known as the "Lion of the North." He needed a navy to transport soldiers to the continent during the "Thirty Years War." For this he commissioned the building of the flagship "Vasa." It was to be the most magnificent warship on the Baltic Sea.

Henrik Hybertsson, one of the great Dutch shipbuilders of the time, was given the task of construction. Oak timbers were chosen which had the right curve. Each piece was checked against flaws. At 200 feet in length and 38 feet wide, it was a large vessel by the standards of its day. A 30-foot bow jutted forward with a lion's head on the prow. It was a dizzy 170 feet to the top of the center sail. The "aftercastle" (top cabin) was 65 feet high. Four decks were built in the Vasa, two of the mounting 64 bronze cannons.

Over 700 carvings of saints and heroes adorned the vessel. No expense was spared for this Goliath of the sea. Just the appearance of such a floating fortress was intended to put terror into enemy sailors. The Vasa was to carry a crew of 135 plus 300 soldiers.

On the beautiful Sunday afternoon of August 10, 1628, the Vasa took its maiden voyage from the royal castle through the canals out to sea. A number of women and children were allowed to ride as it passed through the city. The flagship was a magnificent sight, adorned in gold leaf and colorful pennants.

Suddenly, a powerful gust of wind hit the sails and the ship leaned hard to portside. Water gushed into the open ports. A few moments later, the proud ship went topside and sank in 110 feet of water. About 50 people perished.

What went wrong? The shipbuilder claimed that His Majesty had approved the plans. The Admiral had known of its instability, yet he did nothing about it. It was simply top-heavy. There was not enough ballast (weight) in the hold. If there had been, the first row of cannons would have been under water!

Some of the bronze cannons were retrieved with the use of a diving bell in the 1660s. But it took another 300 years before a successful salvage took place. The Vasa was located in 1956. After a very delicate lifting operation, the Vasa broke surface on April 24, 1961. For the past 20 years it has been housed in a temporary aluminum shelter where visitors can see it. A permanent shelter worthy of the warship is being built. [The Vasa Museum located in Stockholm was opened in 1990 and, according to their website, it is the most visited museum in all of Scandinavia.] Some of the 25,000 recovered artifacts are on display; coins, pewter, pottery, furniture and other items.

The Vasa is housed in warm and humid air to preserve the wood. But even after 333 years under water, it bears a proud look. The wooden carvings remain impressive. Why? Because the tiny termite ("Teredo Navalis") which feeds on wooden wrecks, does not thrive in the low-salt waters of the Baltic Sea.

We don't know what would have happened to the fortunes of the Swedish king if the Vasa had proved a worthy vessel. But one thing is certain. The grand ship would not be on display where visitors to Stockholm can see it today.

SWEDISH HOSPITALITY

by Carol Lind Kindberg

Following the visit of King Carl XVI Gustaf to Jamestown in April 1976, plans were being completed for the First Covenant Church choir to take a concert trip to Sweden in August of that same year. The King had married Queen Silvia in June of 1976. With some contacts from the King's visit, our choir was invited to the palace where we were greeted by the King and Queen in their apartment. They were so hospitable and asked us to sing for them which, of course, we did. They greeted each of us individually, leaving a never-to-be-forgotten memory for every person in the choir.

Gunnard and Carol Kindberg—Scandinavian Festival, 2003

RULLEPØLSE

by Judith Erlandson Cowles

"What do you mean that you're making Rumpelstiltskin?", asked Betty, as she came up the stairs into the kitchen.

Grandmother Erlandson's worn wood cutting board was covered in thin slices of salt pork and chopped onion, but while it was her board, the recipe was not Swedish, but Danish. The Danes have a word for a corned, brined breast of veal, and it is *Rullepølse*. It was the end of November, and using my Danish Grandma Kofoed's recipe, I was starting to assemble this favorite feature of our blended Swedish and Danish family.

Dad's parents, Hilma Johnson Erlandson and Ernest Erlandson, were Swedish, while our Mom's parents, Margaret Nelson Kofoed and George Peter Kofoed, were Danish. While my brother, Tom, and I were growing up, we were closer to the Kofoed side of the family. We always got together at Grandma Erlandson's home on Christmas Eve. Our Mom, Gladys Kofoed Erlandson, usually made and brought the *rullepølse* and Danish red cabbage for Christmas Eve supper. When Mom and Dad took over the hosting of the Christmas Eve supper, she continued to make the *rullepølse*. After Mom passed on, I made and brought the Danish foods to my brother Tom and Mary's home for Christmas Eve supper.

We usually began the preparations for *rullepølse* Thanksgiving weekend. The breast of veal had been ordered at Pearson's Market, and a fresh supply of saltpeter had been fetched from the pharmacy. (It is the saltpeter which gives the meat its pink tinge.) Salt pork was thinly sliced, and we always made sure that fresh parsley and dried dill weed were available for the filling.

Here, then, is the recipe for our family's *rullepølse*:

> 1 large breast of veal, boned, skinned and trimmed to a rectangle
> 1 pound salt pork, rind removed and thinly sliced, like bacon

1 T freshly ground black pepper
2 T salt
1 T saltpeter (from the drugstore)
1 T ground allspice
1 cup finely chopped onion
5 T finely chopped fresh parsley, together with 2 T dried dill weed

Arrange the veal in a neat flat square. Lay the sliced salt pork all over the surface of the veal and sprinkle the remaining ingredients over the salt pork. Roll up the veal, jelly-roll fashion, encase it in a clean white cloth, and tie the sausage at both ends with string, and at several points in between.

Make a brine of additional salt and water. Select a tub or pot that will accommodate the veal, add water and salt until a potato will just float in the brine. Add 1 teaspoon of saltpeter and stir well. Marinate the *rullepolse* for 6 or 7 days in a cool place. Weight down the veal with a heavy plate and a stone so that it is submerged.

Keep covered by the brine. Remove from the brine, place in a large pot cover with water, and boil gently for 1½ hours. Drain, and cool under a heavy weight in the refrigerator for at least 24 hours. Unwrap from the cloth and serve in very thin slices for the cold buffet.

WHO ARE THE "LAPPS"?

by Arland O. Fiske

The first time I saw a Lapp was in Hattfjeldal, a Norwegian city near the Swedish border, a short distance below the Arctic Circle. There was no mistaking these little people in their bright red clothes. There are only about 37,000 Lapps in the world and they live in the frozen regions across the north of Norway, Sweden, Finland, and the Soviet Union. 22,000 are in Norway and 10,000 in Sweden. We later met a beautiful girl in Helsinki who had a Lapp grandmother.

The Lapps call themselves "Samek" or "Samer." The world "Lapp" may once have been a term of contempt. They are small of stature, quick of movement and have a Mongol appearance. Their language is related to Finnish. Four groups of Lapps are identified: Mountain, Forest, River or Lake, and Sea Lapps. The Mountain Lapps have changed the least through time. (They don't have television!) They are totally nomadic and have large herds of reindeer.

Reindeer hides are a big sale item in the department stores and in the open market places. If you travel in the summertime between Trondheim and Oslo, you will find a Lapp encampment near Dømbas in the Dovre Mountains. It's their way to get in on the tourist trade. For a very modest amount of money you can buy a beautiful hide.

In ancient times, Lapps were connected with witchcraft. Viking warriors wore protective leather armor tanned by the Lapps. It withstood the blows of both sword and axe. Lapps were also thought to cast spells and curses on people. One could not be too careful around them.

The ancient religion of the Lapps was "animistic." They believed that "spirits," capable of being good or evil, lived in nature. Sacrifices were made to oddly shaped stones. Bears were venerated because they stood on their hind legs and also for their assumed wisdom. The "intermediaries" in religion were called "noaides" and used drums to produce séances. By means of ecstatic trances, noaides traveled to the other world for help.

Some Lapps became Christians as early as the 13th century. It was not, however, until the 18th century, in the age of "pietism," that the conversion of the Lapps to Christianity became a serious undertaking. Thomas von Weston, a Norwegian pastor, was called the "Apostle to the Lapps."

In Sweden and Finland, a Christian movement called "Laestadianism" developed. Named after Lars Levi Laestadius, a Swedish Lapp clergyman, the Laestadians declare "absolution" to each other during the worship service. Their meetings become highly emotional. They do not use loudspeakers for preaching as they believe the Holy Spirit speaks only through the natural voice.

After the "Black Death" (1349), northern Scandinavia was abandoned by its regular inhabitants. The Lapps and their reindeer moved into this vacuum and were the only people in some areas until the 1820s. Formerly exploited with unjust taxation, the Lapps are now given government protection and public education.

RENEWING AN OLD FRIENDSHIP

by Norma Carlson Waggoner

Our daughter Sue married her husband Jeff on October 26, 1985 in San Jose, California. Dad and Doris (my stepmother) flew here, and we then drove up to San Jose together. The rehearsal dinner was held at Jeff's great-aunt and great-uncle's restaurant. They had always referred to the restaurant as "Val's," so I was surprised when we arrived there and I saw the name was "Vahl's." Jeff's parents told Dad that he really needed to meet Jeff's great-uncle Eric, as he had also come from Sweden, finally settling in California with his brother. The brother was then killed in a vehicle accident. Dad thought for a bit and then said, *"I tink I know dat man."* Dad came from Sweden in 1923, I think, but he never lost his accent. Well, someone went to the kitchen and brought Eric right out. Sure enough, Dad and Eric had known each other when they were first in Jamestown, had been friends, even double-dated. Everyone was so excited that they had been reunited. They spent a nice evening become reacquainted and reminiscing. We all really enjoyed it. It was nice that they had this time together because within the next year Eric passed away. Dad passed away in 2002 at the age of 97.

YOUNGBERG—
MARTINSON FAMILIES

by Mary Wright

Otto Sigfrid Youngberg (Ljungberg in Sweden), his wife, Helena Sofia Carlsson Youngberg (known as Sofia), and their daughter, Astrid Andrea Youngberg, age three, came to the United States in 1903. Otto was born February 18, 1878, in Halmstad, Halland, Sweden, and died October 20, 1969 at age 91 in Jamestown, New York. Sofia was born January 18, 1868 in Laholm, Halland, Sweden, and died January 13, 1943 in Jamestown. They embarked on "Invernia" from Liverpool, England on April 29, 1903, and arrived at Ellis Island on May 6, 1903. Their first destination was Ridgeway, Pennsylvania, where Sofia's sister and brother-in-law lived. They also lived in Moline, Illinois for several years before moving to Jamestown.

Otto worked as an engine polisher *(lokomotio putsare)* for the Swedish Railway Company in Halmstad from 1896 to April 1903. He worked in the shipping department at Art Metal Plant #1 in Jamestown for more than 35 years. Both Otto and Sofia are buried in Sunset Hill Cemetery.

Otto and Sofia had two children: Astrid Andrea Youngberg, born August 14, 1899 in Snostorp area of Halmstad, Halland, Sweden, and Carl Gunnar Youngberg born August 9, 1905 in Ridgeway, Pennsylvania. Astrid died December 13, 1989 in Jamestown and Carl died March 1976 in Long Island, New York. Both are buried in Sunset Hill Cemetery.

Astrid married Carl Bertrand Martinson (*Martensson* in Sweden) on May 21, 1927 in Jamestown. Carl (better known as Bert) was born May 4, 1893 in Skogaby, Veinge, Halland, Sweden and came to Jamestown by way of Copenhagen, Denmark on the "Oscar II" and arrived at Ellis Island on January 25, 1912. Carl was a U.S. Army veteran of WW I, serving in France with the 77th Division. His mother, Bina Martinson Carlson, born in Skogaby, Sweden on July 27, 1865, came to Jamestown before Carl to care for the husband and six sons of her friend who had died, leaving Carl to work to earn enough money for his passage to the U.S. As was common in those days, Carl had been "farmed out" to work as a young boy, and he did not have any pleasant memories of his life in Sweden. Bina died in Jamestown on June 13, 1939.

Carl was a carpenter in Jamestown until he lost his hand in an accident while working during the winter months making Army canteens when the machine malfunctioned. He could no longer work as a carpenter but found work for the Village of Celeron and the VFW Post in Jamestown.

At the time of their marriage, Carl lived at 222 Barrows Street and Astrid at 11 Tower Street, both on Swede Hill. They moved to a new home in "Fairmount Park" that Carl had built.

Astrid, while only three when she came to the U.S., spoke fluent Swedish and wrote letters in Swedish to her relatives in Sweden and occasionally spoke with them on the telephone.

Carl and Astrid belonged to the Viking Ingjald Lodge IOV in Jamestown. They were both active in the American Legion Herman Kent Post in Celeron and the VFW John W. Tiffany Post in Jamestown. Carl served as commander of the American Legion and Astrid served as president of the auxiliaries of both organizations.

Carl and Astrid had three children, all born in Jamestown:

Ruth Elaine (English) Schilling—born March 18, 1928 and died May 6, 2000. She lived in Southern California for several years but returned to Jamestown where she worked at the Automatic Voting Machine Company (later American Locker) and last worked at Ramco Drilling Company in Jamestown.

Donna Mae Vandewark—born May 28, 1931. She graduated from Celeron High School in 1949 and worked at Bigelow's Department Store in Jamestown. She moved to Southern California in the mid-1960s and later to Bellevue, Washington to be near her son. She died in 2002.

Mary Lynne (Bittick) Wright—born November 30, 1937. She was in the first graduating class from the then new Southwestern Central High School in 1955. She worked for the law firm of Lombardo & Pickard in Jamestown for two years before moving at age 19 to Southern California where her sister Ruth was living. She recently retired as an attorney in private practice and lives in Hemet, California. She has visited relatives on Astrid's side of the family in Sweden on four occasions. She is active in her local Vasa Lodge.

Both the Youngberg and Martinson families left Sweden during the great period of emigration from Sweden—after the famine years and when it was difficult to find work and to support families. Some of the reasons for emigration were poverty, cramped housing accommodations, unemployment, years of poor harvest, religious persecution. And on the other side of the Atlantic loomed a land of "milk and honey," the dreams of a better life for themselves and their families. Homesickness was a heavy burden and knowing they would probably never see their relatives who stayed behind. Although they may have encountered difficulties in their early years here, they were anxious to learn the language and assimilate into their new country, while often living in little communities of other Swedes, such as "Swede Hill," and trying to maintain many of their cultural traditions.

EDVARD GRIEG AND "TROLDHAUGEN"

by Arland O. Fiske

When Denmark's Frederick VI asked Edvard Grieg who had taught him to play the piano, he replied: "I learned from the mountains of Norway." When people think of Norwegian music, Grieg is usually the first name that comes to mind.

Who was this unusual musician that combined romanticism with patriotism? Edvard Grieg (1843-1907) was the great-grandson of a Grieg who had come from Scotland to Bergen. On his mother's side, he descended from the well-known Hagerup family. They were highly gifted in music. It was Ole Bull, Norway's famous violinist, who urged that young Edvard study at the Leipzig Conservatory in Germany when he was only fifteen. There he received a classical training.

The music of the continent did not suit Edvard's nature. Another Norwegian musician, Rikard Nordraak (1842-1866), persuaded Grieg to listen to the folk tunes of his own country. He wrote: "Listen to the unclothed plaintive melodies that wander, like so many orphans, around the countryside all over Norway. Gather them about you in a circle round the hearth of love and let them tell you their stories." Grieg did and he enchanted the whole world with these melodies.

To feel close to the music of Grieg, you must go to Bergen and visit Troldhaugen. There you can walk through the summer chalet where Edvard and his wife, Nina, spent many summers. It's on a lake overlooking the Hardanger Fjord. "Troldhaugen" means "Troll Hill," and the pathway to his home is lined with trolls. He built a small hut by the water's edge where he spent many hours alone with the piano and musical scores. The dampness was not good for his health, but he could not give up Troldhaugen.

In Rome, Grieg was highly acclaimed by Franz Liszt. He was compared to Chopin. Whenever you listen to Grieg, you can hear some notes from Norway's folk dances. This does not find favor with some critics of the classical tradition. One of his favorite authors was Hans Christian Andersen. He wrote the music to Andersen's "Jeg elsker dig" ("I Love Thee"), a favorite to this day.

Grieg had a definite purpose with his music: "My aim is what Ibsen expresses in his drama, namely to build homes for the people, in which they can be happy and contented." Queen Victoria told him: "I am a great admirer of your compositions."

Grieg has done for Norway what Sibelius did for Finland. He took the sounds of nature and put them to music so that the whole world can hear them. The movie, "The Song of Norway," tells the story of Grieg. But best of all, listen to his music and, if possible, visit Troldhaugen. The foliage on the pathway to the house is a lush green. Down by the lakeside, you can see their burial crypt, imbedded into the side of a rock. He was a romantic to the end. And if you listen carefully, you can still hear the piano playing the tunes of the waterfalls and mountain winds.

COUSIN NIA

by Jean Wistean Seastedt

My husband Robert's cousin Linnea (Nia) was born in Jamestown, New York. She and her sister were teenagers when they went to Sweden with their parents and stayed there. Nia's mother died and the father returned to America. By then, Nia was about 18 years old and in love with Gustaf Mobjer. They were married and started their family. So it is through Nia's family that we went to Sweden, and she has come to stay with us.

On our first trip, Nia arranged for us to go on a Swedish bus tour which started in Sweden and went to Germany, Austria, and Italy. Nia was unable to go at the last minute, so we were the only two Americans with fifty Swedes. Thirty years ago not many Swedes spoke English, especially the ones who lived outside the large cities. However, some were learning English, and several of the children and their parents were so excited to try out their English on us. The bus would stop on the side of the Austrian Alps and we would have coffee. We all stayed at a "Zimmer" in Austria and each day we traveled together on the bus. It was the most wonderful ten days ever.

Because of this trip, several relatives have come to the USA and stayed with us. When we go there, we go to their homes and now their children's homes.

We have been to confirmations, baptisms, and several large weddings and receptions. Nia's granddaughter Susanne's wedding was in both Swedish and German, and the priest spoke one verse in English for the two American relatives in the congregation. The wedding reception was wonderful. While at the reception, one relative on the German groom's side told us about his being a POW—he spoke English so well that he was captured by Americans.

Shopping in downtown Falkenberg in center square was heavenly. We have more Swedish things in our home than some of the Swedes in Sweden do!

We have a big *"Valkommen"* sign we put up when our relatives come. It's designed so that we can just change the name to honor whoever is visiting us. David Miller, a neighbor who is a very talented artist, painted it for us.

We are so proud of our Swedish heritage.

LOOKING FORWARD, LOOKING BACK

by Jane Samuelson

In all the time I spent with my father's family, I never heard any of them say, "We should have stayed in Sweden." They had settled in Jamestown in 1913. According to my father, John, and his brothers, Ossie and Tully, they had adjusted to their new life quickly and easily. Once Dad remarked that he didn't even remember learning English! Uncle Ossie said that soon after their arrival he accompanied his mother as the translator when she went downtown to buy a sewing machine. Quite a feat for a boy who two weeks earlier had known only one "English" sentence: *"Ve are going to Yaw-mess-stove-'n (Jamestown)."*

My father, more than the others, enjoyed talking about their earlier years in Göteborg. In their neighborhood park stood huge slippery rocks that the brothers used as slides, much to their mother's dismay because they often came home with ripped trousers. They'd had wonderful vacations on the seashore at their aunt and uncle's summer home. When they lived on the island of Hisingen, in the city's harbor, they went to school by ferry, and just after the novelty wore off they moved to America! Dad insisted that in Sweden the strawberries and blueberries were bigger and more delicious than ours and the sky was bluer.

When my grandmother, Selma Larsson Samuelson, whom we called *Farmor*, and my grandfather, Oscar, emigrated from Sweden along with their five children, she had left her parents, her siblings, and her nieces and nephews in her hometown. I don't recall from my childhood that Farmor ever gave any indication that she might be lonesome for her family and old friends. She was a busy woman. Whenever we stopped by her house, she was never sitting down, always doing some household chore or working in her garden, and often she had something good baking in—or just out of—the oven. She was famous in our family for her snickerdoodle cake and glazed almond tarts called *masariner*. In her later years, after my grandfather died, she moved to Florida to be near her daughter, Linnea, but spent summers with us. Each morning when she came down to breakfast she always smiled as she quoted her favorite verse from the Bible: *"This is the day which the Lord hath made; we will rejoice and be glad in it."*

    One day in the late 1950s Farmor received a letter from her niece Greta that had a black band around the front of the envelope. Ester, Farmor's only remaining sister, had died. Farmor was overcome with grief, and Dad spent the whole afternoon trying to comfort her. That was the first time I realized that Farmor's life was larger than I had known. She loved all of us, we knew that for certain, but she still greatly loved her Swedish family, too, whom we had never seen and knew very little about.

    As I got ready to go to Sweden in 1964 to study for a year, Farmor became more and more excited that I would be meeting her nieces and nephews and their families. She'd written them that I was coming and could hardly stop talking about them. I spent a few fascinating days with these very welcoming and generous relatives before I went on to Stockholm. There was no doubt that I was among my kin—the resemblance of one of my father's cousins to my father had actually startled me at first. No family members were fluent in English, and I, unfortunately, couldn't speak much Swedish, but we had fun anyhow.

    On the second day of my visit, Greta placed a large desk drawer on the sofa beside me. It was full of black-and-white photographs that her mother, Ester, had received from Farmor. "Who are all of these people?" Greta asked me in Swedish. There we were—Uncle Tully in his U.S. Army uniform in France. My sister, Martha, and I swimming in Chautauqua Lake. Cousin JoAnn in her nurse's uniform and cap. My parents, Sylvia and John, on their wedding day. Hundreds of photos spanning nearly fifty years. In my meager Swedish, I related something about the people in the pictures. As I sorted through the photos, Greta and her sister, Kerstin, took turns recounting what had been in the various packages that *Moster* (mother's sister) Selma had sent them over the years: dolls, kids' jewelry, coffee, Jell-O, canned corned beef, and American candy. A big question they wanted answered was, "What is Jell-O exactly?" It was hard to explain.

    After my year in Sweden I returned a few times for visits, and I continue to correspond with Kerstin, now my father's only living cousin. About four years ago Kerstin sent me a photocopy of a lovely and revealing letter that

Farmor had written to her mother's brother, Karl. Farmor had returned to Göteborg for three months in 1924 when her mother was ill and was with her mother when she died. In 1925 Uncle Karl had sent Farmor a telegram for Christmas, and she responded in Swedish with a long letter in which she said that the telegram was the best Christmas present she'd ever received. Farmor told of her yearning for "home" and for all of the dear ones she missed so much. She wrote that she could hardly read the telegram through her tears as she discovered that together they had composed the message on Christmas Eve, missing her as she missed them. She ended the letter by writing, "I know the time will come when we are all together, never again to separate. I wait for that day!"

When Farmor died in 1974, at the age of ninety-four, her personal things were left to Aunt Linnea, and she left them to her son Herb. When Herb died two years ago, one of his friends sent me a box that contained as many black-and-white photos of Swedish relatives as were in Greta's collection of black-and-white photos of American relatives fifty years ago. But I had no one to ask, "Who are all of these people?" I could identify only a few.

I take consolation in the fact that Ester and Selma had known who all of the people in the photographs were, and at one time there were letters, along with the photos, that described in some detail, no doubt, the interests and achievements and concerns of all of us relatives. Ester and Selma's frequent correspondence enriched their lives, and surely in their letters they shared their worries, sorrows, and longings and also reported on the good times, year after year.

Occasionally my far-flung cousins and I get together and the main topic of conversation is always the old days. We remember how Farmor, making one of her little jokes, talked and chuckled at the same time. Certainly we recall how hard she worked to prepare the *smörgåsbord* for Christmas Eve. We really liked most of the food and were encouraged to take tiny portions of what we didn't like. I ended up liking everything. Whenever our family visited our grandmother in Florida and spent a day at the beach, Farmor, in her seventies, swam and splashed around in the ocean with Martha and me while our parents sat in their chairs on the sand. I hadn't known that old people (in other words, people my age now), could still play, but she demonstrated that they could. At eighty she was determined to learn to shoot with our bow and arrows and learn she did, though you wouldn't have wanted to be anywhere in the vicinity of the target when she was shooting.

As a teenager I thought that Farmor's quoting of her favorite Bible verse in the morning was meant to be a reminder to my sister and me to be grateful for the gift of another day and to "be glad in it." But now I think that she was mainly addressing herself—and offering a silent prayer for the continuing of the contentment and joy she'd achieved in her life, which only seemed to grow as she aged. I cherish my memories of Farmor in Orlando in her sweet little house, living next door to Aunt Linnea, and tending her flower garden in all that sunshine!

Guds fred, Farmor. The Peace of the Lord.

Notes from Jane:

I used the expression *Guds fred* at the end, "God's peace," which was often used to close personal letters in bygone days. It must be that people said it to each other too as one might say "God bless you" now. In a Carl Larsson painting of a lovely dining room, the words *GUDS FRED* appear on a hand-embroidered hanging above a door. At the Lutheran church I attend, during "The Peace" some people wish you "God's peace," but most say "The Peace of the Lord," which is how I translated the expression in my story.

The Scripture quotation is from the King James version of the Bible which is the one my grandmother used.

VAXHOLM

by Barbara Hillman Jones

Although my father was an only child, he had lots of first cousins on both sides of his family, a few in America but most of them back in Sweden. Dad was the oldest cousin on his father's side. When dad and I traveled to Sweden in 1974, we visited as many relatives as we could. One cousin we stayed with was Sven, his wife Gunda (Gun), their daughter Anita, and their son Per. They lived in Jacobsberg, a modern city north of Stockholm.

Sven had learned to speak English, but Gun had not. Both Anita and Per spoke English very well since they were required to learn English in school. I did not speak Swedish, at least not more than a few words here and there. I could understand it better than I could speak it. Fortunately, my dad spoke Swedish extremely well, and he was a wonderful translator for me.

Even though Gun and I could not speak much to each other, we quickly found that hand signals and gestures are almost as good as actual words, and we learned to communicate quite effectively that way. Gun knew I missed my husband during that trip, and whenever she heard an airplane overhead, she'd point upwards, look at me with a twinkle in her eye, and say, *"Har comer David!"* (Here comes David!) Then we would both break out in giggles.

One evening Sven and Gun decided they would drive us to a town called *Vaxholm*. The Swedes used public transportation whenever they could because gasoline was very expensive. So when we went somewhere in their car, it was a special event. Dad, Sven, Gun, and I collected our belongings and piled into their Volvo. We drove along, chatting and enjoying the scenery. Sven and Gun explained to Dad what we were seeing, and then Dad translated it for me. There were some turns and even a couple of traffic circles (roundabouts to the British), and we enjoyed the ride. We went around one of the traffic circles and kept on our way. Later on, we came to another traffic circle, and Gun got a strange look on her face. It seems that it was the same traffic circle we had navigated a few minutes prior. Then she broke out in laughter and said to me and my dad, *"Vaxholm! Tvo gonger!"* ("Vaxholm! Two Times!")

Gun simply could not contain her peals of laughter. Of course, Dad and I joined in with her, but Sven remained unsmiling and silent. It seems that Sven did not think it funny—not in the least.

Well, we did get to Vaxholm that evening, and we enjoyed our visit there. Actually, I can't remember much about the town because Gun and I were trying so hard to keep our composure. In the days to follow, Gun made the mistake of reminding Sven every now and then that we had gone to Vaxholm *tvo gonger*, and it took a very long time until Sven could bring himself to crack a smile. It seems that some men just don't take making mistakes in going somewhere very well. However, Gun finally was able to suppress her desire to remind Sven, and Sven was finally able to see the humor in it. When we got back home to America, all one of us had to say was *"Vaxholm,"* and we'd have another good laugh.

Both Sven and Gun and their children were wonderful people and gracious hosts, and I am so glad that I was able to become acquainted with the relatives in Sweden. I learned that even though we had never met prior to that visit, family is family even when we are separated by an entire ocean and even if we can't speak the language. We know we are loved and accepted simply because we are family.

MOTHER'S LEGACY

by Carolyn Gustavson Johnson

My Mother, Signe Amelia Sjoqvist, was born June 24, 1894 in Vimmerlay, (Småland) Sweden, one of 14 children. She had a very difficult childhood. She was dissatisfied with her life in Sweden and wanted to come to America. She contacted her Aunt in Jamestown, New York and informed her of her longing, but she had no money. Her Aunt sent her the fare with the stipulation that she had to repay her. Thus, in 1911, my Mother boarded the ship in Sweden to come to Jamestown. Of the 14 children, she was the only one to ever come to America to live.

She found employment as a domestic for a well-to-do family on Lakeview Avenue in Jamestown and dutifully repaid her debt to her Aunt.

She met my Dad, Arthur Gustavson, who had immigrated from Örebro (Västergötland), Sweden, with his Mother, Father and Sister. They married and both went to night school to learn the English Language. The proudest day for them was when they received their citizenship papers to the "United States of America." They raised 11 children and we all learned the Swedish and English languages.

We always spoke Swedish in our home. We followed many Swedish customs, especially at Christmas time. Mother was an excellent cook and homemaker and cooked and baked all the Swedish delicacies.

They never talked much about their childhood, but I can still see the look in Mother's eyes when she received those "letters edged in black" announcing the death of a loved one in the "old country."

I married Ralph Johnson in 1955 and he too is the son of immigrants: Axel Hjalmar and Anna Johnson from Karlstad (Värmland), Sweden. Consequently, Ralph and I hold to many Swedish traditions and are members of the American Scandinavian Heritage Foundation in Jamestown.

THE SPINNING WHEEL

by Lois Jones Oster

Although I have never lived in Jamestown, New York, it was the hometown of my Swedish mother (Evelyn Hallin Jones). We visited our relatives on Swede Hill every summer, and so I have many fond memories.

Two of my mother's sisters, Austrid and Adelaide Hallin, were the proprietors of The Spinning Wheel, a needlework shop on East Second Street. Austrid had previously been employed in the needlework department of Bigelow's Department Store and was well respected as a merchant and as an instructor in all forms of needlework.

Each summer I would look forward to spending a day with my aunts at The Spinning Wheel. Aunt Austrid would open the store in the morning, and after lunch Aunt Adelaide and I would board the bus across the street from the house on Chapin Street for the ride downtown. As we approached the shop, I could see the spinning wheel in the window which my great-grandmother, Anna Louisa (Hagg) Peterson, had brought with her to America from Sweden. The window also contained a variety of merchandise as a sampling of the treasures inside the shop.

Along the right wall there were shelves filled with beautiful china tea cups and figurines. Beneath the shelves were drawers stocked with more china and baby clothes. On the opposite wall were shelves filled with a rainbow of cotton fabrics suitable for sewing aprons, tablecloths, and house dresses. Further down the wall behind the counter with its cash register were boxes of yarn of every color.

A row of tables marched down the center of the shop and were stacked with various items. Near the front of the shop a table carried many gift items for newborn babies, artfully displaying an array of pink and blue, soft yellow and pale green. Many items were handmade such as booties and sweater sets. Further on, there was a table with hand-crocheted potholders and colorful tea towels, luncheon cloths or aprons.

At the end of the row of tables there was a room on the right containing a table and chairs, along with racks of pattern books for knitting, crocheting, or Swedish weaving, a popular craft in the 1950s. Trays of embroidery floss were also in this room. Mrs. Bly, an employee of The Spinning Wheel, would sit at the table in this room and work her magic with yarn when the store was not busy. This was the instruction room where customers could sit in a quiet, homey atmosphere to receive help with a difficult pattern or learn a new art.

Throughout the day I was allowed to help the customers from behind the counter, using the cash register and learning how to make change. It was at The Spinning Wheel that I received instruction for my first piece of needlepoint, a small purse. Aunt Adelaide also taught me to do Swedish weaving and provided me with the colorful fabric, the multi-colored threads, and five instruction books. I made tea towels for many family members the following Christmas, and a chocolate brown skirt with a six-inch border of pastel design for myself.

When dinnertime came, we would go to the back room where we would heat our food on the hot plate and drink coffee from a pretty china tea cup with its tiny chip making it unworthy of being sold in the shop. There were a couple of chairs and a clean counter for our table. The back room also had an iron and ironing board, a sewing machine, and rows and rows of shelves for merchandise.

As I write this story, I can almost smell the scent of new yarn and fabric in The Spinning Wheel, hear the squeak of the wood floor beneath my feet, or the tinkling of the bell when the front door opened or closed. However, what is most precious to me is the memory of spending those days with my two wonderful Swedish aunts in Jamestown, New York.

THE SAARINENS: FINLAND'S ARCHITECTURAL GIFT TO AMERICA

by Arland O. Fiske

Everyone has some special place that they like to be. One of my favorite spots is on the first base side of home plate in Busch Memorial Stadium in St. Louis. I admit to being an ardent Cardinal baseball fan. But why do I like to sit there? It's so I can look over the rim of the stadium and see the "Arch," the "gateway to the West."

The Arch, of course, is really the Jefferson National Expansion Memorial. It stands 630 feet high and is the same distance at the base between its two giant legs. It is built of reinforced concrete and is covered by one-fourth inch thick plates of stainless steel. Constructed between 1962 and 1964, the Arch marks the expansion into western USA through the "Louisiana Purchase." President Thomas Jefferson closed the deal with Emperor Napoleon on May 4, 1803, for $15,000,000. The French needed money for their continental wars.

St. Louis became the point of entry to the West for explorers, for traders, soldiers, mountain men, missionaries and settlers. The westward movement attracted some unusual people: Meriwether Lewis and William Clark, Jedidiah Smith, Fr. Joseph DeSmet, and the Choteaus, just to name a few. Until the railroad was built from Chicago to Sioux City, Iowa, as a shortcut to the Missouri River, almost everyone had to travel through St. Louis.

In 1948, Eero Saarinen (1920-1961) won the competition for the best design for the memorial. President Roosevelt had authorized the planning on December 22, 1935. Today, millions of people have visited the Arch and have been amazed at its design and at the museum which it houses. It's built in the shape of a "catenary curve," the same shape a hanging chain will form. Nothing like it had been constructed before and it thrust Eero Saarinen into international recognition.

This was nothing new, however, for the Saarinens. Eero's father, Eliel Saarinen (1873-1950), was already a celebrated architect, both in Europe and in America. The elder Saarinen was born in Rantasalmi, Finland. Educated at the Polytechnic Institution in Helsinki, he was an advocate of modern and functional design. It was his Finnish Pavilion at the Paris Exposition in 1900 that gave him his international fame. In Finland, he is best remembered for the Helsinki Central Railway Station. In 1923, he emigrated to the US and became a professor of architecture at the University of Michigan. His wife, Loja, was also a distinguished designer. Among his famous American buildings are many schools and churches. He became a US citizen in 1945 and was the author of several books.

There probably has never been a father-son combination so famous in architecture. Eero, the son, was born in Kirkonummi, Finland. He graduated from the Yale School of Architecture in 1934. His most famous project was the Arch. At the top of this memorial monument is a gallery for visitors. It's reached by riding in capsules holding five people which travel like an enclosed aerial ski lift. The Arch was built to withstand winds up to 150 mph.

There are many other designs which also brought Eero Saarinen fame. These include the former TWA terminal at Kennedy Airport in New York, as well as the Dulles Airport near Washington, DC, the US embassies in Oslo and London, the hockey rink at Yale University, the Lincoln Center for the Performing Arts, and the CBS building in New York. Other works of Eero Saarinen which appeal to me are the campus of Concordia Seminary in Fort Wayne, Indiana, and Christ Lutheran Church in Minneapolis which has influenced the design of many more churches.

In the years that I lived in St. Louis (1961-1967), I don't ever remember meeting a Finn. But the 630-foot tall Arch more than made up for this. It towers above all the structures of the city's beautiful riverfront. I hope that my grandsons who share in the Finnish heritage will always be proud of this ethnic connection.

And I, as a latter-day Norseman, will enjoy my favorite chair with its molded plywood frame, which is also a Saarinen creation. Then I'll scan the TV programs for a Cardinal baseball game. Perhaps they will show the Arch one more time.

MY DAD

by Dolores Carlson Jackman

Karl Arvid Karlsson became Carl Arvid Carlson when he emigrated from Sweden to the United States through Ellis Island in 1923. He was just 19 years old. During this emigration period, many names were Anglicized.

Dad was one of 12 children born to Karl and Anna Olsson in Dragontorpet, Brattfors in the province of Värmland, Sweden. The sons were Knut, Gustaf, Olaf (Olie), Arvid (Carl), Erhard (Ed) and George. The daughters were Emelia (Emmy), Kristina, Maria (Mia), Hedvig, Selma and Sara. All of the births occurred in their small, two-room house with an upstairs sleeping area. This house has since been registered as a historical site which depicts a farm home in the late 1800's/early 1900's. I was there in 1999 and was excited to sit in the family kitchen and drink cider with my Aunt Selma.

Six of the children emigrated to the United States. In 1922, my Aunt Emmy was the first to leave Sweden. She was working as a cook in a hotel in Karlstad, when the wife of a businessman asked her to come to Chicago, Illinois to work. This kind woman agreed to pay all of Emmy's travel expenses and to set her up in a home in Chicago.

In the 1920's, there was a drought in Sweden. The economy and farming were depressed. Jobs were very difficult to find. Aunts Marie and Hedvig left for domestic work in Chicago during this time. My Dad and two uncles, Olie and Ed, emigrated to find jobs in American factories.

My Dad first came to Jamestown, New York where his Uncle Andres (Andrew) Fredricksson sponsored him. This meant that Andrew vouched for his character and prospects for potential employment. Jobs were not plentiful in Jamestown, so Dad went to Chicago to look for work. Later, he worked for a federal program called the Civilian Conservation Corps (CCC). This job took him to different parts of the Northeast, working at the submarine base in Connecticut and the high school in Auburn, New

York. Dad finally came back to Jamestown where he eventually worked at the Dahlstrom's Metalic Door Company until his retirement.

Many Swedes came to Western New York because other family members and friends were there. The beautiful lakes, woods and rolling hills also reminded them of their native Sweden. Dad loved to fish in Lake Chautauqua and hunt in the woods around Panama, New York. He always shared his lovely flower and vegetable garden with family and friends. Dad's love of his family and his church, Gloria Dei Lutheran, were very important to him. These were the qualities that he brought with him from his beloved Sweden.

Dad lived to be 97 years old and died in the Lutheran home in 2002. Because of him, I am very proud of my Swedish heritage.

Oh, how I miss his Swedish accent and happy laugh.

Dolores Carlson Jackman's Swedish Family—1923

12 unga män möttes i Jamestown, USA, 1927 för att ta den här bilden som sedan skickades till släkten i Sverige. Alla (utom en) hade de utvandrat från de små byarna i norra delen av Brattfors socken. Stående fr v Anders Fredriksson, Verner Elefant, Viktor Fredriksson, Arvid Karlsson, Göran Kristoffersson, Birger Larsson (fr Nyed), Arvid Brattlöv, Einar Pettersson. Sittande från vänster Eskil Pettersson, Karl Henriksson, Per Nilsson och Erhard Karlsson.

Twelve Men from Varmland in Jamestown—1927

MY FATHER'S FAMILY

by John E. Anderson

My father's family can be traced back to 1312 in Västergötland, Sweden. Through those years the only non-Swedish person to enter the family was Adolph Schmitt, who married my great-great-great-great grandmother. The family farm has been in the family since the 1600s and is still prosperous, presently run by a second cousin, Daniel. Two ancestors through the years were members of the Riksdag, the Swedish Parliament, speaking for farmers. It was in Västergötland that my father was born on May 28, 1908, and christened Baltzar Gustaf Andersson.

The story of why my father was born in Sweden was that his father, Evard, had immigrated to the U.S. in 1890 and became an American citizen. He went to work for the election of William McKinley as president and was told, along with the other workers, that if McKinley didn't win the election, not to come to work the next day, as there would be no work for them. As you know, McKinley won and Evard kept his job, but there was a kink in his plan: he wanted his betrothed, Hannah, to come to the United States to join him. Hannah, however, loved Sweden, and I always suspected she used her feminine wiles on Evard, so he returned to the old country. They had four children, with Dad being the oldest and that is the story of why my father was born in Sweden.

Gustaf, as he was called by his middle name, helped work the farm during his early years and decided to go to America in 1929, not the most propitious time for a young man to attempt a new life in a country at the beginning of the Great Depression. He found work first in Ashtabula, Ohio, digging ditches, unloading trucks, and other physically strenuous jobs. Dad maintained to the end of his life that anyone who wanted to work bad enough and who wasn't afraid of hard work could always find a job. Dad proved that, as he was never unemployed. He found work in Mayville, New York, working at the Kling Furniture factory and in 1936 he made a trip back to Sweden aboard the Kungsholm to visit his family. On the ship he met my mother, Helen Sundstrom, who was taking her Swedish-born mother for a visit to the homeland. Mom was born in New York City to Swedes who settled there. Dad moved to Jamestown because he knew that Mom would never be able to go from the City of New York to the Village of Mayville. Mom and Dad married in 1938, and in 1940 I appeared on the scene, followed four years later by a brother, Greger.

After the war my father was offered many jobs (remember his credo that hard workers could always find work) and went to work in the furniture industry. He was a multi-talented man, who was a machinist originally but had an interest in what was then Jamestown's outstanding place in furniture-building in the whole country. He took a job at the Jamestown Lounge Company and was a foreman there until he retired.

In 1952 my brother and I traveled with our parents to Sweden aboard the *Stockholm*, the ship that was later to become infamous for the collision with the Andrea Doria some years later. In Sweden I met my grandfather Evard who, although he was in his 80s at the time, was a strong and commanding presence. We were there for two months, and I rode the hay wagon and the work horses, helped in any way I could around the farm, and came away with a deep appreciation for the farm and for my family who had run it successfully for so many years.

In large part because of their Swedish background, both my parents were thrifty and hard-working, and Mom and Dad had many good years together, traveling a great deal, including several trips back to Sweden. Dad became active in the Viking Chorus, and both he and Mom attended many Swedish events around the area. Dad built the house that they lived in until they went to live at Lutheran Social Services, where Dad died in 1999.

I sometimes wonder if the younger generation realizes the hard work and contributions of the immigrants that made possible the freedoms and many privileges we enjoy. Surely we Swedes should be proud and thankful for our heritage and for the courage, hard work, and foresight of our ancestors.

John's parents, Gustaf and Helen

GRUNDTVIG—THE MOST DANISH OF THE DANES

by Arland O. Fiske

It was the summer of 1954 when the Ox Creek Church near Rolette, ND, celebrated its 65th anniversary. Since it had been founded by Norse settlers, a Norwegian service was planned. One hymn was the unanimous choice of the old-timers: *"Kirken den er et gammelt hus"* (Built on a rock the Church shall stand"). Translated literally, it means "The church is an old house." It was written by one of Denmark's most famous sons, Nikolai Frederik Severin Grundtvig. He was born September 8, 1783, the youngest of five, to a parsonage family on Zeeland (Sjaeland), Denmark's largest island.

Nikolai was taught by his mother to love literature, history, poetry and Norse mythology. At age nine, he left home for boarding schools and did not return to live with his parents until after he had graduated from the University in Copenhagen.

Though he had graduated from seminary, he was not ordained until he was 38. His father became ill and needed help. On his first Sunday, he preached a scathing sermon attacking the clergy of Denmark for unfaithfulness to the Gospel. Later on, he would have to submit his manuscripts to the police for approval.

Over the years, he mellowed and wrote over 1000 hymns. Besides his poetic skills, he contributed much to education in Denmark. While studying at Cambridge University in England, he got some new ideas and returned to become a leader in the Folk High Schools movement. These were residential schools which carried education far beyond the classroom walls. They made education available at government expense to the families of the poor. These schools stressed patriotism, pride in Danish heritage and helped progressive views on agriculture. They soon spread to Sweden,

Norway and even in America. The Danes who settled north of Kenmare, ND, built such a school out on the prairies in Denmark township. These were troubled times in Danish history. Military power and empire were passing. Though "orthodox" in his religious views, Grundtvig was ahead of his time as a folk leader. He had a great appreciation for what was human.

Despite all his talents, Grundtvig was never appointed to any large parish. The State Church was not keen on any pastor who challenged the system. So he spent most of his career as a chaplain in an Old Peoples Home for women. On the 50th anniversary of his ordination, he was finally recognized. The king conferred on him an honorary title of "bishop." He was 89 when he died.

It's an irony of history that many of the best people are not recognized until late in life or until after they have died. Maybe that's better because it keeps them creative. Praise, while sweet, has ruined many a good person. Today, visitors to Copenhagen are directed to the "Grundtvig Church." Designed like a giant pipe organ, it is one of the nation's showpieces.

I like Grundtvig's views on rearing children. He believed that childhood was "fantasy time," rather than a time to stress reason or emotion. Maybe that's why this poet-bishop, the most Danish of the Danes, kept young at heart. And we still sing his hymns with gusto.

TASTES OF HOME

by Norma Carlson Waggoner

My friend Connie Marker and I moved to San Bernardino, California together in October of 1960. When the Christmas season came, it could have been very sad for us had it not been for the fact that my stepmother, Doris, and Connie's mother Elvie, sent us many boxes filled with all their great Scandinavian baked goods and other treats. It was wonderful, but the highlight for me was when my Dad paid $15.00 (remember, this was 1960) to air mail a jar of his special homemade pickled herring to me, which he knew I loved. I was so touched—I know I cried. On Christmas we had an open house and shared our goodies with friends at our apartment complex. Thanks, Dad, Doris, and Elvie, for taking such thoughtful care of your two lonely daughters. You are gone now, but I will always love and appreciate you.

SEARCHING FOR THE GHOST OF MY GRANDFATHER

by Loren G. Carlson

I never really knew my grandfather, but he has been a very strong presence in my life to this day.

I grew up in Jamestown, New York, in the 1940s and '50s. My mother's father was Rev. Arvid Edstam, pastor of Chandler Street Baptist Church in Jamestown from 1926 to 1931. I didn't really get to know him before he died in January 1944 since I was born in 1940. My brother and I were toddlers when our family moved to Florida and then Wisconsin before returning to Jamestown just before he died.

I heard many stories about Arvid from my mother, Linnea Edstam Carlson, over the years. These stories were so strong, so colorful, so well told that they became foundational to my effort to define myself. Based on these stories I constructed a model of Arvid in my mind. These stories became the family myths that we shared at holidays. But over the years I seemed to remember differently or more intensely certain parts about Arvid's early life.

These are the core myths I remembered:

> *Arvid was born in a small town in Sweden and when he was 12 years old he was forced to leave his family and his village because he refused to be confirmed in the state church (Lutheran). He refused the ceremony of confirmation because he said, "I am a Baptist." For this crime he was expelled from his home and had to walk out of town alone and was never to return or see his family again. This young boy left with one bundle of clothes to make his way in the world.*

Somehow this young boy learned about botany and got enough education to enter Bethel Baptist Seminary in Stockholm. After graduation he became a missionary to Russia, which was illegal in Czarish Russia, so he went under the "cover" of being a botanist. He survived and on the way home to Sweden, he stopped in Åland, an island between Sweden and Finland where he met Irene Erickson, the beautiful strong woman who would become my grandmother.

He was invited to be the principal speaker at an international Baptist conference in Chicago, Illinois in the early 1900s. At this conference he met many Swedish Baptist church leaders in the U.S. and he was called to serve a church in Duluth, Minnesota. My mother was born in Duluth.

Arvid served several other churches in Minnesota, Kansas and Missouri and then was called to be the pastor of Central Baptist Church in Minneapolis/ St. Paul. This was the largest Swedish Baptist church in Minnesota and a very long way from the little town in Sweden that he was forced to leave. He retired after a very successful ministry in Central Baptist but was soon called out of retirement to serve Chandler Street Baptist Church in Jamestown, NY, another area populated by Swedish immigrants.

The stories about Arvid's talents and skills as a pastor were often repeated to me by my mother. She obviously idolized her father and probably would have followed his example into some magnificent adventure if she had been born in a time when women had more freedom. My mother emphasized that he was a brilliant preacher, very well read, and able to deliver extemporaneous sermons in iambic pentameter—the language of Shakespeare. He was active in social and civic issues, serving on many boards and always trying to defend and protect the poor.

I remembered these stories when I had my own family and passed them on to my children. I started wondering how much was exaggerated myth, especially the being forced to leave town when still a child and the missionary to Russia segments. How could this child become this man?

But by now my mother and father and their whole generation were gone and no one else seemed to have the same memories. So I decided to see what I could learn about Arvid's early years. I started the search for the ghost of my grandfather.

I was stopped almost as soon as I started. There were no records of an Arvid Edstam in the usual genealogical databases. By pure luck I was contacted by Kjell Bensing, a relative in Sweden I did not know of, who was looking for some information on his great-grandfather's family. He found me through the postings my cousin Pat Killoran (daughter of my father's brother Harold Carlson) made on the ancestry search engines looking for information to help me. He had learned that his great-grandfather had a brother named Arvid Andersson. We were able to confirm that Arvid Edstam was born Arvid Andersson in a small village north of Örebro, called Asker in the province of Nerike in 1872. He grew up in a nearby 'state' named *Brevens Bruk*. There were eight children born to Anders Per Larsson and Kristina Lisa Ersdotter, between 1863 and 1885, all with a first name beginning with "A". So I now had the right name and the birthplace. I planned a trip to Sweden to see if I could find any further information concerning the myths.

My wife Dee and I scheduled two weeks in Sweden in August 2010 and I started to explore ideas for how I would find information. I did a web search for Bethel Seminary (which I learned was *'Betel' Seminarat*). This seminary did exist but was no longer named *Betel*. It was now named *Stockholm School of Theology* and had moved to another location in Stockholm. I sent inquiries to the seminary to see if they had any records that would help. I also contacted the Baptist conference headquarters in Stockholm to inquire how I could learn more about Arvid. After about two months I received replies that would lead to a gold mine of information and help.

The Baptist Conference forwarded my request to Pastor Sören Carlsvärd of Betel Church in Örebro who then put me in touch with Åke Broms, the chairman of the Trevens Bruk church. Åke, his wife and his daughter, Elizabet, were wonderful. They researched the church records and libraries. Before we left for Sweden, they confirmed the essential facts about Arvid, including the fact that he had been forced to leave home and village because he refused confirmation in the state church. They found a book that reported this story (see below). We learned two new aspects of the story, that Arvid was 14, not 12, and that his whole family was threatened with expulsion, not just Arvid. Only the intercession of Pastor Pira with the state church and the factory manager stopped this from happening. The compromise was that if Arvid left alone and never returned, his family could stay. When told of his son's refusal to take confirmation and the threat to the family, Arvid's father, Anderson Larsson, said, "My son speaks for himself and he will make his own decisions."

"A Remarkable Free Church Man—The Life and Work of Claes Fredrik Pira" by J. Byström, published in 1928

Translation by Elizabet Broms

At Brevens Bruk, Asker's Baptist Congregation had a group of members. Brevens Bruk belongs under the large estate of Bystad, with land in three counties: Örebro, Östergötland and Södermanland. Men of power from the families Sparre, Thott, Rålamb, Bielke, Hildebrand, Bonde, Anckarsvärd and Gripenstedt have owned the estate during the centuries.

Towards the end of the 1850s, a preacher named J. P. Lundquist, visited Brevens Bruk and preached there. There were many prejudices against the "readers," and some of the blacksmiths wanted to give the preacher a lesson, after he had reproached them for their sins. So they simply threw him in the water at Brevens Bruk.

. . . .

The ill will against the Baptists at Bystad and Treven continued for some time, and not only from ignorant people. Some Baptists were even driven away from the estate . . . In Pastor Pira's time, the Swedish Church priest in Treven did not take kindly to the Baptists. When the priest and the "almighty" management of the estate and ironworks were unanimous in their resistance, it was not easy for the free spiritual movement.

Under Pastor Pira's later years, something happened at Treven, which illustrates some people's resistance against religious freedom as well as Pastor Pira's care for his congregation members. Pastor August Larsson, who was Pira's assistant in Asker's Baptist Congregation, had baptized a 14-year-old boy at Breven, who belonged to a family Larsson. The boy's name was Arvid. At that time, all children of that age got confirmation education from the priest, who also demanded that Arvid come to confirmation lessons. He came, but after three days he said that he couldn't continue because his parents were Baptists and he agreed with their beliefs. He was summoned to the priest but bravely defended his views. Now the priest turned to the estate management. The next day Arvid's father was summoned to the office and was told that the boy should apologize to the priest and start confirmation lessons again, or he must leave home. If not, the family must leave their home and work at Treven. This was a hard sentence. There were four children younger than Arvid in the family, and their economy was not strong. And where should they go? The father turned to Pastor Pira and asked for advice. At once Pira called for his assistant pastor August Larsson, told him about the case and said: "I suggest that you and I promise to help the boy. We will take care of him in the Lord's name. Can't we do that?" "Yes, we can!" came the answer.

Pastor Larsson says about this: "I will never forget the gratefulness in Pira's eyes, and he shook my hand, saying: 'Go in peace and tell the boy that we wish him the peace of Jesus and deep spiritual openness.'"

Pastor Larsson went to Breven. When Arvid heard what had been agreed, he was very glad. After a few days, he left his dear home. Of course, it was not without fear in him and worries in his mother's heart and tears on her cheek. It probably hurt inside his father, too, but he said that one must be faithful to one's convictions. So Arvid came to the chapel in Asker carrying a small bundle of clothes. Pastor Larsson arranged a situation for him with his sister and brother-in-law, farmers in the village of Fiskinge. Arvid was well taken care of there.

It should be added that the 14-year-old grew and in time became an industrious man for the kingdom of God. He went through the Betel Seminary. After that he worked a couple of years in Finland and since then he has been a successful pastor among Swedes in America. His name is Arvid Edstam.

I also received a reply from Magnus Lindvall, the historian of the seminary, confirming that Arvid Edstam did graduate from the school in 1899 and became a missionary. Note this is the first time that we see the name *Edstam*, a name that he chose during his time in the seminary. I made arrangements to meet Magnus at the seminary when we were in Sweden.

So I confirmed the two most romantic aspects of the myth. I was finding the ghost of my grandfather.

Search in Sweden

Soon after our arrival in Stockholm in August 2010, we met with Kjell Bensing and his wife Madeline. They gave us a wonderful tour of Stockholm and shared photos and stories about Kjell's family. His grandmother was the daughter of Arvid's oldest brother, Axel. In his photo Axel seems to be a very distinguished, strong and stern man! Kjell and Madeline were wonderful hosts and we enjoyed many meals and conversations with them and their family. Kjell had already done much research on the parents of Axel and Arvid and had traced the family tree back several more generations to the 1600s but he did not know Arvid's story. (Note: the parents' ancestors had all come from the same area of Sweden—they were not ones to travel or to marry strangers!)

Kjell took Dee and me to meet with Magnus Lindvall the historian of the seminary that replaced Betel. Magnus had prepared for our visit. As we entered the main hall, he pointed out a very large painting, "The Baptists," that hung in the original Betel Seminary. It is a rather famous painting in Sweden by Gustaf Cederstrom in 1886 depicting a group of people being baptized in the cove of Lake Ekoin at dawn. Arvid would have looked at this painting frequently. (I now have a print of this picture in my home.)

Magnus had done a lot of research including finding photos of Arvid as a graduate in 1899 at the age of 27. He showed us Arvid's graduation photo and various group photos including the group of new missionaries to Finland. Arvid was an exceptionally distinguished and handsome man. We confirmed that Arvid was a missionary to Finland and we surmise that he was one of the missionaries that started a Baptist church in St. Petersburg, Russia—the first Baptist church in Russia. Finland would have been the natural gateway into Russia. I could not confirm that he traveled under cover of being a botanist but did confirm that missionary work in Russia was dangerous. And we do know that he was an expert (self-taught?) on plants and trees so it is possible—and this version fits the imagination of a young boy!

I asked about the persecution of Baptists in the mid-1800s and Magnus confirmed that there was much prejudice against any who did not join the state church, especially in the smaller towns. Apparently it was better if you accepted confirmation in the state church as this would add you to the tax rolls but then you could attend other churches. So Arvid's refusal was not just an offense against the church but also against the state. Arvid's parents were known Baptists in Brevens Bruk and they were left alone so it was more Arvid's refusal to 'just go through the ceremony of confirmation' that got him and his family in trouble and not just the fact that he was a professing Baptist.

After Stockholm we drove to Örebro, which is a very beautiful old city directly west of Stockholm. After sightseeing in Örebro we drove north to Asker to meet Åke Brom and his family at the Asker Baptist Church for Sunday service. This is a beautiful building set in a grove of trees on what is now a side road. The service was in Swedish but familiar, with much commentary from the congregation and an emphasis on prayer. Another family from America was sitting in the balcony and they were also introduced.

After walking around the church grounds we followed Åke to Trevens Bruk, a village notable for its yellow plaster buildings. This is now a restored iron foundry town set on a pretty little river. The whole town is privately owned by a family and the villagers are tenants just as they were when Arvid and his parents lived there. It was a 'company town' and all of the workers lived in company-owned housing. The town was famous for its iron foundry, especially the cast iron stoves that were used for cooking and heating houses. Some of these are still in use today. Arvid's father, Anders Larsson, worked in this foundry. (Note: Brevens Bruk is in the process of being turned into a tourist attraction by the person who owns the town now—still an absentee landlord.)

We left the village and followed Åke up the road a mile or two to an old house that was the actual home of Arvid's family. It is a two-story square yellow stucco building. It is now owned by Lars Bjurstrom and his wife who are restoring it to the late 1800s condition. We were invited in to see it. The house was really a four-family house with four identical rooms, two up and two down. A whole family would live in one room. The original cast iron stoves were in the center of the inside wall and all vented into the large chimney that was in the center of the house. There was a single double bed for the parents. We asked where eight children would sleep and they showed us how the other pieces of furniture in the room, including table and benches, could be converted into beds. I stood in the middle of that room trying to imagine what it would have been like to live in such close quarters. I'm sure that given the 22-year age spread of the children, not all were living in the house at the same time. Outside of the house there were fruit trees and gardens and an earthen 'cold room.'

Åke took us to the church in Brevens Bruk that replaced the original Baptist church and he showed us photos of Anders and Kristina Larsson. Old church records show that they were members #5 and #6 in the original congregation that moved out of the Asker church in 1869 because the walk between villages was too long. Anders was portrayed in the church notes as a leader and a man of very strong will—a man who was willing to risk expulsion of his whole family to support the decision of one young son. He also showed us two silver candlesticks that had been given to the church in memory of Anders by two of Arvid's brothers. Anders and Kristina are remembered in Brevens Bruk.

Then we followed Åke to the state church cemetery where Anders and Stina were buried. (Everyone had to be buried in the state church cemetery.) It is a beautiful, well-maintained cemetery. You enter through two iron gates and proceed down a tree-canopied aisle walk with gravestones on either side. I thought it portended what was to become classic Scandinavian design, simple and elegant. Before entering, I prayed and left a coin for the spirits. Åke and his family had found the gravestones and cleaned them of the moss and dirt so we could read them. Anders was born in 1835 and died in 1905. Kristina was born in 1840 and died in 1910.

Anders' headstone was inscribed:

> *Revelation 22:4: "They will see his face, and his name will be on their foreheads."*

Kristina's headstone was inscribed:

> *Isaiah 32:18: "My people will live in peaceful dwelling places, in secure homes, in undisturbed places of rest."*

Now I was really encountering the ghost of my grandfather!

We knew that Arvid did leave home at the age of 14 and was taken in by a farm family in Fiskinge under the protection of Pastors Pira and Larsson. We visited a farm that may have been the place where he lived. We have found that he was baptized in Asker in 1886 (at the age of 14) and in 1890 he moved to Eskilstuna about 80 km away. He probably worked as a gardener. There are some references to him renting a large garden, which seems strange for such a young person with no money. We lose track of him until he reappears as a student at Betel Seminarat in Stockholm in

1895. We don't know how he gained his education allowing him to enroll at Betel, but it was probably self-study.

This is a question that would be interesting to explore: How does a young man working the gardens learn enough to become a botanist and to preach in iambic pentameter? There is one possible clue. The steamship records for when Arvid Edstam went to America in 1902 have a note saying he was *"returning home"* as his reason for travel. This is a very strange comment and it could be an error—but there is also a record of an Arvid Andersson going *from* America to Sweden in 1891! Could the young man have made his way to America and received training from the Baptists in America and then returned to Sweden to complete his studies at Betel? The chronology doesn't support this hypothesis, but it is a romantic idea. The Baptist Church did start in America and then moved *from* America *to* Sweden in the 1850s. Perhaps more time in the archives at Betel Seminarat and the steamship records would be helpful.

Life in America

Arvid Edstam traveled from Abo, Finland to America in 1902 at the invitation of the General Conference of Swedish Baptist Church of America to give the principal address at the 50th anniversary jubilee in Chicago. Apparently his skills as a preacher and speaker were already recognized. Following the conference he was invited to visit the church in Duluth, Minnesota, and he accepted a call to be the pastor. In 1903 Irene Ericksson came from Mariehamn in Åland to marry Arvid. They were married on June 24, 1903. (Note: The island of Åland was considered part of Sweden although it changed hands several times over the centuries. Irene always said she was Swedish, and "certainly not Finnish"). They served the church in Duluth for seven years, leaving in 1909. (Note the irony of Arvid being born in the iron-mining area of Sweden and then moving to the iron-mining area of Minnesota.) Arvid became a naturalized U.S. citizen on April 23, 1908.

Following Duluth Arvid served as pastor in several other Swedish Baptist churches in the Midwest, including Worthington, MN, Lawrence, KS where a third daughter Viola was born, and Kansas City, MO. Not much is yet known about these years, but I do remember my mother talking about living in a 'sod house' in Kansas.

In 1917 Arvid accepted a call to be the pastor of Central Baptist Church in Minneapolis/St. Paul. This was the largest Swedish Baptist church in

Minnesota. His salary was $1,400 a year. He served nine years there until 1926. The history records of Central Baptist emphasize that Arvid was a "master preacher."

He was also a good leader and manager. While he was pastor, the church grew from 140 to 322; 85 were baptized, and the building debt was paid off. (Even pastors get measured by the numbers!) Closer relationships between the Swedish General Conference and the Minnesota Conference were established. Missionaries were sponsored in China and India. There were frictions with the Twin City Church Federation and there was a split with the Northern Baptist Convention over the issue of supporting the inter-church World Movement. Inter-church politics have always been with us. In 1923 English language services were added on the 2nd and 4th Sunday *evenings*. I wonder if iambic pentameter sounds the same in English and Swedish?

In 1923 Arvid took a trip back to Sweden. We don't know who he visited, but his parents had died by then. Hopefully, he saw some of his siblings and their families.

Central Baptist Church in Minneapolis is a very active church to this day. My wife and I visited the church and were warmly greeted and introduced to the congregation. The original church building is still in use today, but a new contemporary church has been built next to it. The old building is now used for Sunday School and other group activities. I stood where the baptismal pool and podium used to be and pictured Arvid preaching in his elegant, resonate voice to the congregation in the back of the balcony. The building is beautiful with stained glass windows that remind me of Frank Lloyd Wright designs—very prairie. The Sunday morning service congregation is very typical, mostly older white people, but the activities promoted on the hall board and on posters reflect a church that is successfully reaching out to its neighbors. Due to the lack of meeting space, some groups meet at 9:00 PM on Sunday nights! I felt that Arvid was present and proud.

I have not yet been able to confirm my mother's version of the story that Arvid retired from Central Baptist in 1926. If so, it was a very short retirement because he accepted a call to Chandler Street Baptist in Jamestown, NY that same year. He was 54 years old at this point, and it is possible that he intended to retire but felt he had to accept another call.

The new pastor at Chandler Street had become very ill suddenly and there was some urgency to replace him. To say "no" may not have really been an option for Arvid.

However it happened, he did bring his wife Irene and their three daughters to Jamestown. It was at Chandler Street that my mother Linnea met my father, Walter Carlson, son of Emil and Alida Carlson, members of the Chandler Street Church. Arvid retired for good five years later in 1931. The church bulletin remarks that Arvid was a gifted preacher in the Swedish language—a continuing acknowledgment of his intellect and skill.

At the age of 60, in the depth of the Great Depression, Arvid became a successful insurance salesman, and he and Irene were able to travel to Florida in the winter. He continued to "fill in" for other pastors and maintained a busy schedule of civic activities.

My father, Walter, talked about the long conversations he had with Arvid about theology, philosophy and history while fishing on Chautauqua Lake. Walter was a well-read man, and he spoke of Arvid as a mentor, in contrast to his father Emil who punished him for "wasting" his time reading.

My parents were married in 1930; I was born in 1940 and my brother Bruce in 1941. My dad was in newspaper advertising for the Jamestown newspapers during the '30s. My mother, who was several decades ahead of her time as a 'feminist,' was the manager of the Furniture Mart when Jamestown was the 'furniture capital of the world.' We moved to Tallahassee, Florida soon after Bruce was born where my father was the assistant publisher of a local newspaper. Mother hated Tallahassee, and we quickly moved to Racine, Wisconsin where my dad worked for another paper. We moved back to Jamestown in 1943, just before Arvid died on January 5, 1944, just a few months shy of his 72nd birthday. So, I never really knew Arvid, but as I said at the start, he has always been a strong presence in my life. My search for his ghost confirmed the myths I had learned at my mother's knee and the model of the man I had built in my mind.

I think that the strongest legacy a person can leave are the stories told about them after they are gone. Arvid left a very strong and positive legacy. These stories are the true measure of a person's net worth.

Postscript

A further question: Why did Arvid select the last name 'Edstam' when he was at Betel? I've asked about this and learned that it was very common for men to choose a new last name as the patronymic naming system changed. By why *Edstam* which is not a common name in Sweden? I've learned that the two parts of the name have special meaning in Swedish: *"ed"* connotes an oath or commitment and *"stam"* refers to the trunk or limbs of a tree and *"stamlader"* means progenitor—so *Edstam* could mean an oath to be a tree of faith or oath to live by and pass on his beliefs. I rather like this.

Rev. Arvid and Irene Edstam

"The Baptists" by Baron Gustaf Cederstrom

LEIF ERIKSON DISCOVERS AMERICA!

by Arland O. Fiske

Who really discovered America? As a child, I was taught in school that it was found in 1492 by an Italian named Christopher Columbus. There was also a rumor in my home community that a Norwegian had found it long before that Columbus fellow, whoever he was. Recently, Great Britain's Royal Geographical Society reports that a Welshman, John Lloyd, who was trading with the Vikings in Greenland, reached America in 1475 while searching for the fabled "Northwest Passage" to China. Because the trading was illegal, the information was kept secret at the time and later passed on to John Cabot.

This can become quite an emotional issue. Andy Anderson, the founder and president of the "Leif Erikson Society" in Chicago, has been on a truth campaign to set the record straight. He published a book entitled "Viking Explorers and the Columbus Fraud." There is no question in his mind where credit ought to go for finding this New World. In fact, he musters up quite a few arguments to assert that the whole Columbus story is a case of mistaken identity. He claims that the real "Columbus" was a Jewish seafarer from Spain named Christobal Colon. As you can guess, Anderson is not the darling of Italian-Americans.

What is the case for claiming that Leif got here first? There are three main sources. First, Snorri Sturluson, the famous Icelandic saga writer, wrote of Leif: He . . . found Vinland the Good." Second, a story called the "Tale of the Greenlanders." And third, the "Saga of Erik the Red." These writings do not always agree on all points. Erik (Old Norse did not have the letter "c"), also spelled "Eirik," was the father of Leif who was called the "Lucky." Erik had been outlawed in Iceland because of his pagan ways with the sword in settling personal disputes. Fleeing Iceland, he established a colony on the west coast of Greenland which grew into at least 330 known farm sites. Norsemen continued to live in Greenland for over 400 years. That's longer than they've been in North Dakota!

America may have been first seen by Europeans when a Viking boat was blown off course en route to Greenland from Iceland. The Viking ships did not do too well against hard winds with their single sails, though they rode the waves well. The leader, Bjarni Herjolfsson, did not stop to explore the land but turned back to Greenland to tell his story to Erik. Leif bought Bjarni's ship and with a crew of 35 set sail westward about the year 1003. Their first landing was among glaciers, probably Baffin Island, which he named 'Helluland."

The second landing was named "Markland" or "Land of Forests" and was likely Labrador. The place which lived on in their memories, however, was named "Vinland" or "Wine-Land," because so many grapes were found. On board ship was a German winemaker. He became ecstatic at the sight. Wine was expensive in Greenland because it had to be imported from Europe. Here was a paradise of unlimited grapes and abundant salmon in the lakes and streams.

Leif returned to Greenland and became its ruler. He is also credited with converting the people to be Christians. Leif himself became a Christian while visiting King Olaf Tryggvason in Norway. Olaf was an uncompromising evangelist.

The task of colonizing the New World was taken up by Leif's brother Thorvald. All went well at first. But on his first contact with "Native Americans," there was bloodshed. The Norseman acted arrogantly. One of the natives escaped and returned with an attacking force. An avenging arrow killed Thorvald and the rest fled in their boats. He was the first European to be buried in America.

Besides the saga accounts, is there any other evidence that Norsemen set foot on American soil 500 years before Columbus? Attempts have been made to locate Norse settlements all the way from Hudson Bay to Virginia. But there is only one place which many scholars agree is clearly identified. It's on the northern tip of Newfoundland called "L'Anse aux Meadows." Helge Ingstad, a Norwegian Arctic explorer, began excavating in 1961. His findings were confirmed by Dr. Bengt Schonback, an eminent Swedish archaeologist. Evidence of buildings, jewelry, tools, slag iron and coal has been found.

A much publicized map purchased by Yale University has turned out to be highly controversial. Many claim it's a fraud. In 1898, a stone slab written in runic letters was found near Kensington, MN. It told of 30 Scandinavians who had journeyed inland and met tragedy. Most scholars, however, reject the genuineness of the stone. But this has not discouraged nearby Alexandria from erecting a monument to display for tourists. Perhaps other runic slabs will be found and Leif's claim for finding American will turn up some new wrinkles.

MY GRANDMOTHER: MRS. ARVID J. THORSELL

by James Swan

My grandmother, Martha Alida Niord who later became Mrs. Arvid J. Thorsell, left Sweden on a ship when she was 19 years of age. As the ship was leaving the port, she recalled her father waving to her, both of them with the knowledge that they would never see each other again, although my grandmother did make a return trip to Sweden in the early 1950s.

She came to Warren, Pennsylvania and worked there doing housework. My grandfather, Arvid Thorsell, came from Sweden and the first place he came to was Camden, New Jersey, where he worked building ships in the shipyards. He eventually came to Warren, and worked in the logging industry. In later years he was self-employed as a carpenter and worked with Joe Larson [father of Carilyn Larson Wright].

My grandmother and grandfather met one summer at Lake Chautauqua and later were married. They had two children: one was my mother, Ethel, and then Philip, born twelve years later.

My grandmother had a maiden sister Aunt Betty who lived in New York City. Occasionally she came to Jamestown for a visit. She was a staunch Democrat. My grandfather was a dyed-in-the-wool Republican. He hated President Roosevelt. The more he talked about Roosevelt, the madder he got. Aunt Betty liked Roosevelt and told my grandfather that Roosevelt's heart was bigger than his head and that he was a wonderful President. The two of them would argue politics. My grandfather would listen to the radio and Aunt Betty would come over and turn it off.

My grandmother had a cousin whose name was Joseph Ander. He lived in Toronto, Ontario, Canada and ran a diesel factory. He was also the Swedish Consul of Ontario. I remember him saying one time when we visited him, "It's so easy to get to Sweden now. You can jump on a plane and you're there in twenty-four hours." (This was in the late 1940s or early 1950s.)

Joseph Ander in his early years was involved in youth meetings of Peter Waldenstrom who was the founder of what became the Evangelical Covenant Church. I remember in our travels up to Canadian Keswick Bible Conference coming over the Peace Bridge to Fort Erie and the Canadian Customs. My grandmother told the attendant that she was born in Sweden. For some reason he would not let us through Customs. My father told the representative that her cousin was the Swedish Consul of Ontario. At that point there was no problem, and he let us go into Canada.

Joseph Ander denied any contact with Peter Waldenstrom, but my grandmother told us that she knew he did have a part in youth meetings with him.

My grandmother passed away in 1973, and I'm happy to have these memories of my grandma.

A CHANCE MEETING

by Susann Sparrman Gustafson

Soon after emigrating to America from Sweden, Lars Lawrence became employed by Dahlstrom Metallic Door Company in Jamestown, New York, as a private chauffeur for one of the owners.

One day in the middle of May 1929, Lars drove his employer, Mr. Anderson, to New York City to meet a relative who was coming in on a boat from Göteborg. My uncle Håkan Anders Åberg was on that same boat. After disembarking, he was milling around the dock with the hundreds of other passengers. He happened to see a friendly looking man, who was wearing a black chauffeur's cap, leaning against a big black car. The man called out to him in Swedish, and thus the conversation began. "Where are you from?" Lars asked. Håken answered, "I am from Hunnebostrand, on the rocky coast of Bohuslän. There were no jobs there, only if I wished to follow in my father's footsteps and become a sailor or a fisherman."

It wasn't long after the two Swedes began conversing that Lars realized that Håken didn't know anyone in America and also didn't have a destination. So Lars asked his new friend, "Why don't you come to Jamestown? I know they are looking for workers at Dahlstrom's where I work. I'm sure they will hire you."

A few days later, Håken Anders Åberg, who would Americanize his name to Andrew H. Oberg, boarded a train bound for Jamestown. He got settled in a boardinghouse at 339 E. 4th Street, and soon made his way down to Dahlstrom's for an interview. A few days later, on May 20, 1929, he received a Postal Telegraph reading:

REPORT TO WORK FRIDAY TOMORROW MORNING SEVEN O'CLOCK
DAHLSTROM METALLIC DOOR COMPANY

Uncle Andy worked there for a few years and realized that he had an aptitude for and enjoyed working with metal. He decided to move to Cleveland, Ohio where he established "Oberg Metal Products" and began manufacturing metal cabinets.

He attended the Swedish Mission Church, where he met my mother, Ruth Olson's sister, Esther, who was working there at the time as a nanny. They soon married and after successfully operating their business for fourteen years decided to move it to Jamestown where they would be closer to family and by now close friends Lars and his wife Martha, also a Swedish immigrant.

The Lawrences had started the "Lawrence Restaurant" on the corner of Main and Fourth Streets a few years earlier. They later opened the "Kaffestugan Restaurant" one block west on Fourth Street. Both restaurants were known for many years for their wonderful Swedish cooking.

These two young men from Sweden were typical of the entrepreneurship of many of the new Americans who settled in Jamestown. It truly was the "City of Opportunity" for both of them.

Both couples retired to Vero Beach, Florida in the 1960s. There they continued their friendship and Andy and Lars would often reminisce about their chance meeting on the dock in New York City.

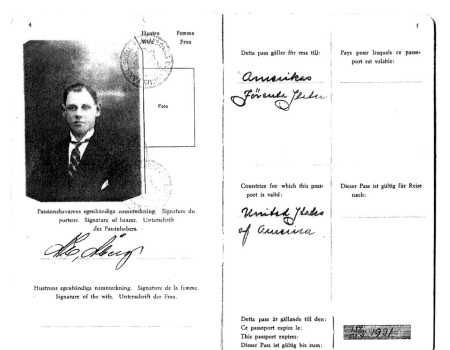

Uncle Andy's Passport

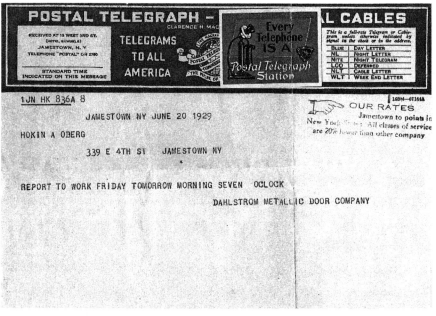

"You Have a Job!"

NIAGARA

by Barbara Hillman Jones

My husband David's mother's family is Swedish. They lived in my home town of Jamestown, New York on what was termed *"Swede Hill,"* the area of Jamestown where the largest concentration of Swedish immigrants built their homes and raised their families. Swede Hill had its own small neighborhood businesses—grocery store, bakery, etc. And it definitely was a *hill*. Willard Street which takes you to that area is a huge hill and it can be a real problem in the winter time. The streets that are perpendicular to Willard Street seem to be built as tiers, and David's family, the Hallins, lived on one of those streets—Chapin Street.

His maternal grandparents had come from Sweden in the late 1800s, his grandfather built a house on Chapin Street for his family, and that was followed by other members of the family building houses next to his. Most of the homes on Chapin Street were occupied by members of the Hallin family, and David tells about how they would visit each other at one house or another for morning *kaffe* (coffee) and fellowship.

David's mother Evelyn Hallin worked at Zuckerman Furriers as a bookkeeper before she married David's father, and she loved being able to buy her clothing at Zuckerman's. She was a pretty, sweet Swede who always looked very chic. Evelyn had three sisters and a brother. Her brother, Delavan, owned and operated a grocery store for many years, and two of her sisters, Austrid and Adelaide, owned and operated a needlework store on East Second Street called *The Spinning Wheel*.

David tells a family story that reminds me of some of the Swedish "Sven and Ole" stories that we often hear. Although most of the pictures of our ancestors portray them as being very stern and serious, we know that they also had a keen sense of humor.

It seems that David's great-grandfather, Carl Snug, had taken a trip to America and during that trip he visited Niagara Falls. He was appropriately impressed as he gazed at the Niagara River thundering down 173 feet below at the Horseshoe Falls. It was a sight he could never have imagined, and he was elated to have had the privilege of personally witnessing the majesty and grandeur of Niagara Falls in America. He returned to Sweden and, of course, proudly told everyone about his trip and especially his visit to Niagara Falls.

In Sweden at that time in the latter 1800s, there was a great class distinction between the nobility and the commoners. I'm not sure if those aristocrats had some sort of identifying mark or if the commoners could just tell by their airs or their attitude what their class was. At any rate, it was an understood ruling that persons of nobility would be given preference over the *hoi polloi*.

Back home in Sweden, David's great-grandfather boarded a trolley in Stockholm and took a seat. After a couple of more stops, the section of the trolley in which he was sitting filled up, and there were no more empty seats. At the next stop, a person of the nobility boarded the trolley and finding no empty seat, he fixed his eyes on David's great-grandfather, fully expecting him to give up his seat to this man of the upper crust. However, Carl Snug did not rise but continued to occupy his seat. The man cleared his throat and glared at David's great-grandfather who again did not move. Finally, when he was unable to ignore the nobleman's arrogant demeanor or warning gestures any longer, Carl Snug looked up at him with an assertive smile, and said: *"Vell, have YOU been to Niagara?"* Taken aback, but still in pursuit of a seat, the aristocrat turned to someone else—undoubtedly someone who had *not* been to Niagara.

OUR CROSSING STORY

by Joan Peterson Shevory

"Darling Mother, your little boy (almost) drowned last night." These were the words of six-year-old Gustaf who crossed the ocean with his twelve-year-old sister, Jean, and a "trusted" servant when they were en route from Sweden to America in 1886.

It is said that every family has a "Crossing Story." This is ours as told to me for a school assignment by my grandmother, Jean Gustafson Carlson, when I was in the 5th or 6th grade (1936 or so).

Jean and Gustaf's parents, Hilda and John Severin Gustafson, lived in a small town called Oskarshamn (translated into English, *Oscar's Harbor*) on the shores of the Baltic in Sweden. According to my grandmother, Hilda was an eye doctor and John was a maker of musical instruments, mainly violins. They had six children in Sweden—Jean, Hulda, Axel, Gustaf, Edna and Edwin—and two children later in America—Mabel and Olga.

In 1886 Hilda and John decided to send two of their six children, Jean and Gustaf, to visit their grandparents, Gustaf and Augusta Gustafson, who had left Sweden for America in 1881. Gustaf and Augusta had settled in Buffalo where it was said Gustaf was a shopkeeper.

According to my grandmother, they were in the care of an "impatient" nurse on this trip. This nurse proved to be in a great hurry to get to America because she boarded the wrong boat which took them to Boston, not their planned destination, New York City. More disasters followed. When the boat made a stop in Hull, mischievous Gustaf ran off and couldn't be found. Luckily, they discovered him just in time to get back on the boat. Then, on the ocean, a tremendous storm washed three men overboard. This is when Gustaf must have thought he was going to drown.

Although they were terrified by the trip, Jean and Gustaf liked living in America and they could not be persuaded to go back to Sweden. In 1890 their parents and siblings joined them in Buffalo. In 1892 the family moved from Buffalo to Jamestown.

Before she left Buffalo for Jamestown, Jean worked for Elbert Hubbard at the Larkin Soap Company. Hubbard later became famous as the author of a very popular pamphlet, "A Message to Garcia" and as the founder of the Roycroft Community in East Aurora, New York. I have my grandmother's book, "Elbert Hubbard's Scrapbook," on which she writes inside the cover: "E.B. was my boss when I was 16. I was his Swedish interpreter and translator."

The Gustafsons prospered in Jamestown. John Severin Gustafson brought his entrepreneurial skills to our community, buying land along the Chadakoin and selling it for factories being built along the river. He started the Swedish Flag Snuff Company in 1895 and later the Jamestown Cigar Company. His sons, Gustaf, Axel, and Edwin, all helped with the family businesses. Gustaf was also a talented musician and the director of the Ideal Mandolin Orchestra.

In Jamestown Jean met and married Elmer Carlson, a watchmaker and jeweler who owned Carlson's Jewelry Shop on Second Street. They had three daughters, Doris, Irene and Lois. Doris was my mother. Elmer was also a member of the Ideal Mandolin Orchestra.

"Grandma Jean," as she was known to me, was a very special person, and I was fortunate to have her for my grandmother. She lived with us for several years during my childhood. She taught me how to sew, using her treadle machine, how to knit, and how to play cards. She told me stories about Sweden and hinted that we were related to Swedish royalty. This was my favorite story, even though I suspected that it was a fanciful tale.

Jean was not your typical Swedish grandmother. After a few years in this country, she had lost all of her Swedish accent and was a modern American in every way. She wore dramatic hats and stylish clothes, smoked using a long cigarette holder, and especially liked going to bingo games. She loved music of all types from Gilbert and Sullivan to Liberace. She was also a radio soap opera fan. I remember "Mary Martin" as one of her favorites.

Grandma Jean did everything fast and was always on the go. With her sisters, her parents, and daughters living in Jamestown, there was constant travel between their houses and much gossip to share over coffee.

If there was one thing Swedish about Grandma Jean, it was her cooking. I remember the wonderful smell of her limpa rye bread when it came out of the oven. I still cherish that recipe along with the bread mixer and the well-used pans she used in making the bread. My other favorites were *kroppkakor* (potato dumplings stuffed with minced bacon and onions), *raggmunk* (potato pancakes), and *kåldolmar* (stuffed cabbage).

I am grateful that Jean and Gustaf made their adventurous "crossing," even though it was traumatic for them at the time. Without it I would not have had a grandmother I remember so fondly and possibly three generations of Gustafsons would not have been reunited in this country. This was not true for many Swedish immigrant families who lived out their lives never seeing their closest relatives again.

> **Editor's Note**: Joan tells about her Grandma Jean working for the Larkin Soap Company in Buffalo. I have some beautiful antique dishes in a pattern called "Azalea" that I inherited from my *farmor*. The dishes came in boxes of Larkin Soap in the 1920s and 1930s, and she had collected them.

Jean Carlson, c. 1940

BROSTROMS AND ULANDERS

by Janice Ulander Johnson

Both of my parents, Oscar Ulander and Elsie Brostrom, were the youngest in their families and were born in this country—my father in 1904 in Collinsburg, Pennsylvania, the son of Emanuel and Emma Sofia Ulander, and my mother in 1910 in Jamestown, New York, the daughter of John and Augusta Brostrom. According to the Ellis Island immigration records, it appears that Emanuel Ulander came to West Newton, Pennsylvania from Sweden in March 1903. His wife, along with five of their children, arrived in October, 1903. My grandmother, Emma Sofia, died of pneumonia in 1910 after being sick for only ten days. Dad was just five years old at the time of his mother's death so he was raised mostly by his father and his sister Gertie in West Newton. It was tough for a small boy not to have a mother to care for him. My grandfather, John Brostrom, came to this country from Sweden in 1892. Augusta arrived in 1894. They were married in Pittsburgh and settled in West Newton for a few years before moving to Jamestown in 1904 where John was a stone mason during the building season and worked at Art Metal during the wintertime. They lived on Swan Street at the top of "Swede Hill."

My parents met at a picnic around 1929 (I think in the Jamestown area but am not sure) and had a long-distance courtship that lasted for seven years. They married in 1936 in Jamestown and lived in West Newton for a few years before moving to Jamestown, where my father was employed at Art Metal.

Many of my childhood memories revolve around my mother's family, the Brostroms. There were eight children—all of whom lived in Jamestown. The oldest was Albin, followed by David, Signe, Evald, Paul, Martin, Ebba, and my mom, Elsie. Several of them attended the Zion Mission Church in Jamestown. The brothers and sisters missed no opportunity to get together for birthdays and holidays, especially Christmas. We would always sing the doxology, "Praise God from Whom All Blessings Flow" before meals were served. On Christmas Eve there would be huge "get-togethers" with all of my aunts and uncles and cousins. Each family would bring a dish for supper, which usually consisted of plenty of homemade korv, ham, scalloped potatoes, sylta, sill, vegetables, limpa rye bread and several kinds of jello. I don't know if jello is a Swedish custom or not, but we all loved it. Of course, there were plates full of Christmas cookies, including lots of spritz and pepparkakor. Mom (with a little help from me sometimes) would spend days making the cut-out cookies and decorating them with colored sugar. She and her sister, Ebba, made korv and sylta together every year. Later on I got to help make the korv by turning the handle on the grinder and watching the long rings of sausage come out. Some years one of my uncles would dress up as "Santa" on Christmas Eve which scared the daylights out of some of us younger kids, and we would end up in tears. With all the people crowded into our small homes, I remember the Christmas tree falling over on at least one or two occasions. There were so many presents and so much excitement. All of us kids got gifts from everyone. Sometimes we would go to Julotta at church afterwards. I remember coming back home late at night on Christmas Eve and seeing the beautiful sparkling snow. It seemed magical, and all was well as we jumped into bed and awaited Christmas morning.

Part of the excitement in preparing for Christmas was, of course, picking out the Christmas tree. We would always go down to Tedesco's, a produce market in Falconer, where the trees were inside. They were all wrapped separately with twine and Mr. Tedesco would cut them open and twirl them around for us to see. They had a big pot belly stove pumping out heat and the whole place smelled like a pine forest. My dad would haggle on the price of the tree and usually we would get a beautiful balsam for about three dollars. On our way out the door we would be given a bag of oranges.

Our family always got big boxes of presents from dad's sister in West Newton and particularly looked forward to the popcorn balls she would make and send us. Since we didn't have a fireplace, we hung our Christmas stockings, which were my dad's work socks, across the pillars going into the dining room. These were always filled with oranges and bananas and some small gifts on Christmas morning.

Going to church was certainly a big part of the Christmas holidays. Every year there was a children's program written and directed by Gertrude and Dolores Johnson. We would go to rehearsals on Sunday afternoons and would be assigned a "piece" to memorize and recite at the program. The church was always filled to capacity for these programs and we kids were always dressed in our finest holiday clothes.

One of the joys of the winter season was the horse-drawn sidewalk plow that would clear our sidewalks on occasion. We loved hearing those sleigh bells as the plow went by our house and we'd rush to the window to try to catch a glimpse of the passing horse and driver. I might add that I don't remember having to walk through a lot of deep snow as I walked to Fletcher School because everyone's sidewalk always seemed to be nicely shoveled or plowed.

> **Editor's Note**: My father's family also lived in West Newton, Pennsylvania and my mother's family lived in Jamestown. Jan's parents introduced my parents to each other. It must have been sometime in the seven-year long courtship of Jan's parents because my parents were married before hers! Arnold Hillman married Florence Tuline on September 14, 1935, in Jamestown, while Oscar Ulander married Elsie Brostrom in 1936. It was a good introduction—my parents were married for more than fifty years.

Elsie & Oscar Ulander, 1936

RAOUL WALLENBERG—
"RIGHTEOUS GENTILE"

by Arland O. Fiske

Raoul Wallenberg is the most famous "missing person" in the world. There's been a million dollar reward for his safe return to freedom. Very few people knew his fate, but most westerners didn't believe their explanations.

The Wallenbergs are a respected Swedish family, distinguished as statesmen, diplomats and bankers. Raoul was born August 4, 1912, in Kappsta, *Lidingö*, near *Stockholm*, into a less wealthy branch of the family. His father, a naval officer, died three months before his birth. Fortunately, he had a strong-hearted mother.

After graduating with distinction in architecture from the University of Michigan in 1935, Raoul tried banking in South Africa and Palestine. He found it to be "too calm, cynical and cold." Architecture was his dream though he went into international trade. The family thought his talents were in politics.

While in Palestine, Wallenberg came in contact with Jewish refugees from Germany. He was moved by their persecution and by the anti-semitism which he found. It touched him more deeply because his great-great-grandfather, Michael Benedicks, was a German Jew.

During World War II, the evidence was mounting that most European Jews were being destroyed by Hitler. Adolf Eichmann, a heartless sadist, came to Hungary in March 1944 to personally exterminate the country's Jewish population. His cunning and cruelty knew no bounds. The Allied powers were slow to respond with help. But finally, President Roosevelt gave his support to save them through the United States War Refugee Board.

Strange as it may seem, it finally came down to one man, 31-year-old Raoul Wallenberg. He joined the Swedish legation in Budapest and assembled 250 Jewish volunteers who were given Swedish diplomatic protection. He rented 32 houses over which he flew the Swedish flag to shelter 15 Jews and set up two hospitals, soup kitchens and a children's home. Portuguese, Swiss and Vatican legations also gave help. Surviving many Nazi attempts to kill him, it is believed that he saved over 100,000 Jews of Budapest by giving them "protective passes." Bribery and threats of post-war punishment were his weapons against the Nazis.

On January 17, 1945, as the Russian army approached, Wallenberg was summoned to the Soviet military headquarters. Though warned against going, he went in hopes of negotiating with them on behalf of the Jewish people. Soviet paranoia and treachery, however, regarded him as a danger to their rule. That was his last day of freedom.

Until late 1987, there was hope that Wallenberg was still alive. Then the Kremlin advised his family that he died of a heart attack in a Soviet prison in 1947. Despite this report which has been accepted by his family as factual, there are former Soviet prisoners who have returned to the West who claimed they had seen him and spoken to him since that time. The new Russian republic is reported to have recently turned his file over to his family.

The government of Israel has declared Wallenberg a "Righteous Gentile." The United States government has made him an "honorary citizen." He is only one of three foreign nationals ever to be granted such recognition. As a part of the "New Sweden '88" celebration, Gustavus Adolphus College had a special lecture on Wallenberg by Ambassador Per Anger who had been a personal friend and colleague of Wallenberg.

A tree has been planted in his honor at Yad Vashem, Israel's memorial to the Holocaust victims near Jerusalem. It was with deep emotion that I paused before that tree, silent in my heart for the Holocaust victims, but proud that a great Scandinavian had sacrificed his life in this mission of mercy.

OUR SWEDISH B&B

by Carilyn Larson Wright

My Swedish heritage is very important to me. The stories that my Mom told were so clear, I could almost believe I was walking with her in that tiny little town of Wilcox, Pennsylvania, when they would meet the train for yet another family from Sweden, giving them a start in their new homeland.

My Mom's parents were born in Sweden, her father coming when some of the family was already here and working. Her Mother (Selma) had two brothers who both married Selmas, and they had a sister Mandy. Her father's family had five boys—some remained in Wilcox, others relocated to Jamestown. They lived in a company house, called Tannery Red Row, which was close to the railroad station. Their families bought tickets directly from Sweden to Wilcox, knowing that there would be a Swedish family who would take them in, (sometimes having the whole family sleeping in the dining room), until they could secure a job and a rental house in which to live. [It was just like a Swedish bed and breakfast.] Mom would tell of a stream of people that would follow them home and the forever friendships that were made at that time. When Mom's father died, the family purchased the Mission Church parsonage, and therefore the family became the ones to house all the pastors that served the little church. Grandma and my Aunt took care of the church and when we spent days there, my sister and I would clean along with them. She and I knew every corner of that little country church, playing Sunday School and preaching ... also enjoying the oak pump organ that was retired to a corner when someone donated a piano.

My father's family came from Anita, Pennsylvania. My Grandfather (a widower) had been here for a few years when he returned to Sweden to find a wife, which he did. However, in order to persuade his chosen one, she had to bring her Mother with her. My Grandfather worked in the coal mines, as did my Father for several years, starting when he was 12. He had only five winters of schooling, then had to enter the mines to help with the family finances. At 15 he helped a carpenter build the Presbyterian Church, and carpentry became his lifelong occupation. At 16 they traveled to Jamestown, on their way to California to live on the land Grandpa had purchased some years before. But relatives here in Jamestown convinced the family to stay, and Grandpa started to work at Art Metal, as did so many other Swedes. My father built his first house at the age of 16, so that his family would have a home to live in. He shingled his last roof at the age of 77. As did so many immigrants, the Swedes had a very strong work ethic because of the hard life they experienced in the old country, and they really wanted to make a different life for their families in their newly adopted country.

My parents instilled a strong sense of family and religion in us. They belonged to Zion Covenant Church which did not convert to total English until 1945. We celebrated holidays with the same customs that our ancestors did, and I still decorate with my many, many Swedish Christmas items. Our daughter is the one who will carry on the traditions, for which I am grateful. We all need to remember that our heritage is only as distant as yesterday and where we came from makes us who we are.

G. ELVING LUNDINE, A BRIEF BIOGRAPHY

by Stan Lundine and Barbara Lundine Goldman

Gustaf Elving Lundine, the youngest of eleven children, was born in Sweden in January 1914. Two years later, his mother, Hulda, took him and his 5-year-old twin sisters, Margaret and Martha, to the United States. Although she could not speak a word of English, Hulda and the children made it through immigration and traveled to Jamestown, New York where her husband had been residing, along with their eight other children, and working for about two years.

Elving attended Jamestown public schools until sometime in his high school years when he had to drop out and work at two different jobs to help support his family. Later, he passed the equivalent of a GED to get his diploma. Still later, he took a number of correspondence courses in engineering.

In 1936, Elving married Ruth Nelson who lived on the corner of Camp and Juliet Streets. Since he grew up on Juliet, he presumably knew Ruth for most of his life. They had two children: Stanley Nelson and Barbara Louise in 1939 and 1943, respectively.

Elving eventually became a sales representative for a Jamestown company in New York City. He and Ruth lived in Brooklyn from 1939 until 1940 which Ruth found very troublesome. About 1940, Elving became an engineer for Steel Partitions Company located in Falconer, New York. That company, which manufactured metal office partitions and other specialized products, became a defense contractor during World War II. In fact, they made the metal casings for atomic bombs. Elving made several trips to the Manhattan Project which designed and produced these weapons. As a result of this critical job, he was exempt from military service during the war.

Al, as almost everyone called him, was a very friendly, outgoing person with a wonderful smile. As a young man, he was a very good baseball player with a team called the Ashville Merchants in the local semi-pro league. He even got a tryout with the Chicago Cubs in their spring training in Los Angeles one year. But he "threw his arm out," as they said in that day, and gave up the game for golf which he played for the rest of his life. He joined Moon Brook Country Club around 1943 and won several tournaments there over the years. In the winter, he was a bowler in local leagues.

Around 1950, Elving left Steel Partitions and took his family on a trip to the West Coast, visiting his brother, Nels, and his family in Los Angeles as well as relatives in Seattle. Shortly after returning, he invested in a small metal fabricating company in North East, PA. In spite of working 16-18 hours a day, this venture did not succeed. He returned to Jamestown and worked as sales manager for Jamestown Metal Products, a hospital and kitchen cabinet manufacturer, owned by a character named Hugo Lindgren.

In 1960, Al and a small group of former Steel Partitions employees founded Dowcraft Corporation. He was the President and the driving force behind the founding of this new enterprise that purchased one facility and retained some of the customers of the former Steel Partitions. They manufactured office partitions, which comprised roughly half of their sales, and metal specialty products including casings for Feedrail, a continuous electric current for the undersides of bridges and other places where wiring was impractical. The first few years were such a struggle that it was sometimes difficult even to make payroll. But by the late 1960's, the company was so successful that they acquired Ellison Bronze, the nation's first manufacturer of balanced entrance doors for office buildings and other structures such as the domed stadiums in Syracuse, Minneapolis and elsewhere.

He was delighted with the birth of his grandsons—his son Stan's boys—John and Mark, in 1974 and 1976, respectively.

Elving had an extraordinary command presence. He never shouted at his children or others. You just knew that you would do as he said. The one exception to this was in later life, with his dog Watson. The dog did whatever he wanted, including jumping on Al's lap. When Mike Goldman asked to marry Barb, Elving said, "You can have my daughter, but you can't have my dog."

During the 70's, Dowcraft adopted an employee stock ownership plan. When Elving died in 1979, virtually all of the company's workers owned some stock. After his death, Ruth sold all of the family's stock back to the corporation so it became almost 100% employee-owned. This seemed to be a fitting testament to Al Lundine's business and personal philosophy. Dowcraft was sold to a Canadian company in the 90's, but Ellison Bronze continues as a separate, successful employee-owned company to this day.

This is a very brief and inadequate summary of Elving Lundine's life, but it may give a glimpse into the background and character of an extraordinary human being.

'SYTTENDE MAI'—NORWAY'S CONSTITUTION DAY

by Arland O. Fiske

May 17—"Syttende Mai"—is Norway's happiest holiday. How did it start and what does it mean? On that day in 1814, 112 men signed a new constitution for Norway. They had been elected from the Lutheran state church parishes. They had traveled by foot, skis, horseback and wagons from every part of Norway except the far northern parts, Nordland and Finnmark. Travel was not possible from those wintry areas. The delegates met at Eidsvoll in the home of Carsten Anker, a wealthy merchant. Eidsvoll is about 40 miles north of Oslo.

The constitutional assembly met for worship on Easter Sunday. It consisted of 47 officials, 37 farmers, 17 town representatives and 12 from the military. It was called by Christian Frederick, the ruling representative of the Danish king. The purpose of the assembly was to save Norway from an uncertain future. The majority of the delegates favored declaring Norway an independent monarchy with the Prince Christian Frederick as the new monarch. He was not unwilling.

It was an age of revolutions and a time for redrawing the maps of Europe and the New World. A new nation, the United States of America, had adopted a constitution in 1787 based on freedom and justice for all. The might of Britain had been repulsed. In France too, a once powerful monarchy had been overthrown and a new constitution was adopted in 1791.

An international crisis had started the chain of events rolling. As "punishment" for siding with the French, England and its allies had forced the Danish king to give up claim to Norway at the Treaty of Kiel on January 14, 1814. This ended a joint rule begun in 1380 and which lasted 434 years. The Norwegians had not even been consulted! Ironically, Norway's possessions, Iceland and Greenland the Faroe Islands, were overlooked in the treaty and became Danish colonies by default. Norway was promised to Sweden as compensation for the loss of Finland to Russia in 1809.

The Eidsvoll assembly was a bold stroke for independence. Why couldn't Norway be free? The delegates studied the new American and French constitutions. It was also known that Karl Johan of the Bernadotte family in France, who had become Sweden's new crown prince in 1810, would rather have returned to France as its new king than to wait for his future in Sweden. He never did learn the Swedish language. The French, however, restored the Bourbon family to power and Karl Johan chose to cash in on his fortune in Sweden with Norway as a bonus.

Brave talk, however, is not enough to secure freedom. The British navy blockaded Norway and cut off its needed food supplies as well as all exports. The economy crumbled. By the end of July, Karl Johan personally took command of his battle hardened troops. They were superior to Norway's "home guard" in numbers, training and equipment. Fighting lasted less than two weeks. The pro-Swedish faction in Norway's Storting (parliament), headed by Herman Wedel Jarlsberg, held sway. They were no less patriotic, but were realists about international politics. During this time, they were also lobbying in London for more favorable terms. Christian Frederick renounced his claim to be king of Norway and returned to his homeland where he became King Christian VIII, 25 years later. On November 4, 1814, the Storting unanimously elected and recognized Karl XIII, the king of Sweden, as Norway's monarch. Norway, however, remained a separate nation from Sweden and was only beholden to the king.

The Norwegians negotiated a favorable agreement with their new king. The constitution was respected, they were not required to supply troops for Sweden's foreign wars, they could elect and run their own Storting, and a representative of the king would reside in Oslo.

Four years later, the French-born Crown Prince of Sweden became King Karl XIV Johan. He would have liked to have had November 4 celebrated as a holiday in Norway in recognition of his rule. As in so many things proposed by the Swedish kings, the Norwegians were not agreeable. Instead, a group of students led a demonstration on May 17, 1829, a symbol of their determination for full Norwegian freedom. Still hoping to win the Norsemen over, the king good-naturedly allowed "Syttende Mai" to be celebrated.

The "Unions Perioden," as the union with Sweden was called, lasted until October 26, 1905, when the Swedish King Oscar II gave up all rights to Norway. He concluded that it was a hopeless task to govern Norway from Sweden. It was also a time of bad economy and heavy emigration to the New World.

"Syttende Mai" has become as much a symbol of freedom to Norwegians as July 4 to Americans. Norsemen are still celebrating May 17 as their Constitution Day, even though independence didn't come for another 91 years. When independence finally came in 1905, they revised and updated the Eidsvoll constitution and declared it to be "Kongeriget Norges Nye Grundlov" (the Kingdom of Norway's New Constitution). The Eidsvoll assembly had done its work well. Long live the constitution and freedom for Norsemen and their neighbors everywhere!

JOHAN AUGUST HALLIN

by C. David Jones

Sometime during the last part of the 18th century, there was born in Sweden a soldier, Johannes Paff, who had seven sons, five of whom would also become soldiers like their father. One of these sons, Soldaten (soldier) Anders Snugg, born in 1821, married Stinat Hellena Cathrina Nicolaidotten. Anders and Hellena Cathrina had three sons and four daughters. Among these children was Carl Johan, who was born in 1841 and who took as his wife Hallina Christina Ecklund (born in 1838). Carl Johan Anderson (Ander's son) and his wife Hallina had a son, Johan August Carlson (Carl's son) born March 8, 1874. Fate was not kind to Johan, whose mother died when Johan was a small boy. His father remarried, and his second wife was jealous of Johan and his sisters, Ida and Albertina. Johan's stepmother was cruel to him but not to her children—Gustav, Oscar, Anna, and Elmer. Johan decided to leave home and to seek his destiny in the new world of America, so he left Hakarp-Søsken, near Husqvarna, Småland, Sweden, and at the age of twenty, he made the trans-Atlantic voyage to America aboard a sailing vessel, spending seven weeks in passage at sea.

Like thousands of other immigrants, the young *Svenska poika* Johan August Carlson, landed in America almost penniless, not able to speak the language of this new and strange land, but yearning for the freedom from want and suffering which America promised to the teeming masses which thronged to its shores. At Ellis Island, Johan was asked to register with the Immigration Office. Disappointed and sad over the cruel treatment given to him by his stepmother, Johan decided not to take his father's name: he would not be Johan Carlson (Carl's son); instead, he would adopt his mother's name, "Hallina," but he would omit the feminine ending of her name and he would take the name *John August Hallin*. When his younger brothers and sister came to America, and even when his half-brothers came later on, they all adopted John's new surname, and they would become known as Gustav Hallin, Oscar Hallin, and Elmer Hallin.

John (Johan) Hallin made his way from Ellis Island to the Swedish settlement of Jamestown, New York, on the shores of Chautauqua Lake in the western part of that state. There John found employment as a woodworking craftsman in one of the numerous furniture factories in the Jamestown area. Developing and refining his woodworking and finishing skills, John energetically became an entrepreneur and President of Elk Furniture Company in Falconer, New York. He and his partner developed a noble manufacturing business with a fine reputation for creating excellently crafted furniture worthy of the credit given to old-world master craftsmen.

When he first moved to Jamestown, the young Swedish craftsman found room and board in the home of the Swedish immigrant family of Carl Johan Peterson and his wife Anna Louise Hagg Peterson. The Petersons' ancestors, like those of John Hallin and most Swedes, had been baptized and raised in the Lutheran State Church of their homeland. But somewhere they had come under the influence of the Anglican Englishman, John Wesley, and had become devout and staunch Swedish Methodists. Carl and Anna Peterson had five sons and a daughter, Anna Marie (born April 4, 1876). Carl, who was a steward in the Epworth Swedish Methodist Church in Jamestown, was determined that no man would court his daughter unless he was a Swede and a Methodist! John August Hallin attended the Epworth Church with the Peterson family, and it was not unpredictable that he would fall in love with their beautiful and demure daughter, Anna Marie. The couple was married in the Epworth Church on October 8, 1896, and to their union were born a son, Delevan, and four daughters—Mildred, Austrid, Evelyn and Adelaide. It was the third daughter, Evelyn Marianna, who married the Reverend Glenn David Jones, pastor of the Calvary Assemblies of God Church, Jamestown, NY, and to their union was born the Rev. Dr. C. David Jones who is the husband of the editor of this book.

MY STORY

by Rheba Brumberg Carlson

I have always been fascinated with my paternal grandfather, Peter Brumberg, and how he met his future bride, Hulda Maria Hemmingsdotter. My father, Edwin Brumberg, told me their story when I was ten years old.

Peter and Hulda lived in Småland on the Baltic Sea. Peter was a Navy sailor. They met in a favorite restaurant of Peter's where Hulda was a waitress. They became close friends that soon turned into an engagement when they both emigrated from Sweden on the same boat.

From reading the genealogy book, it seems to be the year 1836 when they had the courage to leave Sweden, a year of financial disaster. My grandparents chose Pennsylvania because of the similar farms in that state and the beautiful Appalachian Mountains. Peter made a huge success as a farmer and also a coal miner in the mountains. Hulda and Peter had a large family: five boys and two girls. My father was the second oldest of the seven children.

My parents first lived in Buffalo, New York but left when my father lost his job during the Depression. They moved to Jamestown, New York and urged many Swedish emigrants to move there with them. In Jamestown they were only 90 miles from the farm of Peter and Hulda Brunberg. Note difference in spelling. Peter wanted to "Americanize" the name.

Because of this romantic story, I recognized my own love for Rolland Carlson, who happened to have the same last name as my mother—Hattie Carlson (Brumberg). I will always remember Hulda and Peter. They were blessed by God in a very special way.

We are still in touch with the Erlandssons, the Brumbergs, and all their children. We are lucky to have a genealogist in the family, and there is still travel back and forth from America to Sweden, and we maintain very close connections.

MANNERHEIM—
A NAME THE FINNS TRUST

by Arland O. Fiske

In Finland's short history as a free nation (since 1917), its determination for freedom has often been tested. Its most dramatic moment was in the "Winter War" in 1939-1940 with the Soviet Union. The free world cheered as the gallant Finns successfully resisted the first Soviet invasion attempt. Unfortunately, they did little else.

One leader stood out in that struggle: Carl Gustav Mannerheim (1867-1951). The Mannerheims had come to Sweden from Holland and were made "nobles." During the reign of the Swedish king, Gustavus III (1771-92), they moved to Finland. They were politically conservative, aristocratic and were confirmed monarchists. There was nothing unusual about that in those times. The one Mannerheim who stands out as a national hero, Carl Gustav, went to Russia in 1889, at the age of 22, to seek a career in the military. At that time Finland was under the control of the Czar's government. He distinguished himself in the war with Japan (1905).

When the Russian Revolution of 1917 took place, Mannerheim returned to Finland at the age of 51 to drive out the Bolsheviks. The German military gave aid. In 1918, he became "Regent" of Finland and ran the government until a new constitution was ratified on July 17, 1919. Then Mannerheim retired to private life.

By 1931, the Finns feared that the Soviets may try to reclaim the lands controlled by the Czars, Mannerheim returned to public life at age 64 as Chairman of National Defense. The "Mannerheim Line" was built 20 miles in depth, consisting of concrete bunkers, tank barriers, and artillery.

In August 1939, Hitler and Stalin made a secret treaty to divide Eastern Europe. In October, Stalin demanded that Finland turn over areas sensitive to the Russian borders. He offered other land in return. Mannerheim advised the Finns to accept, but the government in Helsinki felt confident that help would come from Britain, France and their Scandinavian neighbors. Stalin's patience ran out and on November 30, 1939, bombs fell on Helsinki. Instead of rolling over, the Finns surprised the world and gave the Soviets a bloody nose. The Russians were unprepared for such determined resistance.

Unfortunately, the free world (and Hitler too) miscalculated the ability of the Soviet military. Mannerheim knew better. When a second Soviet offensive began, the Finns fought valiantly before being overwhelmed by massive numbers of weapons and troops. Mannerheim bargained for the best possible terms. When the Nazi invasion of Russia took place, Mannerheim's forces retaliated against the Soviets in Finland but would not commit themselves to aggression against Russian territory. The aging commander was "Mr. Finland" during those days. He served as president from 1944-1946 when he retired due to ill health. He died in 1951.

Mannerheim will live in Finnish memory as a name to be trusted. Small nations need strong people. Long live the Finns in their determination to be free.

THE SWEDES IN ZION

Excerpted from a talk by Russell N. Chall in celebration of the 100th anniversary of Zion Covenant Church, September 25, 1994

Submitted by his daughter, Cynthia Chall Holt

... In order to survive in a new land with its strange customs and language, they [the emigrants] drew upon what they regarded as their richest cultural base: their religious heritage. Their faith which was paramount for them sustained them in the sometimes painful adjustment to American life. The earliest newcomers organized and built churches immediately.

The first Swedish church in Jamestown was built in 1852. Others followed and by 1894, the year Zion Covenant Church was organized, there were six Swedish churches all within two city blocks bordering Chandler Street—two Lutheran, one Methodist, one Baptist, and two Covenant churches, also including a Swedish Salvation Army downtown. With so many choices one could not only sample but also choose a fellowship they felt most comfortable and at home with. All of the churches prospered and all are still in existence today. Language was as important at that time as it was on the day of Pentecost when God ordained that everyone in Jerusalem would hear the Gospel in their own language, regardless of nationality or origin. Our thanks to the Swedes who were concerned about the religious well-being of their fellow countrymen.

From this background came the 57 Swedish immigrants who organized and built the Swedish Zion Church on College Avenue opposite the old Jamestown High School. Today the building housing the swimming pool is where our church stood. Organized October 4, 1894, they met in the old Gifford Building at the foot of Main Street until the church basement was complete. Then they met in the basement until the church was finished, no doubt in order to save the rent paid for the space occupied in the

Gifford Building. The sacrifices, labor, prayers and dedication in building and paying for our church can only be imagined. There were some who even mortgaged their homes. Their faith, coupled with stubborn will and determination, resulted in a church that has won many to a living faith in Christ and nurtured them on their life's journey. The charter members would rejoice to see how faithful we have endeavored to fulfill their dreams as we worship in our present beautiful location, edifice, educational wing and facilities. And we are now celebrating our 100th anniversary!

There were problems that had to be faced and dealt with. One very important one was the gradual transition from the Swedish language to English. This began in the early 1920s, using Swedish for the morning and English for the evening service. By the mid-1930s it was one Swedish service a month. By the late 1940s, the change was complete. The only Swedish heard thereafter was a Swedish and an English sermon at "Julotta," the early Christmas morning celebration, Easter Sunday, and on our church anniversaries. Swedish choir anthems and hymns were then included, also. That too was short-lived. There were many discussions, arguments, and opinions expressed during this change, but looking back, it was all settled in a peaceful, Christian spirit. The original challenges that the founders faced and took care of so nobly and the problems that faithful members later had to settle were all prayerfully met with a spirit that has bonded us together as a loving fellowship . . . .

> **Note**: Russell Chall was the organist at Zion Church from 1949 until he retired in 1979. Cindy tells about her dad playing the organ the Sunday of that 100th anniversary celebration after he had been retired for several years. She remembers how nervous she and her brother Wesley were for him because they knew their father wanted to do such a good job, knowing that would be the very last time he would play the instrument he loved so much. Cindy says he did a wonderful job and afterwards he told Cindy that he felt "Someone" guiding his fingers over the keys that morning.

A SWEDISH FAMILY'S HISTORY

by Arthur (Pete) Thorstenson

If you will look at a map of Sweden, on the West Coast you will find Göteborg. The international name is *Gothenberg*. Approximately 90 miles north you can see where the Norwegian border comes down, jogs west a short distance, then jogs north to a narrow strait of water. If you look to the left of these two jogs, you can find a town named *Skee* (fway). This is the province of *Bohuslan* (Boo us lahn). Keep in mind when a "w" appears, it is pronounced as a "v".

Here a gentleman named Edward Ericksson Walback, a sailor and eventually a Naval Officer, was born on October 18, 1836. He married a lady by the name of Carolina Andersdotter who was born in Hogdal on July 16, 1827. How they came together is unclear because these two places are quite far apart.

They had three children and Carolina died at the age of 41 years. All three children were born in Nasinge. One daughter named Amellia Serafina, moved to Norway in November 1887. The other daughter, Hilda Ablation, died in 1953. My cousin Errol Bergendorf mentioned he had met her once.

After Carolina died, Edward married a lady by the name of Maria Ericksdotter who was born in Nasinge on April 23, 1838. They had two boys and three girls. One was named Anna Carolina. In 1890 the family moved to Skee. At that time Anna Carolina was almost 15 years of age. The younger boy, Erik Olof, had died at the age of 9-1/2 months, six months prior to moving.

On May 17, 1874, a person by the name of Joseph Torstensson was born in Quidinge. His father was Torsten Nilsson and the mother was Oliva Johnsdotter. It is felt her name actually was Olivia. There is no record of when Torsten Nilsson died.

Joseph grew to be a very tall and husky man and became a stonecutter. He married and lost both wife and child in childbirth. It is presumed there were no other children. In fact, little is known about his family, even though his mother lived with them. Eventually, he married Anna Carolina Walback and they had nine children.

She went by the name of Carolina. The first three children were born in Skee and in 1905, they moved to Kulhult. The firstborn was Thorsten on July 4, 1900. He was followed by Agnes on September 28, 1901. John was born May 29, 1904.

Kulhult was an area south of Osby, Skåne. Thorsten was five and John was about one year at the time of moving. Joseph's mother accompanied them and resided with them in Skåne. It is believed by cousin Errol that Olivia may even had paid for the farm. The mother and mother-in-law resided on the farm, tending the garden, chickens, cows and horses. Of course, as the children grew, they became the ones to do many of these chores. The mothers and children were very self-sufficient. The father worked in Osby and came home on weekends. There were many churches and public buildings being built at the time, and being a stonecutter, he had ample work.

Like most families at that time, the oldest kids had it the hardest. Thorsten worked, at times plowing gardens and other crops for neighbors and turned the money over to the family. At the age of 19, he purchased a bicycle and his father and he had quite a row over that.

Having grown up on a farm he was very good at handling horses. Sweden had compulsory conscription (draft for military service), and he was inducted into the cavalry. After service time there wasn't much work (early '20s) but farming. Most Swedes had large families and when the parents died, these farms were split up. Eventually, these farms became too small to make a living on. What saved the young men was the migration to the United States. Here there was plenty of work. In those times there was a quota on immigrants. As it had been filled he could not stay in the United States but could go to Canada. Thorsten migrated to Canada in or about 1923. He worked at three different jobs; one was in a gold mine, another on the railroad, and lastly as a lumberjack. After being there a short time, Thorsten sent money to his father, and he migrated to Canada. Shortly after arriving in Canada, he received word his infant sister had died. After being joined by his father, money was sent to John who also joined them.

The lumberjack season usually ends in the spring because the ground gets too soft to skid the logs. With that, Thorsten and John applied for visas to the United States and the father returned to Sweden. Thorsten worked on the Weland Canal while he was waiting for his visa. His visa came through first, so he went to Jamestown. The reason he went to Jamestown was that he had been to Niagara Falls. He heard a couple of Swedes sitting on a park bench talking. He approached them and inquired if they knew of a place in Buffalo where he could get a job. Their reply was, "You want to go to Jamestown. That's where the Swedes are." So when the visa came through, it was off to Jamestown.

When he arrived in Jamestown by train, the station was located on First Street at the bottom of Cherry Street. Upon disembarking from the train, he walked up Cherry Street and turned towards Main Street. Again, he heard a couple of Swedes talking. He inquired if they knew of a place where he could stay. Their reply was, "Yes, we'll even go with you so you get to the right place." They took him over to Lafayette Street between Second and Third Streets. Apparently, it was a boardinghouse.

The next morning he ventured down to Brooklyn Square and entered a restaurant. A person by the name of Olof Person worked there, and they struck up a conversation. Olof suggested he go around the corner where they were building Market Street. Thorsten followed his suggestion, and he was hired. This was only a short-term job and on completion of that, Olof suggested he go to Jamestown Veneer and Plywood because they were hiring. I guess it was always called The Panel Company. Well, Thorsten was hired and the boss was another Swede. After maybe a day's work he asked the boss how much he was going to be paid. When he was told how much, Thorsten asked him if he would get his pay for him. The boss calmed him down, and he stayed. After a period of time, this boss and another person left and formed Chautauqua Plywood located on Jackson Avenue in Celeron. For years after the war they built cabinets for Zenith television sets.

While working at the "Panel," he became acquainted with a floor sweeper by the name of John Chindstrom. He learned that John took in boarders, and by that time brother John had arrived. So they moved in with the Chindstrom family. One day Thorsten's boss asked if his brother had a job yet. John had applied, but they weren't hiring at that time. Thorsten answered that John had secured a job at the Crescent Tool Company. The boss said it was a good place to work and he would probably be better off working there.

It was while boarding at John Chindstrom's place that he met John's niece, Greta. After a time he acquired a Chevy Phaeton which was succeeded by an Overland 6.

Thorsten tells of the time as a youngster when he was to get his driver's license. His test consisted of going on South Main Street to the city line. The testing officer asked him to turn around, which he did. As they approached Cole Avenue, he was asked to turn right on Cole Avenue. He did and went over the curb, but he got his license anyway.

Thorsten married Greta and the following April I was born. The first place they lived was on Harrison Street in the area of J V Restaurant. From there they moved to the corner of Barker and Hazzard Streets, just a few houses from John Chindstrom's. They were thinking of having a house built, but for whatever reason, instead purchased one at 122 Ivy Street. This was behind where the Southside Plaza is today. There were only three houses above Cole Avenue, and we lived in the last one. From there on, there was just a trail.

As Betty and I grew up, we could walk to the south and pick all sorts of berries. Between that and Pop's garden, we were provided with enough food. I can remember when as a kid our parents sent us to the store on Sunday to buy a pint of ice cream. That was a real treat. It had to be eaten the same day as purchased because we didn't have a refrigerator. When Thorsten purchased the house on Ivy Street, he sold his car and didn't have another until 1948.

Betty was born in 1929 shortly after the stock market crash. The following years were tough years in which to be living. Work was very spasmodic and there were terrific doctor bills in 1936 and 1941. It was like walking a tightrope.

My godparents, Carl and Mary Johnson, lived for a time on South Main Street. At times we visited them and at times they visited us. Friday nights were fight nights. I can remember the excitement created over these fights. There was Joe Louis, Max Baer and Max Schmeling. Of course, there were others, too.

By 1941 World War II was approaching and Thorsten went to work at Jamestown Metal Corporation. He eventually became a belt sander. This job seemed to be where he really shined. All the fussy jobs were his as well as rework jobs that might have ended up as scrap. He was missed for years after his retirement.

This gets us years ahead of where we should be. In the late '30s, his mother sent him a letter asking him to return to Sweden. She wanted him to take over the farm. My sister and I never knew about this until years later. After seeing what a God-forsaken place it was, I'm glad we never lived there. We think of how it would have changed our lives, especially if we had lived there during World War II.

In 1944 the house on Ivy Street was sold, and the family moved to 213 Curtis Street. While residing there, my sister got married in 1948. My turn came in 1952. In 1956 Thorsten and Greta moved to 36 Roland Road where they resided until 1986. They designed the house and had it built—they finally got their new house!

It was tough for many folks going through the Depression. I can remember guys sitting around my folks' kitchen, cutting out cardboard to put in their shoes because they had holes in their soles. They never felt safe for very long. Thorsten financed only one car in his lifetime, and that was in 1958 or '59, and he couldn't sleep at night. He had the money in the credit union and could have paid cash, and after a few months he withdrew the money and paid off the car.

Thorsten retired in 1967; he did some gardening for others, and he was a janitor in a store for a short while. The reason he did this was because Greta was seven years younger and didn't qualify for Social Security.

Thorsten and Greta were very good money managers. In their retirement years in addition to his gardening, he and Greta would pick grapes. This gave them extra money which they really needed. While retired they purchased a new carpet, refrigerator, a washer, dryer, and a new car and returned to Sweden twice.

After about 20 years of retirement I asked how much money they had. Their answer was they had about as much as when he retired. While living on Roland Road, they attended Camp Street Methodist Church. They were active there and participated with appropriate groups in their age level. Sadly, after leaving Roland Road they never returned to the church.

THE HERRING FESTIVAL

by Barbara Hillman Jones

When some people travel, they go to Alaska, Hawaii, the Grand Canyon, or some exotic place that they have been looking forward to visiting for a very long time. We have friends who have gone on an African safari and to the Arctic Circle, my nephew and his wife have climbed most of the highest peaks in Colorado, my sister and brother-in-law have conducted numerous mission trips to Peru, Kenya, and Syria, my two nieces toured the pyramids in Egypt. We envy them the trips they have been privileged to take. We know that we will never live long enough or have the financial wherewithal to see all of those places ourselves, and so we love to see their pictures and hear their stories.

We feel very blessed to have visited just a few faraway places, however ordinary ours might seem in comparison to theirs. We did take one, though, that we are sure not many of our friends or relatives have taken—in fact, we don't know anyone who took this one!

Several years ago we were privileged to go to Scandinavia on a tour arranged by a minister friend of ours, who was also a professional travel agent. To us, it was rather exciting since I am 100% Swedish and David is 50% Swedish. We arrived in Copenhagen, Denmark, then toured Stockholm in Sweden where we were delighted to be able to spend a little time with some of my relatives, we flew to Oslo and Bergen in Norway, and we took a boat ride on a fjord in Norway, to name a few things we did.

None of that was terribly unusual—we know many people who have seen those same sights, and we know many people who have taken extensive cruises. However, we had never been on a cruise ship, but an overnight cruise was part of our tour, and we were anxious to see what that was like. We embarked on a ship of the Silja Lines in Stockholm where we found our stateroom on the 5th deck of that 10-deck ship. We left Stockholm at dusk one evening, and that huge ship slipped noiselessly through the Swedish Archipelago in the Baltic Sea toward our destination of Helsinki, Finland. We were told that there are approximately 3,500 islands between Stockholm and Helsinki, some of which are no larger than to accommodate a very small red *"stuga,"* (*house* in Swedish). Most of these homes flew a Swedish flag. We were impressed that there was almost no yard around the *stuga*, and the sea came almost right up to the house. Then we learned that there is no tide in the Baltic Sea, so they did not have to worry about the sea rising and falling. It remained constant. We finally fell asleep in our stateroom, arriving in Helsinki just as the sun was rising.

Having never visited Helsinki, we had no idea what to expect, but fortunately, some of the other more experienced travelers in our group had previously toured Helsinki. One of the Lutheran pastors for whom this was a repeat trip kindly took us in tow and showed us many of the sights.

An extremely memorable event for us was to attend a worship service at the Rock Church (Lutheran) which was held in English. The underground Rock Church, completed in 1969, is built inside of a massive block of natural granite in the middle of an ordinary residential square. The structure is barely visible from outside, with only its copper dome poking out of the rock. Inside, the church is circular and enclosed by walls of bare rock, and the ceiling is a giant disc made of copper wire. The interior is lit by natural light streaming through 180 vertical window panes that connect the dome and the wall. A solid copper-colored balcony provides a nice view of the church interior from above. The combination of natural and man-made materials in the Rock Church is striking and explains its popularity.

After the service our Lutheran minister guide pointed out some things we could do and then left us on our own until evening when we would again board ship to return to Stockholm. Since David loves the water, we headed in that direction. As we got closer, we could see quite a commotion. There were lots of people milling around and then we saw what seemed like hundreds of fishing vessels backed up to the shore. As we read the signs, some in English, we realized that we were in the midst of the *BALTIC HERRING FESTIVAL!*

Now a Herring Festival intrigued both of us because of our Swedish heritage and because we were used to eating herring *(sill)* in our homes. My grandparents always had pickled herring on their table, a perfect complement to Grandma Tuline's limpa rye bread! A young woman who obviously recognized that we were Americans approached us. She spoke

English very well and we shall always be grateful to her for her kindness and patience with these Americans who had never been to Helsinki. She told us that Finnish herring are smaller and more delicate in flavor that what we might find in America, due to the Baltic Sea's comparatively low salt content. Herring, a small oily fish, is found in the shallow, temperate waters of the North Pacific and the North Atlantic oceans, including the Baltic Sea. Herring move in vast schools where they are caught, salted and smoked. The fishing season draws to a close in October, and fishermen come to sell all of their catch directly from their boats, but during this Festival, it's all about herring! You can choose between mustard, citrus, garlic, chili, herb and fruit flavors. You can eat them "on the go" as they are with a wedge of local, dark bread, or enjoy them prepared in many strange and bewildering selections of dishes.

Of course, we couldn't wait to sample something from the Festival, but not knowing what to select, we asked our kind guide what she would recommend. We never quite understood the name of the dish, but she pointed us to what she said was the most popular, a small round loaf of dark bread into which several herring had been baked, which we thoroughly enjoyed.

We returned to our ship and smuggled the leftovers into our stateroom, although I suspect the not-so-secret aroma of freshly-baked herring and bread may have wafted through the air.

The next morning I awoke to find David already up, spellbound as he gazed out of the picture window of our stateroom. The sun was just rising with its vivid shades of orange and pink as we passed through that Archipelago on our way back to Stockholm. That huge cruise ship barely made a ripple in the water as it again noiselessly made its way past those tiny islands with the tiny red *stugas* with a flag in the yard and a boat tied up at each dock. People waved to us as we passed them, and we waved back. I could not get David to leave the window, even for breakfast. He was mesmerized by the beauty of that experience.

We often reminisce about that trip—Sunday worship in The Rock Church, the beauty of the Archipelago, and the fun we had at the Baltic Herring Festival. We've met other travelers who worshipped at the Rock Church, and we know others who've been enthralled by the Archipelago, but we've never met anyone who has attended the Baltic Herring Festival. If perchance we had, I doubt that they could have had more fun than we did!

HARD TIMES IN THE NEW WORLD

by Tom Erlandson

It is well known among Scandinavian-Americans that their ancestors emigrated from their homelands to their new homes in America in part because of hard times in the "Old Country." In his book "Saga From The Hills—A History of the Swedes of Jamestown" (Fenton Historical Society, Jamestown NY, 1983), M. Lorimer Moe lists economic difficulties as the first of six factors causing the Swedes and other Scandinavians to leave their homelands. According to Moe, between 1820 and 1920 one million Swedes, 730,000 Norwegians, and 300,000 Danes immigrated to the United States. The economic opportunities offered by *det forlovada landet*, the promised land, were far greater than those they left behind. That was true in part because class distinctions were less important in America. Three of my four grandparents were among the many.

My Grandmother Erlandson was born Hilma Sophia Carlson (changed to Johnson when her widowed mother remarried) on October 9, 1874, in Kalmar Län, Småland, Sweden, the eldest of 17 children. She died in May, 1966, in Jamestown. During her 91 years she grew up in Sweden, met and became engaged to my grandfather, worked briefly in Copenhagen, came to America, married my grandfather, had seven children, lost her husband in her mid-'60s, worked much of her life, and made many friends. She was employed in private homes and at Jamestown's Gretchen's Kitchen, Nordic Kitchen, and the Harvey-Carey Drug Store. Among my fondest memories are those of Christmas Eve at Grandma's 3rd floor walkup, with Dad's siblings and our Erlandson cousins, enjoying the Swedish holiday foods. It was a privilege to know her.

Although I have wonderful memories of Grandma Erlandson, her husband, my Grandfather Ernest Robert Erlandson, died in September, 1938, a few months before I came along. Born in Sweden in 1869, he came to this country on a sailing ship in 1890, choosing Jamestown because an older brother, Frank, lived here. Unable to find work in Jamestown, he went to Bradford, PA, where he worked in the oil fields for a time. Returning to Jamestown, Ernest worked for the city laying bricks to pave the city streets. Having met my grandmother and having become engaged to her in Sweden, he sent for her and they were married on May 5, 1895, in the First Lutheran Church. Before he died, he worked at the Broadhead Worsted Mills and later at the Automatic Voting Machine Company, both in Jamestown.

I recently learned that a surprising number of people with Swedish surnames in the Jamestown area have Danish relatives on their mother's side, and that is true of my family also. My maternal grandfather, George (Jorgen) Peter Kofoed, was born in 1880 and grew up on Bornholm, a Danish island in the Baltic Sea. His family lived in Rønne, the island's largest community, where my Great Grandfather Andreas Peter Kofoed lived at 15 Stengade (Stone Street). When my wife Mary and I visited Bornholm in 2007, we were unable to find that address, but that is another story. The family had a grocery store in the front of their house and a butcher shop at the rear. Great-Grandfather Andreas picked up dead cattle outside of town and processed them for sale in the store. His son, my grandfather, helped in the family business while growing up, but then trained to become a furniture maker.

Grandfather Kofoed came to America at the age of 17, settling in Jamestown because relatives from Bornholm were established here. Although they were in the furniture business, Grandfather's relatives had no work for him at the time and he took a job in nearby Warren, PA, making axe handles. He lived in a boarding house run by Mary Nelson, who had a daughter Margaret (Maggie), who became my Grandmother by marrying young George Kofoed on July 5, 1905. Margaret Christina Nelson was born in Lander, PA in 1882 and died in 1949, five years before her husband. Shortly after their marriage, my Grandfather found work in Jamestown as a furniture salesman. The couple had 3 daughters, the youngest my mother, and a son.

Once established in Jamestown, and having good jobs, my grandparents on both sides of my family were able to have new homes built, not far from each other as it turned out, on the city's south side. In addition to their home, my Mother's parents also had a small farm just outside of town. Considering this story so far, readers may wonder why the title contains the words "Hard Times." As it did for so many others in that era, the answer for my grandparents involved "The Great Depression."

On Dad's side, the Erlandson home in those pre-depression days was on the corner of Beech Street and Everett Avenue, near Allen Park. My Grandfather owed $3000 on the mortgage for the home and, when city officials decided to pave the streets, they notified my grandparents that they had to pay their part of the paving bill. Because the house was on a corner and both streets were being paved, they were faced with a double bill, which amounted to about $3000, the same as they owed on the mortgage. Being conscientious citizens, they paid the city bill in full, continuing to pay the mortgage in the usual gradual way. This occurred not long before October, 1929, and after "The Crash" on Wall Street, the bank holding the mortgage wanted it paid, which they could not do. The bank foreclosed and my grandparents lost the house. I find it ironic that paving the streets with bricks, a job my Grandfather had in his early days in Jamestown, was part of the cause for losing his house.

On my Mother's side, prior to the 1929 depression Grandfather Kofoed had become a very successful furniture salesman for Jamestown and area companies. Mother remembered having a Willys Knight automobile which they used to go to their nearby farm and to visit relatives in Lander, just south of the PA line. Her father was a member of the local Masonic lodge and the family was, in the words of the day, well-to-do. He regularly invested in stocks, including many holdings in area furniture companies with which he was affiliated. (I have several of those large and colorful stock certificates, now worthless.) Then came "The Crash" and, with so much invested in stocks of little value, the family lost their town house and country farm.

Just as the Scandinavian heritage and early success in Jamestown of the Erlandson and Kofoed families are similar, so are the story sequels: neither family in my grandparents' generation ever owned their own home again. Both families rented apartments, and Grandfather Kofoed lived with my parents for a time when my sister Judy, also a contributor to this volume, and I were teenagers. Times became better as Judy and I grew up, and we both graduated from college and had families of our own, held good jobs and own our own homes. However, the stories we heard when young, including those about The Great Depression, have forever influenced our thoughts and our actions.

George & Maggie Kofoed & Daughters, 1911

Hilma & Ernest Erlandson's Wedding

SIMPLY SCANDINAVIAN

by Ann Nelson Quackenbush

One of the delights of getting to know the man who would someday be my husband was discovering that we shared Swedish ancestry. His last name of *Quackenbush* bespoke Dutch blood, though there were Irish forebears on his dad's side as well . . . Barretts and Dolans, mainly. His mother's people, however, were Nordic, most sailing to America much earlier than my four grandparents. Who knew at that moment that our first overseas retirement trip nearly thirty years later would include an attempt to locate Ölbo (near Gävle, Sweden) where Pat's great-grandmother had lived until 1880? Sadly, by the way, we would be unsuccessful. Though Ölbo clearly showed on a Google Earth map, neither local government nor bus transport officials in the area had ever heard of it.

In those initial months of dating, the two of us conversed incessantly. How fortunate we were that Sambo's Restaurant stayed open all night! Among the interesting items that came to light was that Pat had Swedish relatives in Ridgeway, Pennsylvania, a town not far from Dagus Mines, Pennsylvania, where my maternal grandparents lived for some years. Turns out his great-aunt, Linnea Rydquist Beck, owned a women's apparel shop on Main Street and three generations of "Tulines"—my grandmother, mother, and I—had browsed and bought there. Another coincidence was that Linnea's first cousin was a neighbor to my grandparents during their time in Dagus Mines. Jennie Swanson remained on their Christmas card list for decades. Small world indeed.

Patrick was not only a good talker, but also a good listener. During his growing-up years and well into adulthood, he spent much time with his maternal grandma, Agnes Beck Saylor. In high school, he often lunched at her apartment and with six siblings at home, happily accepted invitations to spend occasional weekends there. Pat loved to get his grandmother reflecting on days gone by . . . early life in logging camps, a romantic honeymoon at Chautauqua Lake, Swedish celebrations of Christmas that included Julotta services, special foods, and unique decorations. No wonder Pat approached our first Christmas as man and wife with such anticipation. We'd be going to Jamestown, and my mother and grandmother still adorned the holiday with abundant Swedish touches.

Pat seemed enchanted with the way his new in-laws' home looked and smelled as we walked through the door after our two-hour trek from Hornell. At last, he'd be getting to taste classics he'd heard about for years like *korv, lutfisk, bruna bönor, sill, gröt,* and homemade root beer. He was certain he impressed the family with a near-perfect recitation of their Swedish table grace. The meal was off to a great start! The korv came out first, browned and beautiful, just the way he liked his meat. Lutfisk screamed fishy, so he quickly sent it along in spite of multiple cries of "just try it" directed his way. One glance at the *sylta* made him reject that outright . . . and the *sill* as well, once he recognized his grandma's precious side dish was nothing more than pickled herring. Thanks, but no thanks. The beans were fine, the root beer a mite yeasty. Deciding the *korv* "needed something," Pat politely requested mustard. That's when the room went silent. Eventually, Uncle Arnold queried, "Whatever would you put that on?" I had warned my sweetie ahead of time about the "who'll-get-the-nut rice porridge" knowing his aversion to anything custardy, but he wasn't stressing about dessert as he'd seen tins of cookies stacked high on the kitchen counter. Pat rather fancied himself a cookie connoisseur. I might label him an addict. This was one occasion when "I never met a cookie I didn't like" simply did not apply. He told me later he was absolutely incredulous to have so many platters with so many varieties come his way and to find not a single one of them was frosted. He attempted one with a shortbread base but found it difficult to finish. Meanwhile, the rest of the diners were oohing and aahing over them all. I am convinced that if McDonald's had been open on Christmas Eve, we'd have made a quick detour on our way to church that night. Fortunately for him, Christmas Day dinner was much more "American" and to his liking. He would have plenty to say to Grandma Saylor upon our return to Hornell!

All these years later, we still look back on that holiday and laugh. My husband continues to reject many of the traditional Swedish specialties, but has developed quite the taste for brown beans, lingonberries, potato *korv* sans mustard, *pepparkakor,* and *mandelskorpor* [almond rusks or Swedish biscotti!]. The coffee habit didn't kick in until he turned sixty, but at least we're finally sipping together. After a while, Pat began taking his own frosted cut-out cookies to Jamestown at Christmas. There were plenty to share, but no takers. No offense taken. Oh, and one more thing . . . when we took that glorious trip to Sweden in May of 2008, guess what I found in our suitcase between Pat's socks and his underwear? One large jar of creamy peanut butter! He wasn't taking any chances. Can't say I was surprised; are you?

H. C. ANDERSEN—DENMARK'S BELOVED STORYTELLER

by Arland O. Fiske

In New York City's Central Park, there is a statue of Denmark's favorite storyteller. Around it gather crowds of children to hear his fairy tales. Many suppose him to be American, but Hans Christian Andersen is still the pride of Denmark. Next to the Bible, his writings are the most widely read and translated in the world. Who is this Dane that so many people have come to love?

Hans was born April 2, 1805, at Odense on the island of Fyn, the son of a shoemaker and a washerwoman. His father died when he was only nine and his mother died twenty years later. How did this boy, reared in poverty and obscurity, rise to become so famous that when he died on August 4, 1875, his funeral was held in the Copenhagen Cathedral? Nearest the coffin sat the royal family, foreign ambassadors and other impressive guests.

Great writers have a streak of loneliness in their souls. Despite his fame and his welcome into the homes of the most famous people of Europe, he never owned a house nor did he marry. There were loves in his life, but it was usually fantasy. His self-centeredness and his strange appearance got in the way. He was his own "ugly duckling." Even his most friendly critics noted that he wrote mostly about himself.

Despite his loneliness and outsider role, Andersen was a great entertainer and reporter of his times. He had a love-hate relationship with royalty. At the time, kings were held to be above criticism, except in France where Louis XVI was beheaded. He enjoyed royal favor, but in his writing he showed contempt for the vanity of blue-bloods. In private papers found after his death, he wrote: "I maintain that the Shoemaker's Guild is the most famous, for I am the son of a shoemaker."

Andersen was a deeply religious man, despite his father's atheism. He did not, however, accept conventional creeds. When questioned about his beliefs, he claimed: "I have become convinced that what Christ teaches in fact comes from God." He was at odds over theology with two other famous Danes, Bishop Grundtvig and Soren Kierkegaard.

Andersen was a legend in his own time and was the most photographed person of his day. He was one of the most widely traveled Danes, but never visited America. He wrote: "What a pity that America lies so far away from here." He was a pen-pal of Longfellow in Massachusetts and visited Dickens in England. He made 29 journeys abroad and wrote 156 fairy tales and stories.

Some of his works include "The Emperor's New Clothes" and "Red Shoes," as well as "The Ugly Duckling." My favorite Andersen fairy tale is "The Snow Queen." It's the story of a little girl named Gerda who rescues her friend Kaj from the ice castle of the wicked Snow Queen.

If we could rescue the world's political and military leaders from their fears for a week and gather them to read Andersen's fairy tales, there just might be a chance for peace in our times.

> **Editor's Note**: Maybe "The Snow Queen" is Arland Fiske's favorite because his wife was named "Gerda."

CARRYING ON THE TRADITION

by Donna Nelson Johnson

My father, Torsten Axel Bertil Nilsson, was born on April 3, 1912 in Tjallmo, Brunneby Östergötland, Sweden to Axel and Sigrid Krentz Nilsson. He came to the United States in March of 1930. An older brother, Hilding, had immigrated to Jamestown a few years before, as had an uncle and aunt, Fred and Amelia Berguson.

He grew up in Borensberg, Östergötland along the Göta Canal and had worked the locks on the canal and also worked in a glass factory. His family consisted of three brothers and four sisters. As a young boy he danced with a Folk Dance team and enjoyed music and dancing all his life.

He worked at various jobs until he was employed by the Crescent Tool Company and later with Jamestown Metal Products as a welder. He soon became a part of the Jamestown Swedish Community, playing soccer with the Swedish Workers Soccer Club, singing with the Viking Male Chorus and, of course, attending the many Swedish Dances that took place around the area. He met my mother, Ebba Cathrine Olson, at one of the dances, and they were married on December 23, 1933.

My mother's parents, Jacob and Maria, were from Linhamm in the Province of Skona and had come to Jamestown several years before my mother was born. Mom's family also loved music and dancing and any time the family got together, someone would bring out an accordion, harmonica or whatever and the dancing and singing would begin. They belonged to the Skona Lodge and I can remember what fun that was as after the meetings or programs it was time for dancing! My father was a great teacher, so it didn't take long to learn all the gammal dances!

Dad became a U.S. citizen in 1938 and at that time he changed the spelling of his name to Thorsten Nelson.

I was born April 17, 1936, and it was said that I was "born dancing" and I probably was. Knowing my Dad, I am sure he was waltzing with me around the room anytime he held me. My earliest memories are of standing on his feet hugging his knees while he danced with me. My sister Sandy joined our family in 1938 and she, too, was brought up on dancing. In fact, she went on to become a professional dance instructor with Arthur Murray Studios in Miami, Florida. Our brother LeRoy was born in 1941 but lived a very short life. He tragically drowned in Chautauqua Lake near our home the day after his second birthday. Thankfully, God gave my parents another boy a year later who was named Jon after my Dad's youngest brother in Sweden.

Dad had a terrific sense of humor, always clowning around or dressing up in funny outfits. I remember when my mother was ill once, he volunteered to scrub the kitchen floor and strapped scrub brushes on his feet and skated around the kitchen entertaining my sister and me. It wasn't until years later when I was reading Pippi Longstocking to my grandchildren that I learned that is what she had done, and I wondered who had the idea first?

He was also very musical; he played the piano "by ear" and also the harmonica, but his specialty was playing the spoons. If he wasn't out on the dance floor, he would be with the musicians playing his spoons. Even in later years when he was a resident at Heritage Green Nursing Home, whenever there was live music for a program a nurse would run to the kitchen for spoons for him to play.

We always listened to the Swedish Hour with Inge Killburger on the radio Sunday afternoons and that was probably when we learned most of the Swedish dances. My sister and I would fight over whose turn it was to get to dance with Dad.

My first experience with actual Folk Dancing came when I was probably 10 or 11. Dad taught my sister and me to do the Ox Dance, a dance usually done by men—a fight over a girl. It was for the Thule's Midsummer Celebration at Hillside Park. I don't remember too many details about the day other than that I was extremely nervous and there were an awful lot of people there!

Dad kept in touch with his sisters and brothers in Sweden and every time he received a letter from one of them he would cry. My Mom knew how much he wanted to go back for a visit so she took a job and my sister and I tried our best to help around the house so my Dad's dream would become a reality, and it finally did. I had a hard time saying good-bye to him when the time came—I was so afraid he wouldn't make it back! When he returned, he brought back many wonderful mementos from Sweden, including many pictures and greetings from his family. I remember thinking how much I wished I could go to Sweden myself to meet all these relatives.

It took many years, but in 1971 I accompanied my parents on a special group tour from Jamestown to Sweden—my dream come true! It was wonderful to meet all my relatives and see where my Dad had lived as a boy. We were there for Midsummer and went to a local town to watch the Midsummer celebration with the Maypole and all the folk dancing and the next day we had a family Midsummer complete with the Maypole and dancing until dawn. I was enthralled with the folk dancing and. determined that someday I would learn how! It was so hard to bid all the family good-bye, and now I knew why my Dad always cried when they sang *"Halsa Dem Darhemma"*—now I do, too! Since then, several of the aunts, uncles and cousins have visited us in Jamestown, and I went back with my Dad in 1987 to celebrate his 75th birthday.

Needless to say, I soon gathered a bunch of my Swedish descendent friends to try our hand at folk dancing, and while it was a lot of fun, we lacked a real teacher and were thrilled when we learned the Thule Lodge Folk Dance team, which had become inactive, would be happy to have us join them. It didn't take long to realize I had found my life's calling. In 1975 I was appointed to be the Thule Lodge's Children's Club Leader and reactivated the Three Crown Children's Folk Dance Team and have continued with that for over 35 years. We have presented programs for many events and nursing home in the area and take part in the Midsummer Festivals and the Scandinavian Folk Festival. My three children have been a part of the Children's Dance Team and now my two granddaughters are part of it, the fourth generation of Swedish Folk dancers!

The highlight of my Folk Dancing career came on October 22, 2011 when the Children's Dance team was invited to perform for the King and Queen of Sweden while they were in Jamestown for the 100th Anniversary of the Norden Men's Club. Queen Silvia even joined us in doing one of the folk dances! Later in the program five of us representing Scandinavian organizations in Jamestown were called forward and presented plaques of recognition for our contributions to the Scandinavian culture by the King himself! Mine was particularly for working with the Children's Club and the Folk Dancers. That was a "Mountain Top" Experience. If only my Dad could have been there to share it with me.

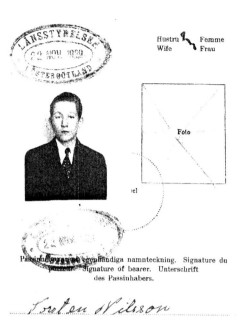

Dad's passport

Three Crown Children's Club with the King & Queen
of Sweden and Svenska Spelmän

Donna with grandson Colin Johnson wearing his great-grandfather Thorsten Nelson's folk dancing costume

MOSTER ANNA

by Karen Thorstenson Canfield

My grandfather, John Swanson, who had come from Sweden to work for a few years to save money, returned to Sweden to get his fiancé and bring her back to the home he had made for her in Jamestown, New York. My grandparents sailed on the Lusitania, which was sunk by the Germans in World War I, a fact that I found fascinating. Grandpa had a cousin in Jamestown and a brother in Sheffield, Pennsylvania, and Grandma had no relatives at all in the United States. When my grandmother, Emma, died unexpectedly in the summer of 1923, she left behind her husband and five children: my mother Alice who was the oldest at 12; Doris, 10; Gilbert, 8; Mildred, 5; and the baby, Dorothy, who was only 8 months old. It was a very difficult time without the support of family; however, my grandfather hoped that his unmarried sister from Sweden would be the person to help them through this trying time, so he went about bringing her to the States.

Moster Anna soon proved she was not quite the godsend that Grandpa had expected and my mother had stories of her that were as humorous as they were shocking.

Mom remembered coming home from school for lunch some days only to find that she and her siblings had been locked out of the house while Aunt had gone shopping. Not only did they miss their lunch, but Aunt had also decided her shopping would be easier without baby Dorothy accompanying her. Mom recalled hearing the cries of her baby sister coming from the house and being unable to help her. Certainly something that would never happen these days without serious consequences!

Mom also humorously recalled the day that Aunt took Grandpa's car out and had a flat tire in Celeron. Not knowing how to change it, and apparently not finding anyone to help her, she walked all the way home with the tire around her waist. According to my mother, she was quite the sight!

The story that always amused me the most was the time the entire family, including my grandfather, went to the circus down in Falconer. They were all having an enjoyable day until Aunt came upon the man with the big snake wrapped around his neck. Muttering words something like *"Min herre Gud,"* Aunt ran out of the circus grounds and walked the rest of the way home to the west side of Jamestown. Since I am not very fond of snakes myself, I am able to muster up a bit of sympathy for her on that particular occasion.

She also recalled the time that all the kids, with the exception of the baby, went downtown on a Saturday afternoon. While I have personally never witnessed anything like this, I have heard tales of the people who marched with signs claiming that the end of the world was at hand. Imagine the fright young children would feel! The kids ran home and came upon a sight that my mother never forgot—there sat Aunt in a rocking chair, one ankle resting on the other knee, reading from her big old Swedish Bible and smoking a cigar! She had also heard the news and was making her own preparations.

Grandpa soon realized that his sister was not particularly nurturing and was going to be of little help to him and his children, so he sent her back home to Sweden. Following that, mostly because I don't believe he could afford hired help, Dorothy went to live with a cousin of his, who I always knew as just "Mrs. Ellison," and stayed there until she married. My mother became the "surrogate mother" to the other three and was helped by Mrs. Lillian Rhodes, who was the next-door neighbor and was referred to by my mother and her siblings as the "closest thing to an angel that they ever knew."

DAG HAMMARSKJOLD: SWEDEN'S "APOSTLE OF PEACE"

by Arland O. Fiske

What can small nations do for peace in the world? A great deal. That's what we have learned from the life of Sweden's Dag Hammarskjold (1905-1961), pronounced *"Ha-mer-shold."* According to historian T. K. Derry, he "exercised an influence in world affairs as no citizen of a minor European state had yielded before him."

It was a fateful day in September 1961 when the plane carrying Hammerskjold on a peacekeeping mission mysteriously crashed over northern Rhodesia. The world had lost its greatest apostle for peace in our times.

Hammarskjold, son of a Swedish Prime Minister, had a brilliant career from the beginning. A success at college, in teaching and in government service, by age 36 he was chairman of the National Bank of Sweden. Outwardly, he had everything going for him.

At age 48, in 1953, he became Secretary General of the United Nations, the most difficult job in the world. He soon distinguished himself by securing the release of U.S. prisoners in China (from Korea) and by helping to solve the Suez crisis of 1956 between Israel and Egypt. In 1960, he gathered 20,000 troops from 18 countries for a successful peacekeeping mission in the Belgian Congo.

What kind of man was Hammarskjold? Usually, we think that such a person must have been an international "wheeler-dealer," both "compromising" and "compromised." After his death, a book called *Markings* was published. It was his private memoirs of religious reflections. Many people found it hard to believe that Hammarskjold could have had such deep Christian convictions while serving in world politics. The manuscript was found in his New York City apartment together with a letter to a friend giving permission for publication. He called it a "white book concerning my negotiations with myself and with God."

Hammarskjold traveled in the highest circles of the world's power brokers. He would necessarily "compromise," but no one called him a "compromised" person, not even the Soviet Union. They did call him a "murderer" and an "agent of imperialism," but not a "self-seeking" dictator.

The truth is that Hammarskjold was a tender-hearted person with strong feelings for the poor and dispossessed, though he had never been either. He felt deeply the criticisms that went with the job. Two convictions motivated his actions: First, that a person has to forget his ego to fulfill life's calling as an instrument of God; and second, that the "way of the Cross," with suffering, sacrifice and humiliation, was the price that he would have to pay. In *Markings,* he wrote: "Goodness is something so simple: always to live for others, never to seek one's own advantage." A few months after his death, Dag Hammarskjold was awarded the Nobel Peace Prize.

When we say, "Blessed are the peacemakers," we should remember Dag Hammarskjold. He was one of them. Sweden and Swedes everywhere can be justly proud of this man whose kind is so desperately needed today.

THE HEAVY COATS

by Katie (Cathy) Peterson

As a young girl, I was raised in Fort Lauderdale, Florida with my three other siblings. I remember mom and dad loading us into the old green Buick to take us to the train station to meet my grandparents from Sweden. As we anticipated their arrival, dad let us put pennies and nickels on the train track. Secretly, I feared the train would derail.

When the train came to a halt, two unusual-looking people with fair skin came over and hugged us. They were dressed in layers and they wore bulky winter coats. It was 85 degrees in Fort Lauderdale! They also had a lot of suitcases and a trunk or two. Both spoke with an accent, and they were very happy to see us. This was my first recollection of my grandparents.

Grandma and Grandpa crossed the Atlantic about 26 more times: first by ship, and then later by airplanes and trains. They kept a residence at Verkstadsgatan 20 (Work Street) in Oskarshamn, Sweden, even while they lived here. They must have loved us a lot to make so many trips. Grandma wanted to live in America and be with her family. Grandpa was torn between family and his love of Sweden. On one visit to the US, Grandma carried, on her lap, a large bakery box of pastries from Sweden to give us. Swedish pastry is the best! On another visit they brought us all matching Scandinavian sweaters. I still have mine to this day.

Grandma was always a working girl but still found time to make us *kroppkakor* [potato dumplings], *kåldormar* [stuffed cabbage], and Swedish meatballs. My mom, daughter, and I all know how to make *kroppkakor*. Although not hard to make, it is time-consuming and messy. Grandma never drove a car, but she knew the bus routes from one end of Fort Lauderdale to the other. Grandma always took me shopping and said I was the "apple of her eye."

Grandpa was the family historian and knowledgeable about family genealogy. He possessed the desk of a relative who was a judge in the

17th century. He had an extensive coin and stamp collection, but his real love was the outdoors and gardening. His garden was planted between the rock boulders in his back yard in Sweden. His flowers were beautiful and abundant. There was also a sauna in the back yard which all the neighbors shared.

I was the first person from my family to go to Sweden. I felt a very strong pull in my heart to go to the land of my ancestors. When I got there and placed my feet on the ground, I felt that I belonged. It is hard to explain the oneness of the land. I was so eager to learn that I had Grandma make out a grocery list and send me to the store alone. It was fun figuring out the products. On my second trip I presented a coin from the past trip to the cashier; however, the coin had a hole in the middle and was not in circulation any longer.

That first trip started my addiction to my Swedish heritage and the culture. My children danced with Thule's Three Crowns Children's Club and learned cooking and crafts at the Scandinavian Studies Programs. I am presently involved with the Thule Folk Dance team, ASHF secretary, and the Norden Club, and I'm volunteer coordinator for the Scandinavian Folk Festival. I plan to be involved for a long time to come!

"A LETTER TO MY DEAR ONES"

by John A. Anderson (1872-1953)

Written to his family on Father's Day, June 15, 1947
Shared by his grandson, Dan

A letter to my dear ones,

I was born in Sweden one Swedish mile from Legungby on a farm named Kastebrag. My father was well off when he married my mother. He had three farms that were well stocked. But in 1869 there was a crop failure in Sweden so dad had to start to sell off the stock on two farms and then he sold the two farms so that he was left with only one, but that was very good.

When I was about five years old, my father took sick and had to go to the hospital, and when I was about six years old, he died. Mother was left with seven children, all under twenty years old, two younger and four older than I. The neighbors around our home told mother it would be best for her to sell her farm and go to America because everything was so much better there. But her father who was quite elderly was living with us, and so mother continued to work. However, my grandfather died about two years later.

My mother then wrote to her brother who lived in America and arrangements were made so she could come. She sold the farm and got enough money to bring us all here and still had enough to make a first payment on a house. So she started out with her children.

It was not so nice and easy as they told her it was. She did not find as many eggs as potatoes and she did not find any gold lying around loose, so we missed the farm.

Jamestown was nice but no sewers, no city water, only for a few fire hydrants, no paved streets, only wood sidewalks on one side of most of the streets, no natural gas. There was a gas plant for a few street lights but they were about two blocks apart and they were not any larger than a candle lit, so when anybody stood by one light and looked at the other, it looked like a star was shining over there. No street car, no busses, no cab company, no hospitals, no relief organizations, no fraternal groups.

All the branch schoolhouses were one room like on the farm. No government buildings, no government help, no city buildings, no help. If you belonged to a certain group, you could get a sack of flour and some salt pork now and then, but you had to belong to a certain group.

Well, the two older girls went out and got housework, and all they could get went for clothes and so on. That left five and mother so it was six to feed and pay on the house: Ernest, 15; Anna, 12; John, 10; Mary, 8; Frank, 6.

Ernest got a job and he got 50 cents a day for nine hours of work. Anna got a job taking care of children for her eats. I (John) started to work as a doffer in Broadhead's mill for 25 cents a day for ten hours (60 hours a week for $1.50). I had to get up at 5:30 in the morning and I came home about 6:30 or 6:45 PM. Mary and Frank went to school, so that left mother with 75 cents a day to feed the other five and take care of the house and buy some clothes. That did not work out, so mother let the house go.

There was a man named Mr. Willard who wanted to adopt me. He said he would put me through school and see that I was taken care of in a very good way. It looked as though that would be fine for me because I only had about three months in a country school in Sweden before we came here. But mother could not let John go, so that's all of that!

Now I am about 11-1/2 years old, but there was something I cannot explain that took care of me. Then they gave me a job carrying water for the weavers for 30 cents a day that was good but hard work. I had to go two blocks to a spring for water and carry two 10-quart pails and then go up and down four flights of stairs. When the next Christmas came, the weavers took up a collection and then they told the loom fixer to take me uptown and fix me up. He took me up to John A. Peterson's Clothing Store and picked out a suit for $15.00. Fine. And then, they picked out underclothes and then a shirt and collar and tie, a pair of stockings, a pair of mittens, and a cap. I was some man now, and then he took me down to John T. Peterson and they picked out a pair of shoes. Well, how about it! Pretty nice now. Then he took me down to the factory a half-hour before they quit work. This was on Christmas Eve. Do you think they knew me? I seemed to get along as good as the other boys who had fathers, if not a little better. But it was quite hard to get up every morning at about 5:30 so we could get to work at 6:30, and in the winter, we were the first ones out and there was no snowplow in the morning.

Well, I am now getting close to 12 years old, so the weavers asked the boss to let me have a job setting bobbins. That was a better job, and it paid 45 cents a day. I was very happy now that I was going to start in the morning. So I am going home to tell mother. Well, then Ernest came home and he said I could have a job setting springs up to Martin Upholstering Company. The boss said he could help me now. This job seemed a little better. Ernest made $5, $6, and $7 dollars a week, and it looked better for the future, so I was up the tree and did not know what to do. I asked mother, but she did not know what to say. She had not seen any of the places and did not know very much about conditions here, so she told me to do what I thought best and then God will take care of the rest.

Well, that was very hard for a boy of 12 years old to do, but when morning came, I went to Martin's and started to set springs. In a little while after I started, Ernest got a chance to go to Sherman's and learn to upholster, and he took that job. Well, the boss did not like it so he thought if he let me go, Ernest would come back, but he did not. That was not so good, but in about ten days, I got a job at Sherman's, too, to set springs. Good! OK now! I started to earn about $6 or $7 a week, so I started giving mother $5 a week for board and then bought my clothes. Ernest gave mother $5 a week and Anna got a job in the factory, so she gave mother $3 a week. Well, now mother got busy and bought another house. It was going good because most of the men only got about one dollar a day at that time.

But now, I am 13 years old and they have made a law so it is compulsory to go to school. Well, now mother cannot make it without our help, so what's going to happen? There is no relief of any kind, and it looks very bad now. But I kept on working and the days went. One day the inspector came around. He was very late, my birthday had passed so that left me out for that year, and our home was safe for this time. The next year the inspector came on time. However, the first two years the inspector did not look over the books very carefully. He just went around the factory and if they found a worker that was not old enough, he just told him to go home. But it happened that Mr. Fred Sherman had sent me uptown on an errand the day the inspector came, and when I got back, he had gone, so it went on at home just the same.

But now I am 14 years old and I am beginning to feel the handicap that I am getting into. What shall I do? Mr. Fred Sherman wanted to help me along some. He was very nice to me so he wanted me to learn to upholster, but I had no chance to be outside since I was ten years old, so I was not very big. I told Mr. Sherman I did not think I was strong enough because the old way was very hard. Now it is more like a tailoring job. But he asked me again and again, and it was only a week or two apart, so the answer was the same.

But it seemed that he was bound to do something for me, so he changed the idea and asked me if I wanted to go setting spring edge jobs until I got stronger. Well, this was something new and as I was working piece work, I did not know what to say, but he said he would give just as much a day as I was making piece work, so I took that they had only four styles and they were big ones so they sold only two or three a month. Well, I set springs in all the frames they had in the factory. I believe this was the best thing for the trade up to this time for all the upholsterers and also for the upholstering firms in Jamestown and probably in the country because I haven't heard of any that started before.

Arthur Greenlund one of the four men that started the Jamestown Lounge Company and who worked at Sherman's when I came there, picked it up and put spring edge in jobs that they could sell for less and that started a fire for the trade. The lounge company taught 12 young men to set springs and they turned the jobs out by the hundreds.

Now at 16, I started to learn a trade. It was the best paying job at that time around here, and it looked very good. So I went on upholstering and I seemed to have good luck, got along fine with all walks of life, good and bad, so time slipped along, had some time to play. I was like all the boys at that time when we had worked 9, 10, 12, or 13 hours a day, we liked to have some fun.

But now in 1891, my mother passed on to her heavenly home. I am now 19 years old, but brother Ernest took over the house so we all five stayed at home. Anna stayed at home, Mary & Frank went to school, the two older girls got married. So Ernest and I (John) had to bring home the bread and meat and so on. Now I just had to settle down to real work, so very little play. Now two years after mother left Frank passed on and then one seemed to go about every two years. It was mother, brother, sister, their children, and now there were 17 graves. Amanda and John used to gather flowers for all the graves every year, but now Amanda and Uncle

Charlie are gone, so now there are 19 graves, and I am the only one left of mother's and father's folks, so after me it will have to start another generation.

Well, now at 19, I met a nice little girl. Her name was Amanda Nordstrom. She was very nice but only a little over 17 years and all alone. She came here with her father, but he died shortly after they came over, so she was all alone here. I had lost everything, so we were in the same boat, but we had good times together, and three years later I had saved up $125 dollars, so we got married, and we had seven nice children—four boys and three girls. Amanda took very good care of them. She saw to it that they got to school on time, and they all went to Sunday School, and some of them became very faithful church workers. I was now making $12 or $13 a week. I tried to make a home for us and with Amanda's help, we got a place for us to get into. All our friends said it was very nice. This house was not as nice when I bought it as it is today. It had only six rooms and a cellar under one room, but it was a very nice lot that had nice shade trees and fruit trees, rose bushes, pines, and about a dozen different kinds more, and a good space for a garden, a fence all around it so we all liked it very much. It was sister Anna that I give very much credit for the house. She was always looking out for us, always ready to help. This was at 34 Charles Street.

But now comes another knock. The School Board wanted this lot for a school house and I did not like that but did not want to stand in the way. I gave them an offer and they said it was all right, but the next day, I withdrew it. I did not want to give it up, but they gave me another offer, so I took that. Then I bought the lot at 20 Charles Street. Then I had the city surveyor give me the grade down there, then had the cellar built and laid a nice sidewalk, planted shade trees, put in the sewer, then had the house moved down. We started to take down trees, bushes, fence and everything else that we wanted. Some job. Now we needed some more room, so I made arrangements to have the house built like it is now. The neighbors around here were very good to us. They gave us meals and sleeping rooms while the house was being built. I would like to thank them again for their kindness. This was another hard job. But we lived here and enjoyed it very much, had many happy days, but after a few years, the city alderman came around and changed the grade and that we did not like but made the best we could of it. We got a little help from the city and then did a lot of hard work ourselves. In 1913, we all went down to the Biederwolf meetings. One night we were nine there and took the first prize for the biggest family.

I was making $18—$20 a week and the house was very nearly paid for at this time. I did not feel very good. I was just about all in. Did not know what was the trouble, could not think of anything I had done that wasn't all right. Everybody was very nice to us if we needed anything we could get it. We were welcome wherever we went. But one night I was down to the Biederwolf meetings and something came to me. The next day I started to see some things that I was doing that I did not care for any more, so I just passed them by and after that they did not bother me anymore.

Now I got a chance to get another job. Four men started a new firm. Three of them were from the Jamestown Lounge Company. They picked me to lead the men, get out samples, and so on. Well, they did not have very much money, so they decided to make some changes, so they picked me for superintendent. Well, now comes the time when my handicap is bothering me. What can I do?

I hired second graders and helped them so we got out the best jobs in town, and we called them the best made line in America and got away with it, but it took lots of my time, so I had to have somebody to take care of the time cards, order sheets, and a dozen other little jobs. But on account of the finances, they would not let me hire anybody that wanted much money. Now Raymond had got up in high school some, so it began to take a little more money than I could gather up. Money was not so easy to pick up as it is now, so he said he'd like to get a job and help dad so he got a job to learn the tool making, and he got along very nice, but he always seemed to like to be with his father, so I asked him if he'd like to go and work for his dad, and he said yes. Well, now the factory was pretty well lined up for that time because Ray turned out to be what they call three in one or something like that, so now I am ready to go again. This was another time I received unseen help. Now we were ready to go and OK, I did not know we had so many friends. It seemed that half of the town wanted something that we made. Well, now it seems to go just fine. Everybody is making a little more money, and so are Ray and John so I can give Amanda a little more so she can have some more for herself and for the children and I can give some more to the church for the Lord's favors to me.

Then Mabel got a job and that helped some more. Then J. Leonard got a job. We are just going to town now and Pearl went to Cornell University and then Kenneth started to work for his dad, so now we are three of us working together and it is going fine. Then Jeanette went down to Pearl at Cornell University and then Bob got a job so the whole family is OK now.

But now comes the depression and our factory got hit very hard. The office help and John and Ray got cut to half pay so now I am back in the dumps again. They said it would not last, only a short time, but that short could have been left out. But the days went and another one came and Raymond stayed with me, so we pulled along. It was very hard but after some time, we began to pull out again, and now we are all right again. But Ray is a faithful help to me, and that's what brought us out of the mess than helped all of our family because without his help at that time, I would not have been able to do what I did for the home.

Amanda and John had to give up lots but we did not let it be known.

I am writing these lines just because there have been times when I would like to have known something about my dad but on account of shifting around, all records disappeared, so if any of Amanda's and John's folks would like to look up something in the past, this might help them along some. But of course, most of these things are in between the lines or stepping stones. Some of this in between are something like this. I would come home and have supper and then Amanda would clean up in the house. I would go outside and do some work and when I'd come in, Amanda would have the children in bed and was fixing up their clothes, stockings, shoes, and so on. Well, that would be 10:00 or 10:30. Amanda would go and get the frame for making a quilt and then she would stretch out the goods and cotton and then I would help her tie it together and when we'd get it off the frame, she would look it over a little and then we'd look at the clock. Well, it is 1:30 AM—time to go to bed. Well, the next night there would be a bushel of peaches to can and some berries—18 or 20 bushels of potatoes to take care of and so on. This just gives a little idea of the things in between the lines. But someone happened to see some of the work so some of my friends had the WJTN broadcast the following:

> *This certifies that John A. Anderson has been designated a distinguished citizen of Jamestown for outstanding service.*

Behind the lines, this was after World War II. To whoever may read these lines, do not think I am complaining. I do not mean it that way. I am better off than I ever expected to be because I realized in my earlier days that I was up against it. But as a retired man, I am getting a monthly salary big enough to keep me going, and I am the first one in trade in Jamestown to receive that, so I am thankful for that.

My life has been mostly taken up with some kind of work, but now and then, the men would get together and talk things over and I would be asked to help out, too. But on account of not having any schooling, I would pass it on to somebody that could do it better, and I would do what I could in some small way so these lines are just a little reminder of my past life.

I pray to God for strength when as life's love and labors find surcease, cares, crosses, burdens to lay down at length, and so with joy's increase to die if not in triumph in thy peace.

Men herre Jesus lär due mig att lepva mera helt för dig på vägen hem till himmelen.

John A. Anderson

"ST. OLAF"—NORWAY'S BEST REMEMBERED KING

by Arland O. Fiske

When I first learned the nursery rhyme, "London Bridge Is Falling Down," I had no idea that it was about Norway's most famous king. He is best known to us as "St. Olaf" or "Olaf the Holy" (Heilige Olaf). He had other names, too: Olaf II, Olaf Haraldsson, and Olaf the Stout or Thick. What is the connection between this Olaf and the London Bridge: And why has his fame survived?

Olaf Haraldsson, who ruled from 1014-1028, was Norway's second king by that name. The first was Olaf Tryggvason (995-1000). The present king of Norway, Harald V (1991-present), is descended from this line. The "Olafs" (now spelled "Olav") came from a Swedish royal family called the "Ynglings." They entered Norway shortly before the Viking Age (793-1066). The first king to claim rule over all Norway was an Yngling, Harald Finehair, about 890. Olav V also traces his ancestry to Gorm, the founder of Denmark's royal family who lived about 940.

Olaf Haraldsson's father descended from Harald Finehair, but he died quite young. His mother remarried a farmer-king named Sigurd Syr. Olaf was not a model child, unless one should be thinking of a young "Viking." He was pagan in all his ways and showed little respect for his foster father. He was of average height but very stout. He had medium brown hair and eyes that no one could face when he was angry. He also excelled in athletic contests and in oratory.

Olaf was only 12 when he went with an uncle on his first Viking cruise. He was especially hostile to the Swedes because they had killed his father. Olaf's craving for adventure brought him to England and to service under King Etherlred. There he fought against the Danes who controlled London and most of England. During an attack on London, it was his idea to fix grappling hooks on the piers which held up the London Bridge. His rowers pulled hard and the bridge collapsed. London, however, remained with the Danes.

With just 120 followers, Olaf invaded Norway in 1014. He had swift success. Many joined him because he had descended from King Harald. His chief opposition came from the large landowners (bønders) who were against a centralized government. But Olaf outwitted them in both battle and diplomacy.

During a stay in Normandy, a part of France settled by Scandinavians, Olaf became a Christian and was baptized. He took his conversion seriously and became a relentless missionary. Charlemagne (d. 814), the Christian emperor of France, was his model for a ruler. Like his hero, Olaf employed non-compromising methods of evangelism. First, he would speak gently to the people, imploring them to leave their idols and to believe in Christ. Then he invited them to be baptized. But he was firm in demanding decision. He warned them that if they refused, they had three choices: Go into exile, become slaves, or face him in battle. In a short time, Norway became a part of "Christendom." Clergy from England accompanied Olaf to instruct the people.

King Knut (Canute), the Danish ruler of England, forced Olaf into exile with the Viking rulers of Russia in 1028. Two years later, Olaf hastily returned with a small army to reclaim his kingdom. He expected that people would join him in rising up against the Danes. King Knut, however, made many promises and most of the farmers marched against Olaf.

On July 29, 1030, Olaf met the enemy at Stiklestad, north of Trondheim. By this time, he had changed in many of his ways. He no longer burned the homes of his enemies, as was the custom. He listened to the reading of the Bible and partook of Holy Communion every morning. But on the day of battle, he was greatly outnumbered. The swords began to clash at noon and by three o'clock Olaf lay dead. His friends secretly buried his body in Trondheim, called Nidaros.

Many people claimed that the dead Olaf performed miracles for them. Even those who struck his death blows praised his virtues. Olaf had become a folk hero against the broken promises of King Knut. A year later, Bishop Grimkel examined the corpse of Olaf. When he opened the coffin, "there was a delightful and fresh smell . . . his cheeks were red . . . his hair and nails had grown." Live coals did not burn his beard. Both bishop and the "things" (the ruling councils) were convinced that

Olaf was "holy." They did not wait for approval from church authorities in Rome. The Norwegians knew a saint when they saw one. The body was moved to the spot where Norway's national cathedral stands today near the Trondheim harbor. This is also where Norway's kings are consecrated today.

A few years ago, I visited with a pastor from Norway. He was interested in my family name because it originates from only a valley southwest of Trondheim. He asked, "Did you know that the Fiske farmers fought at Sticklestad?" In surprise, I said, "Really?" "Yes," he replied, "but they fought on the wrong side."

A COAL MINER'S GRANDDAUGHTER

by Karin Hillman Oeffling

All four of my grandparents came from Sweden at the turn of the last century. Both grandfathers were able to find jobs working in the Pennsylvania coal mines: Grandpa Tuline in Dagus Mines, and *Farfar* (father's father—Grandpa Hillman) in West Newton. Farfar, one sister, and one brother from the large family in Sweden were chosen to go to America. If the entire family were unable to go, they sent the strongest to the new country, the ones they believed could survive. My dad, Arnold Hillman, told me this story about his father only once. The emotion that accompanied his brief words is something that I feel even today.

There was no OSHA [Occupational Safety and Health Administration] in the early 1900s, and earning a living in the coal mines was dangerous and uncertain. Dad was born in 1908, and he was under ten years of age when his world was shaken. There was a cave-in at the mine where his father was working in West Newton. He said he remembers that his mother took him by the hand and they walked silently to the mine, however far that was from their home. They waited for hours. (Dad paused as he remembered the fear.) Farfar was one of the men who walked out of that mine alive on that unforgettable day.

The pay wasn't much, so *Farmor* (father's mother) took in laundry to supplement their income. Dad's job was to deliver the clean and ironed laundry to the customers in his wagon. One day the wagon wheel hit a rock and the laundry tumbled out onto the dirt road. Dad said that Farfar gave him "a good lickin'." I think that lickin' still hurt years later.

Farmor and Farfar lived in West Newton until they died in the early 1950s. My sister (the editor of this book) and I saw the coal mine where FarFar worked when we visited West Newton in the 1990s.

EARLY SWEDE HILL FAMILIES

by Carolyn Pearson Volk

My Great-Grandfather Gust Pearson was born in Walda, Halland, Sweden on March 11, 1836 to Per Larsson and Berta Svenson. He married Johanna Johanson about 1875. She was born January 18, 1850 in Hanhult, Halland, Sweden.

This is my story. Gust emigrated to America April 6, 1883 aboard the "Orlando" out of Göteborg, Sweden to Hull, England. He left Johanna in Sweden with four children and expecting another. He worked for two years, and we assume that he earned enough money to send for Johanna and the children.

In June of 1885 she left Sweden with her five children, Johan Edward, age ten; Hilman Dorthea, age seven; Julia Agusta, age five; Ellen Maria, age three; and Hilmar August, nine months old. She carried with her a small trunk and wooden chair, so she would have something to sit on during her voyage. In her trunk she had a pair of candlesticks and her precious little wood button box.

They landed in Castle Gardens, New York. While gathering her family and belongings, Johanna stopped the kidnapping of Johan by some men who would search the docks looking for young boys to take to work in the factories.

Gust had built a small shack on the top of Swede Hill for his family and here is where Johanna took her children until a better home could be built. Unfortunately, we have no knowledge as to how they traveled from New York City to Jamestown.

They went on to have four more children: Carl James, Josefina Wilhemia (Minnie), Theodore Oscar, and Alma Evelina. Eight of the children took the last name of Parson while Johan spelled his "Pearson."

The oldest son Johan, who name was shortened to John, met and married Caroline Crena Lindholm who lived on the next street. Crena, as she was known, had a son William who was five years old at the time. John and Crena had seven more children, three sons and four daughters: Gustav, the oldest, John Edward, and Allen Burdette, the youngest. The daughters were Olive, Lillian, Allene, and Carolyn, none of whom ever married. Of the four sons only three were married and John was the only one to have a child—me.

John and Crena lived on Anderson Street the rest of their lives. They built a new home just down the street from the family homestead.

The Lindholm family homestead was on Swan Street. Gust Lindholm was born in Sweden, June 6, 1843. No record has been found yet as to when he came to this country. Gust and Maria Mains Lindholm brought their sons, Frank, Harry, and Herbert, to Jamestown from Boston, Pennsylvania, where he had a boardinghouse for miners. Crena was already living in Jamestown. They left behind a daughter, Olive, to live with other family members. William drowned when he was only twelve years old, and another son, Hennigg, died at just one year old in Boston, PA. Two daughters, Hattie and Julie Esther, were born in Jamestown. Hattie married Hjalmer Berquist. Julie died when she was only a year old.

My father, John Edward, met Dorothy Emma Casselman at Keller's Store at Vukote on Chautauqua Lake. Dorothy was a twin born to Charles Hawley and Elnora Keller Casselman. This union of John and Dorothy produced one child, Carolyn Mae Pearson, the writer of this narrative.

I have fond memories of sitting on Grandma Pearson's front porch helping her shell peas for a meal and being scolded for eating too many for fear there would not be enough for everyone at supper.

Grandpa Pearson was a very proud man. He would spend an extremely long time combing his beautiful wavy hair in front of the mirror in the only bathroom in the house. One can only imagine with four daughters trying to get ready for work how a schedule would have been important. He was always dressed neatly and very often wore a bow tie.

My family spoke only English, never Swedish. I often wondered why they did not use any Swedish vocabulary around the house. I remember my Aunt's mentioning that they were only allowed to speak English. I think they were very proud to be Americans and felt that speaking English was better for all of the family.

Putting my memories in writing has been a wonderful experience that I look forward to sharing with not only the readers of this book, but with my children and their families.

Gust & Johanna Pearson, c. 1900

Pearsons' New House—27 Anderson Street

THE DOGGIE BOX

by Barbara Hillman Jones

Dad's youngest cousin Sven in Sweden worked for Phillips Electronics, and because of his position, Sven learned to speak and write English, although he never quite mastered the technicalities of grammar and spelling. He liked to write letters in English, but when a letter from Sven arrived, it sometimes took my parents a while to decipher its meaning.

Some years after our visit Sven retired and his wife passed away shortly after that. Although my dad had also died, Sven wanted to come to America to visit his relatives here. Not wanting to travel alone, he invited his granddaughter Camilla who was about 22 years old to accompany him. He planned to visit us in Georgia, my sister and her family in Colorado, other cousins in Salt Lake City, Utah, and then for fun, he wanted to go to Hawaii—an ambitious itinerary for that grandfather and granddaughter.

We had discovered in 1976 when another of dad's cousins came to visit that they had no idea how vast America is. Their notions are formed and influenced by their only reference—Europe—how close those countries are to each other and how quickly people can go from one country to another. But perhaps Sven and Camilla had been prepared because we never heard them express surprise or complain about the length of travel time.

To our way of thinking, they had chosen a rather circuitous route to these destinations, going first to Hawaii, then to Georgia, on to Colorado and then to Utah, but perhaps that was the most cost-effective way for them to make the trip.

When they were to arrive in Georgia, David and I drove to Hartsfield Airport and waited for them to come through the International Arrival area (we could still do that then). They arrived safely, and we had a wonderful reunion there in the airport. We spent our time showing them our favorite places in Georgia—historic sites, museums, parks, malls, and any other places we thought would interest them. However, we could not compete with the wonderful history that is everywhere in Sweden, and we didn't try.

Sven was one of those people who had been taught that much of America was desert, cactus, and cowboys and Indians. I think we finally convinced him that it is much more than that, but we did dress him up as a cowboy and take pictures just for fun. He was a delight in David's cowboy shirt, hat, belt, boots, and six-shooter, but he refused to put on the long pants to complete the outfit. Even in the middle of summer in Sweden, temperatures are very moderate, and Georgia in the summer is extremely hot and humid. Not being used to that, Sven and Camilla were very hot, and Sven didn't want to part with his shorts, even for a Western cowboy photo opportunity.

One evening we met David's son and daughter-in-law at a restaurant for dinner. We had great fun helping Sven and Camilla order from the menu, explaining to them what each dish was. At the end of the meal, as so often is the case in restaurants in this country, we had food left over and asked for a "doggie box" to carry our leftovers home to be eaten at a later time. Camilla, who is a lovely young lady and with whom we had so much fun becoming acquainted and who fit right into our lives, flabbergasted us when she passionately (that's putting it mildly) objected to our getting a doggie box and taking food home. We discovered that what for us is just a way of life is simply not done in Sweden! It was embarrassing, shameful, humiliating to her, and she let us know very quickly that should we visit them in Sweden and go to a restaurant, under no circumstances were we to ask for a doggie box or even give it a thought. That was just not part of social customs in Sweden, and no civilized person would make such a request.

Whenever we go to a restaurant, even now, and ask for a doggie box to take our leftovers home, it's rare that we don't remark about Camilla's reaction, and we tell ourselves it's a good thing we're not in Sweden right now or that Camilla is not here! While remembering that incident tickles us, we know that it's important before visiting a foreign country to learn and observe the customs of the people who live there. We remember that we are guests, and we want our hosts to be glad we came.

ANNA LAWSON

by Larry Koplik

My family is not Scandinavian, but, growing up in Jamestown, I had many connections with Swedish-Americans. My best friend from age two through elementary school was Martha Anderson, and it is a story about her grandmother, Anna Lawson, that I want to share.

Mrs. Lawson lived next door to our family. She was my brother's and my babysitter, and she did occasional ironing for my mother. She was also my gardening muse. I am now 58, and I tell everyone who asks that I've been gardening since I was five. Well, it was Mrs. Lawson, whose vegetable and flower gardens adjoined our driveway, who first inspired me. I would watch as she turned over her garden every spring with a pitchfork and then planted her vegetables. I would also listen as she told me about her red currant plants.

Anna Lawson's currants were famous among the kids in our neighborhood, for whom a taste of a handful of them was a test of one's mettle. They were so sour!

Mrs. Lawson would tell us the story of how her very large patch of currants came from a single plant that she brought with her from Sweden when she came to America as a young woman of twenty in 1912. Somehow I've always pictured the little plant secreted in her pocket, but perhaps back then, one did not have to be so circumspect about bringing in foreign plant material.

Anna Lawson died in 1972 when I was 18, and we soon had new neighbors, who actually turned out to be lifelong friends of our family. But back then, I was quite annoyed with them when, soon after they moved in, I found that they had ripped out the whole currant patch! I noticed that there were still some small broken currant shoots in the dirt, and I asked the neighbors' young son if I could take a few of them. He, of course, said yes, though his parents later scolded me for not seeking their permission.

In any case, I was able to salvage a few viable plants which I planted in my garden. I didn't want the plants because I particularly liked currants (they were still too sour for me, and I didn't know anything about making jelly, which is what I think Mrs. Lawson used them for); I wanted to preserve the plants to honor her memory.

Soon after this, I went off to college, and my passion for gardening was put on hold. But many years later, now married with my own home and garden in New Jersey, my childhood interest in gardening was reawakened. I learned to make pies with the many kinds of berries I grew on my property, and I remembered those long-lost currant plants at my parents' home in Jamestown. When I went home to visit my father, I found that, underneath a lot of weeds, the currants I had rescued so many years before were still alive, though looking a bit scraggly!

I brought some of the currant plants back to New Jersey with me and also planted some at our family's property on Lake Chautauqua. The ones at the lake have thrived, but it turned out that New Jersey summers are just too hot and dry for currants. So, when my wife and I visit my father in Jamestown, every summer, we harvest currants there and at the lake for delicious pies. (They do require a <u>lot</u> of sugar!)

One final note: I'm still friends with Martha Anderson, and years ago, I gave her and her brother, Martin, some of the descendants of their grandmother's currant plants.

So, Anna Lawson's currants from Sweden and her memory live on.

RETURN TO SWEDEN—2012

by Donna Close Johnson

Years ago I had heard of the journey that my mother's sister and her cousin had taken while visiting Sweden in 1978. They visited the Svensson family in Vaggeryd, Sweden, who were distant cousins. I thus learned more about where my maternal grandfather, Paul (Magnuson) Lundquist, and his family lived before he emigrated to the United States with his sister Ruth where they resided in Jamestown, NY, and he married Anna L. Abrahamson. After our daughter, Laurie, graduated from high school, she and her cousin took a trip to Sweden and visited the Svenssons while also visiting with my husband Ed's "Johansson" family in the Varberg area. Our children, Laurie, Dan and Cindy, have since been able to visit with this family at other times, and a few of the Swedish family have been able to visit us in the US, so we have kept in touch with many of them over the years.

In 1989 Ed and I visited Varberg, Sweden and met his father John's large family. He had been one of twelve children. In 1923, he emigrated to Jamestown as did eventually three of his brothers and one sister. He married Stella who was also of Swedish descent.

Ed's cousins, the Steners, took us to visit the Svensson family and the Skoghall brothers, who were also relatives of my grandfather and lived on the property where my grandfather's home used to be. We enjoyed meeting them and seeing the lovely area where they lived. We hoped to return one day.

This year, our children gave us a special anniversary gift of airline tickets to visit Sweden, and we can't thank them enough for it! In July, we made the journey along with our daughters, son-in-law David and grandchildren, Carly and Axel. We had a great time staying with relatives, the Werners and the Bengtssons in the Varberg area and spending four days in Stockholm. Ed and I were able to again visit my relatives, the Svenssons and one of the Skoghall brothers that we had met many years ago in Vaggeryd. Many of the older relatives are no longer alive, but we met a whole new young generation of our families. Our journey was truly a memorable experience.

BERRY BERRY SWEDISH: SWEDISH BERRY LORE

by Jay T. Stratton

Berries hold a special place in the heart of a Swede. There may be fond memories of gathering berries from field and forest. There are certainly food traditions relating to the berries and their preparation. Swedish pancakes are not served with maple syrup as in America, but with raspberry or lingonberry jam, and perhaps a dusting of powdered sugar. Sugar maples don't grow in Scandinavia.

Even the Swedish names for the berries seem to tell us something about the Viking culture behind them. These words all end in "on" or "-bär" (berry), and the singular form is the same as the plural. For example, *Hallon* can mean one raspberry or many. Does this mean that just one is not enough?

Are you feeling a little Vitamin-C starved up there by the Arctic Circle? Have some rosehip soup. Who but the Swedes would consider rosehips to be a fruit? They're called *nypon*. Are nips related to hips?

Lingon are the signature Swedish berry. This may be because they grow throughout the Swedish forests and are a gift of nature rather than a "crop" from a farm. A landowner did not have a right to exclude peasants from harvesting lingon on his property, although a small patch could be marked off for his own exclusive use. Lingon grow on low bushes like cranberries, but have a very distinct and sweeter taste. The berries are generally not available in America, except at $5.00 to $6.00 a bottle for imported Swedish jam. Pay close attention to the botanical illustrations on the bottles at a Russian store and you may pick up some Byelorussian lingonberries, mistranslated as "cranberry," for $3.50 or $4.00.

Hjortron are called "Cloudberries" in English, for what reason I do not know. They are similar to yellow raspberries and grow on low bushes in the far north (in Newfoundland as well as in Scandinavia). They are wild gathered, rarely farm-produced. Their higher price represents the greater difficulty of harvesting them. In Swedish, a *hjort* is a hart, a stag, or a male deer. Deer would prefer the plant's foliage to its fruit, I imagine, but for some reason our ancestors associated them with this berry.

Smultron are wild strawberries, from "smul," meaning a small bit or crumb. Yes, they are tiny! These would be the so-called Alpine strawberries, not the *Fragaria virginiana* wild strawberries known by many Americans. The kind of strawberry we eat today was unknown in the past. It was produced by crossing the North American wild strawberry (for taste) with a South American cousin (for size). This kind of berries is know as *jordgubbar*, which appears to mean "old men of the earth." That is a very puzzling word, and the only berry name that has a separate plural form. Perhaps the berry was seen as an old man's pink nose sticking up out of the earth.

Blåbär are blueberries, meaning exactly that, but the kinds of blueberries we eat in America, whether wild, low-bush, half-high or high-bush, are not the same as those found in Sweden, which in England are called "bilberries." A number of different kinds of berries share the same common name. That's why Linnaeus, the famous Swedish botanist, came up with the binomial system of Latin names for scientific nomenclature.

Körsbär are cherries. The Vikings considered the cherry to be a berry, which we do not. The name appears to derive from *köra* meaning "to drive," originally by wagon or cart. This is one berry whose harvest is so bountiful you'll need to drive it off home to dry as fruit or to ferment into wine or brandy.

Apples are the only fruit I know of to be mentioned in Norse mythology. Apples, cherries, plums, pears, some grapes and even peaches can be grown in southern Sweden, whereas the other berry fruits are hardier across a greater area of the North, and were available to the peasants. You might pick your lord's lingonberries, but you couldn't make off with his apples or pears!

Björnbär are blackberries, or "bear berries" if you translate literally. I doubt that deer prefer cloudberries *(njortron)* but bears really do love to eat blackberries. Björn and Björna (feminine) are popular Swedish first names! Blackberries include over a dozen different varieties with a dozen different scientific names, so the *björnbär* they eat in Sweden are probably a different species from those in Minnesota or here in New York. I reckon I have at least four different species of blackberry growing on my wild picking grounds alone.

Stickelbär is the old word for gooseberry, derived from the fact that you may get stuck by its thorns. The name used in more modern books is *krusbär*. "Krus" means a ceremony, or a fancy curl or decoration, referring to the withered brown curl at the end of each berry, the remains of the flower, known in English as a beard. The plant's English name comes from the shape of the leaves, which resemble a goose's webbed footprint.

Currants. Have you ever wondered why the name "currant" is given both to those little raisins and also to a kind of small red berry? They have no English name, but if you dry them they look exactly like high-priced Corinthian raisins. Many an unethical trader has used the dried berries to adulterate his imported raisins, which get their name from a corruption of "Corinth," from where they originally came.

In Swedish, raisins are *russin*, and currants are *vinbär*, literally, "wineberries." Wild currants grew all across Europe and were eaten long before the 1500s, when the bushes bearing the sort of currants we eat today began to be sold in England and France. They come in black, red, white and champagne colors.

English has lost the original word for "currant." Perhaps they didn't grow wild in Britain. Sweden has a tradition of using undomesticated fruits like *lingon*. Does the word *vinbär* indicate a Viking tradition of making wine from currants or using currant juice to flavor mead, as in ancient times, or is it a more modern word from Victorian England, where it was common to make "table wine" from crushed white currants (the improved modern cultivars) and water fermented for a few weeks?

If *vinbär* is an ancient word, then currants were widely known and gathered wild before the domesticated currant bush came along. Where do wild stands of currant exist in Europe? Are there enough of them to produce wine from the wild? How much fruit would an unimproved bush give? And how many currants would one use to flavor mead? I have more questions than answers.

Scandinavia has a long tradition of gathering wild fruits. Wild berries were a staple of the peasant diet, and are a cultural icon today. *Lingon* and *hjortron* were certainly basic foods; *smultron, blåbär* and *vinbär* were probably used as well. For the most part, America lacks such traditions of fruit-gathering. Around here we gather the wild blackberries and elderberries and seldom consider planting the improved cultivars. In New England, folks can go cranberrying on the bogs. In the Adirondacks they pick blueberries on the plains of the Oswegatchie. Some may even make part of their living that way, but that's not the same. Most American lands have "private property" and "no trespassing" signs posted everywhere, and unlike in Scandinavia, strangers have no right to the fruit that grows there.

But in Sweden, berries are more than a sweet snack—they are a way of life.

Berry Good Recipes

Fruit Soup

Fruit soups are uncommon in America, but very popular in Scandinavia, both hot and cold. Most recipes feature apples, raisins and prunes, but this one is for berries:

4 cups berries (raspberries, blueberries, blackberries or some combination)
½ cup sugar   1 wedge of lemon
1 cinnamon stick   2 quarts water

Combine the ingredients and simmer for one-half hour at a low boil until the fruit begins to break up. Then mix 4 tablespoons cornstarch and another ¼ cup of water thoroughly, and add to the berry mixture. Allow the mix to simmer until it thickens. You may also choose to add wine or sherry, or to serve with whipped cream or ice cream on top.

Vinsärspie (Currant Pie)

En kopp mogna och fint pressade vinbär, en ditto socker, en half ditto vatten, två äggulor ochen matsked mjol. Bakas i underdeg.

Combine one cupful of ripe currants crushed fine, one cupful of sugar, one-half cupful of water, the yolks of two eggs, and one tablespoonful of flour. Bake with an undercrust.

From *Svensk-Amerikansk Kokbok,* Carl Grimsköld, 1888. This vintage cookbook has no trouble distinguishing *russin* (raisins), *korinter* (Corinthian raisin currants) and *vinbär* (red currants). This recipe recommends making a meringue from the leftover egg whites, but I prefer to serve it plain with ice cream. You'll have to grow your own currants or gather them wild, as they are no longer sold fresh. The currant is going out of fashion. That's too bad, because this odd little one-crust pie is one of the most delicious things I've ever tasted! Enjoy!

>*Article reprinted by permission. First published in *Idunna*, A Journal of Northern Tradition, Issue #85, Autumn 2010, New Haven, CT. Mr. Stratton is a Chautauqua County native who lives in Westfield, NY.

CARL LARSSON'S HOME

by Arland O. Fiske

It's a "miracle," how a talented artist can take what is plain and ordinary, and transform it into a thing of exquisite beauty. Carl Larsson (1853-1919) was such an artist. Carl and his wife Karin took a small house "laying bare on a heap of slag" and turned it into one of the best known and most beloved homes in Sweden, if not "of all times," according to Ulf Hard, author of *Carl Larsson's Home*.

It was in 1889, when migrations to the New World from Sweden were claiming most of the country's attention, that Larssons moved into a house which they named *"Little Hyttnas"* (cottage) in the village of Sundborn in the province of Dalarna in the central part of the country. The house was a gift from Karin's father. It had just two rooms, an attic and an attached woodshed. Over the next two decades many rooms were added, and it still has not lost its quaint appearance of comfort and warmth, but no one would have recognized it.

Nineteenth century Sweden was an underdeveloped country and its capital, Stockholm, was a relatively small city with many poor neighborhoods. It's a wonder that a boy born in *Gamla Stan* (Old Town) should become the outstanding representative of the "new art." I've visited the community twice. Today it's a model of cleanliness and beauty. The old buildings have been renovated in magnificent style.

Carl's father has been described as a "ne'er-do-well" who abandoned his wife and family when Carl was a small child. His mother supported the family by washing and ironing. They were forced to move into a slum-section in the East End of Stockholm. Things were so bad that Larsson wrote: "If I say that the people who lived in these houses were swine I am doing those animals an injustice. Misery, filth and vice—every kind of vice flourished there—seethed and smoldered cozily; they were corroded and rotten, body and soul." He later wrote that he could remember nothing of happiness from his childhood. No wonder that he loved the peaceful woods of Dalarna.

When only 13, Larsson was encouraged by his teacher in the "poor school" to apply to the school where his maternal grandfather had studied art. Because of his background in poverty, he was shy and handicapped by an inferiority complex. After about three years, his shyness wore off and his artistic ability began to blossom. It was when he was editor of the school paper that his talent was discovered. He was hired by a humor magazine to draw cartoons. It wasn't long before he was earning a respectable salary. Then he supported his mother and a younger brother who was also artistically talented.

It wasn't long before Carl was traveling all over Sweden and even abroad as a sketching reporter. It soon became noted that wherever anything of importance happened, two people could be counted on to be present—Larsson and King Oscar II. When one of the students who had been a great inspiration to Larsson in Sweden died in 1877, he went to Paris with a heavy heart. Going to France was the fashionable thing to do for art students in those days. France was in low morale too, having been disastrously defeated by Germany in the war of 1870-71. Larsson traveled to France several times before finding his niche. On one of his return trips to Sweden he drew illustrations for August Strindberg, a famous playwright.

Larsson continued to be afflicted with depression. A turning point in his life seems to have been when he made new friends at Gretz-Armain-villiers, a village outside of Paris where Scandinavians used to get together. He also made the acquaintance of some of Sweden's finest future artists there. Gretz was a quaint village "full of charm," with an ancient arched bridge, a medieval church with moss-covered walls, and the ruins of a castle. Stone walls in front of houses, gardens with flights of stone steps and trellises with grapevines, plus fruit trees, made the village an artist's paradise.

It was at Gretz that Carl met Karin Bergoo, who had come from a well-to-do Swedish home with a liberal outlook on life, evidenced by the fact that she was allowed to be educated as an artist. They were married in 1883.

Larsson described the site of their house in Sundborn as having just a few small birch trees and some lilacs, plus a potato patch. Having limited means, they improved it by putting away extra savings whenever they could. With the help of some village carpenters, a blacksmith, a bricklayer and a painter, they put together a house which has become part of Sweden's pride. At first, it was just a summer house, but eventually, it became their permanent home. Today it is known as "Carl Larsson's Home" and has become a noted tourist attraction.

Carl and Karin were internationally oriented, but retained their romantic views of Sweden. Besides Paris, Carl had also gained artistic impressions of Berlin, Vienna and London. While Carl became famous as a painter, Karin gained her fame for weaving and embroidery.

The rooms in the Carl Larsson home look small to visitors today, but Larsson's painting had the effect of making them look larger than they were. Simplicity marked the interior planning. The main additions to the original log house began in 1890. It included an art studio with pictures to the front, and a large fireplace which added elegance. By 1900, more space was needed for the studio, so the original one was turned into a family room where Karin could do her work while the children worked with wood or played.

Sundborn became their permanent home in 1901. The woodshed was torn down and a two-story addition was added to make room for eleven persons. In 1912, a cottage was attached to the studio for the display of paintings. Author Ulf Hard claims that their home "became unique and exemplary and has so remained" as "a vital part of the culture at the turn of the century." Since 1943, the buildings have been administered by a family society. Above the door there is a wood carving, commonly done in Scandinavia, which reads: "Welcome to this house, to Carl Larsson and his spouse."

We're fortunate to have several books on Carl Larsson. In addition to the one on his house, he wrote six others. The best known are *Carl Larsson—On the Sunny Side* (1910) and *The World of Carl Larsson*. *On the Sunny Side* contains pictures of his paintings of the rooms in the house, about the children. Flowers were everywhere in the home. It reads as an autobiography and a story of life in the home. I have never run across anything quite so charming. *The World of Carl Larsson* deals with his art works, which are displayed in museums around the world.

I'm always amazed at human potential popping up in unexpected places. Here was a poor boy who became Sweden's greatest painter and illustrator of all time and has been acclaimed internationally. Known as the "sunshine man," Larsson occupies a place in Swedish consciousness which is shared by no other artist.

MY MOM, THE COOK

by Yvonne Thorstenson McNallie

My mother, Alice Swanson Thorstenson, loved to cook, and because she was the daughter of Swedish immigrants and because she married a man from Sweden, she cooked many traditional Swedish dishes.

We all remember *kåldolmar*, *lutfisk*, pickled herring, homemade rye bread, *korv*, meatballs, wonderful pastries and pies and cookies that melted in your mouth. Although I am not fond of some of those foods (who can eat *lutfisk*?), it sure brings back memories of the kitchen on City View where my sister and I grew up.

Mom didn't just cook for the immediate family; there were always people dropping in near dinnertime and there was always enough for everyone. She would fill out with pickled beets, Wasa *bröd*, and homemade jams and relishes. When the table was literally groaning with the food, she would say, "Help yourselves, this is all we have." My kids still laugh about that when they recall the table that didn't have a spare inch of space.

Holidays, of course, as in every Swedish household, were a time for baking and cooking. *Smörgåsbord* was an absolute necessity and we had a meal that would have served a family for a week, followed up with wonderful cookies—spritz, *pepperkakor*, and *drömmar*—and homemade sweet rolls. And the coffee! The Swedes make a wonderful cup of coffee (in fact, one of my earliest memories was the smell of the coffee brewing when Mom took me to Cradle Roll at the Salvation Army—heavenly!)

Dad was always a meat and potatoes man, so almost every meal had those as the main course, but Mom went far afield occasionally, such as when she made spaghetti. Her spaghetti would not be recognized by a true Italian food lover, but I liked the sauce she made with home-canned tomatoes and fried bacon instead of meatballs.

My mother's mother died when Mom was twelve, and she was the oldest of our other children. She learned to cook pretty much by trial and error and with the help of their next-door neighbor, a woman whom my mother idolized. Maybe this is the best way to learn cooking, because as I remember she had no catastrophes in the kitchen when I lived there. And she must have taught her sisters cooking, too, because I remember the meals we had at family reunions and my Aunt Doris saying, "Those Swanson girls sure can cook, can't they?" Nobody argued.

Mom's rye bread was a work of art. Someday I will try to make her recipe but I'm afraid that I and everyone else will be disappointed. She did it so easily and didn't need a recipe—grated up some orange rind and threw in, and sometimes used stale beer (which wasn't hard to find because Dad drank little and Mom not at all) for the liquid. My mouth waters just thinking of fresh rye bread just out of the oven—what a treat!

Mom didn't stop with cooking and baking—she also made, with of course the help of Dad, root beer (I do remember a few catastrophes regarding root beer that exploded) and their own wine. Elderberry and dandelion were their favorites, and while I was too young to sample them for many years, I do remember them as being tasty but not very strong, which suited them fine.

Mom continued to cook meals for herself daily even after Dad's death until she died at the age of 87. She was in the kitchen making soup out of the turkey carcass the day after Thanksgiving when she had a fatal heart attack. She couldn't have chosen a more fitting way to go.

Mom, Dad, Karen & Yvonne in City View Kitchen Where Mom Cooked & Baked for 55 Years

JAMESTOWNIAN REMEMBERS NORWAY UNDER SIEGE

by James Sorg
Submitted by his family

At the age of seven, Sorg traveled with his mother to Norway to visit an ailing grandmother some months prior to the Occupation of Norway. His grandmother had passed away before they arrived, but his mother thought they should visit the other relatives before returning home. However, on the mornings of April 8 and 9, German paratroopers descended from the skies, and warships were already in the harbor and the fjords. They were under siege and could not return to America.

During this time, one of the happier moments during Sorg's day was to play soccer in a nearby field with other boys his age. But one day his joy was greatly marred. There was one Jewish boy on their team, and one afternoon a huge canvas-topped truck drove up and three members of the Gestapo jumped out. A quisling soldier singled out the Jewish boy and the Gestapo captured him and drove away. They never found out what happened.

There was a great lack of food, and school children were required to work on the farms four times a week. Lawns were turned into vegetable gardens, and every family living in one dwelling had an equal part of that garden. Once when there was a party where relatives were invited to dinner, everyone thought they were eating rabbit but later learned that a cat had been prepared for their meal.

A very young Russian prisoner greeted Sorg every day from a prison he passed eachday. One day Sorg asked his mother if there was some bit of food she could give him to take to this young prisoner, and she gave him part of the heel of a loaf of bread. After that, whenever Sorg saw this young prisoner, he waved more vigorously and smiled considerably more than previously. One day the prisoner motioned for Sorg to come to the fence, and when he reached out his hand through the fence, he gave Sorg a wooden sculpture made by a small stone. As he did, Sorg noticed that the boy's fingers were bloody as a result of having his fingernails pulled out.

There was a great emotional upheaval suffered by the people because of the frequent bombings, air raids, and the rigid rule to adhere to the curfew each night.

During their seven years in Norway, there had been no contact with his father in the States. The father's letters to them had all been returned stamped "unknown." When they returned to the United States, his father met them at the pier when they discovered another scar from the war—because his dad had not heard from them, he had presumed Sorg and his mother to be dead, and his father had remarried. His mother understood. His father stayed with his second wife and eventually Sorg's mother remarried.

Sorg said that these are some of the things that can happen when war comes—and they learned to adjust over and over to the unexpected.

Note: The above was excerpted from an address by James Sorg to the Scandinavian Heritage Foundation, May 18, 1990. He was a member of the Norden Men's Club and his widow, Carol, is a member of the Norden Women's Club. Mr. Sorg passed away in 2008, two years after his first return to Norway. He planned to make another trip, but poor health prevented it. We're grateful to Mr. Sorg's family for this account of being under siege in Norway during World War II.

GUSTAVUS ADOLPHUS—
"LION OF THE NORTH"

by Arland O. Fiske

Who is the greatest Swede that ever lived? There have been many suggestions, but King Gustavus Adolphus (1594-1632) usually wins the popularity poll. Though only 38 when he died, he changed Sweden from an isolated kingdom in the north to a modern nation respected by its neighbors. Rarely has one person shaped a nation so much.

My interest in famous people centers on their childhood influences. What made Gustavus such a dynamic leader? He was an exceptionally bright child and was trained from infancy to be a king. By age five, he had seen both battle and shipwreck and had learned to speak both Swedish and German. Under the guidance of a famous tutor, he studied literature, philosophy, theology, music, military science and gained skills in twelve languages. He was taught thrift and a strict moral code. His father, Charles IX, died when Gustavus was only 17, before the legal age to receive the crown. Axel Oxenstierna, one of the nobles, arranged for early accession. Before assuming power, he signed a charter of guarantees for the rights of the people. By sharing power, he gained more power.

Those were not good times. The political conflicts of Europe were deeply rooted in religious tensions. The "Thirty Years War" (1618-48) pitted Protestant against Roman Catholic. No war is good, but religious wars are the worst of all. Greed, jealousy and fear on both sides of the conflict have a way of turning theology into tragedy. Into such a struggle, the Swedish king came to the aid of the Protestant princes of Germany.

On June 17, 1630, Gustavus sailed with 13,000 men. Once in Germany, he was joined by an additional 26,000. What made him effective in battle was the superior training of his troops and the best artillery in Europe, plus mobility, discipline and a faster firing musket. But there was more.

Each company of soldiers had its own chaplain. There were prayers twice a day and a sermon once a week. Hymns were sung in battle. Gustavus led the only army in history to have no "camp followers." This kept them free from venereal disease.

On November 6, 1632, Gustavus fell at Lutzen near Leipzig, while winning his last battle. His heart was wrapped in a silk shirt and returned to Sweden. Visitors may see the shirt in Stockholm today.

Important as the military victories of Gustavus are regarded, his domestic policies and administrative improvements were even more important. Sweden became one of the most efficient and well-organized governments in Europe. Oxenstierna guided the government while the king was away.

Gustavus Adolphus is honored in America by a college in St. Peter, MN, which was founded in 1862 and bears his name. His statue watches over the campus.

It is difficult for us who live today to judge the military heroes of the past. But there is no question how the contemporaries of Gustavus regarded him, even his enemies. They called him the "Lion of the North."

HERITAGE AND GOOD MEMORIES

by Karen E. Livsey

Augusta Sofia Svensdotter left Sweden for America in 1895 at the age of 15. She was born in Svenstorp, Korsberga, Jönköping Län, Sweden on September 15, 1880. Her parents died in 1892 leaving five children in Sweden between the ages of 4 and 15. The oldest girl, Maria Lovisa, had already gone to Jamestown, New York, where her mother's brother and family had settled. The two older boys, Emil and Oscar, went to Jamestown in 1894, joining their then married sister and her husband at their home on Chapin Street. Augusta joined her sister and family, eventually married in 1900 and went to night school to learn English. Her husband, John August Anderson, had come to Jamestown with his parents in 1887 from Linköping. He worked at Art Metal Construction Company. He caught a cold that developed into pneumonia and died in 1912 leaving Augusta and their son, Henry. The last two siblings left in Sweden, Emma and Gustaf, arrived from Sweden in 1904. All but Emma remained in the Jamestown area the rest of their lives. Emma went to nurses training at the Swedish Covenant Hospital in Chicago because she had not learned enough English to be able to go to another school. She never married and remained in Chicago until her health forced her to quit nursing and return to her family in Jamestown. The men all married, and they all worked with wood, either as carpenters or as furniture factory workers. They used the surname Swanson, while Emma used Swenson.

Augusta worked for a while as a caterer/cook for a family in Bradford, Pennsylvania, while her son continued to live with his aunt and uncle. John August's parents lived on the Trask Road in Busti. One of their neighbors knew Augusta and also knew a widower who lived down the road on a farm. They were introduced and eventually married in 1915. Augusta and Henry moved to the farm in Busti. Augusta and her second husband, Andrew Anderson, had three girls, Doris, Helen, and Martha. Martha was my mother. During World War II my mother moved back to live with her mother and half brother and after I was born we continued to live there. Andrew's daughter, Bernice, from his first marriage had married and moved to California. Doris married Carl Levin, stayed in Busti and they were both school teachers. Helen married Earl Raines and lived most of her life in the west, returning to Busti after her husband died.

As I grew up, we continued to live with my Grandmother Anderson. It was in those early years of my life that I was introduced to Swedish food and traditions. Every Christmas I was able to "help" soak the lutfisk, grind the veal for sylta, cook the liver for liver pudding, watch the long strands of spritz dough spread across the cutting board as it was squeezed out of the large metal tube by the wooden plunger tucked under and pushed by my Grandmother's arm and my favorite job—testing for holes in the casings that would hold my favorite Swedish dish, korv. I was allowed to turn the crank only a few turns to stuff the casing. I was born too late, thankfully, to hand stuff the casings with the help of the hollowed out and cut down cow's horn which I still have.

Thanks to my Great Aunt Emma, I was introduced to good Swedish coffee at the age of 6 weeks! I was brought to the nursing home where Aunt Emma was living. As always my Grandmother brought coffee and her wonderful cardamom biscuits for refreshments. As Aunt Emma was holding me she fed me a teaspoon of coffee. I did have coffee most of the days as I was going to school, but I am sure that it was mostly cream and sugar in the early days. Grandmother Anderson made cardamom biscuits every week so I soon learned that Swedish coffee required "something to go with it", especially cardamom biscuits. While she was mixing the ingredients for the biscuits, it was my job to remove the cardamom seeds from the pods and then to grind the seeds using the old coffee mill, which I still have.

My biggest regret was that by the time I came along, my Grandmother Anderson was "an American" and would not teach me Swedish. I heard some Swedish as my Grandmother often spoke with her siblings and some neighbors in Swedish, but I learned only a few words. My own interest is genealogy and having learned Swedish at an early age would definitely help make my work easier now.

"JUL MÖNSTER"

by Barbara Hillman Jones

My sister Karin and I both love needlework of all kinds. We probably inherited our love of needlework from our grandmothers and other relatives both in Sweden and here in the United States. Our mother did not do any needlework that we know of, but perhaps that was because she had two girls to care for, she helped my dad in his grocery store, and later she worked in Lockwood's and then Bigelow's in our home town of Jamestown, New York. Both grandmothers crocheted expertly. Grandma Tuline made edgings for sheets and pillowcases, doilies, chair sets, and she crocheted a bedspread for each of three daughters and three granddaughters. *Farmor*, my grandmother Hillman, crocheted beautiful doilies and edgings on handkerchiefs, among other things. We come by our love of needlework honestly.

When Karin and her pastor husband Steve were first married, they lived in a very small farming community in Iowa where Steve served a local church. They both learned lots of valuable things from those farm folks. Steve learned how to plant a garden, take care of it, and when and how to harvest his crops. They learned how to prepare and cook pork and beef that parishioners so generously gave to them. Karin learned how to can and freeze produce from their garden, she learned to cross-stitch, and she learned how to do the ancient art of Norwegian Hardanger embroidery. Hardanger is an intricate kind of needlework that combines a unique kind of stitch with cutwork. Karin taught me to do it, also, and it's absolutely beautiful and great fun. In 1988 she gave me a large piece of Hardanger embroidery that she had made during the time that dad was in the hospital at the end of his life. While he was ill, we flew back and forth several times, and there was lots of down time, both on the airplanes and in the hospital. When Karin gave that beautiful piece to me, she said that she simply couldn't give it to anyone else because there were so many memories of dad's last days connected with it.

Karin lives in Colorado and I live in Indiana, so we don't see each other very often, so when we are able to visit one another, something we love to do is have "show and tell" with all the projects we've made or that we're working on. We know that we can't live long enough to make all the pieces that we'd like to make, so we spend time looking at the patterns we've collected. One of the ladies in Iowa always told Karin that she had to live to be 187 in order to make all the things she had lined up. We've decided that it's almost as much fun to look at the patterns as it is to actually make them.

One of the books I have in my collection is one containing various traditional Swedish patterns. On the cover of the little book is a Swedish Christmas tree and the words *"Jul Mönster"* below the picture. Karin borrowed the book from me to make some of those patterns for herself, and when she returned the book, she had carefully and lovingly stitched that Christmas tree for me, complete with the words *"Jul Mönster"* neatly stitched below the tree and delightfully framed so it could be hung on my wall. Later, I became curious about the word *"Mönster,"* so I looked it up in my Swedish dictionary. To my utter surprise, the definition was *"pattern."* *"Jul Mönster"* turned out to be the title of the book—*"Christmas Patterns"*! My sister had thought it was a Christmas greeting!

When I told Karin, we both burst out laughing! Ever since she made the *"Jul Mönster"* for me many years ago, we have had so much fun with it. I wouldn't miss for anything the opportunity to hang it up along with the other Christmas decorations, and often when we're talking to each other on the phone, one of us will mention the *"Jul Mönster,"* and then we have another good laugh.

From the *"Jul Mönster"* we learned that when something doesn't turn out quite the way we think it should, often the result can be more enjoyable than if it had been carried out perfectly. Maybe that comes with age . . . .

MY EMIGRATION FROM NORWAY

by Vorin Hansen Johnston

We were not the first of my family to travel to America. My mother's father was in America for ten years working in the Northwest. He then traveled back to Norway and married my maternal grandmother.

My father Hermod, my mother Jeanette, and I arrived in America soon after the Second World War. Norway had been occupied by the Nazis for a number of years, and my father and uncles were in the military during that time. My father's older brothers and two older sisters had emigrated from Norway to America years before and wanted my paternal grandparents to come to America now that the war was over. My grandparents were afraid to travel alone, and so they asked my mother and father to travel with them. My father was very keen on going, my mother not so much. The visit to America was to be just that, a visit, although a long one, with no intention of staying.

We sailed on the Stavangerfjord, seven days across the Atlantic to New York City. We were met by my father's older siblings. The noise and hustle-bustle of New York were a bit overwhelming for my parents as we were from a small town on the Strand, near Sigerfjord. I was little, and my mother was afraid of losing me as we toured the city with my aunts and uncles, so they purchased a child's harness to keep me close. That is one of many stories they shared about our first experiences in America.

From New York City we took the train to Jamestown, New York. My mom and dad were very glad to find the large Scandinavian population in Jamestown at that time. We stayed with my aunt and uncle who lived on Superior Street, and they introduced my parents to many people from Sweden and Norway. With the culture and language from both countries so similar, they felt very comfortable being able to converse and share traditions with these new friends and acquaintances.

Eventually, my grandparents returned to Norway, and I am sure my mother would have liked to have returned as well as all of her family was there. However, my father wanted to stay, appreciating all the opportunities America offered. My mother appreciated that as well, and so we stayed.

My father started to work at Ellison Bronze and we moved to Forest Avenue within walking distance of my aunt and uncle's house. My parents went to night school to learn English, and I started kindergarten at Fletcher Elementary School.

After starting school and playing with my new friends, I soon became more conversant in English. I remember learning about new foods and telling my mother about them after coming home from lunch with one of my new neighborhood friends and my mother trying to make that dish. The one that stands out is French toast. After a few tries with making toast in the toaster and drizzling Karo syrup on top, she decided to ask my friend's mother how to make this special toast. As she was learning English herself, she worried she would not be understood. But all went well, I guess, because we had real French toast after that.

Norwegian was spoken at home and with our relatives, traditions were followed, and Scandinavian foods were ever present. It was easy in those days to find those foods because of the large Scandinavian population. English was spoken outside of our home, and we soon learned about the American traditions and began to become Americans.

We joined the First Lutheran Church, and I have many memories of those early Sunday School days, and in the summer, the Bible School days. There were many Swedish members at First Lutheran who became friends and acquaintances of my parents, and there were children with whom I went to school and later with whom I was confirmed.

After attending Fletcher School, I went to Jefferson Junior High School and then graduated from Jamestown High School in 1962. I went on to become a registered nurse and later returned to school to become a teacher.

My husband Rick and I still carry out the Scandinavian traditions and at Christmastime we cook all the special foods, except for the Christmas *lutefisk* [Norwegian spelling]. Rick is Swedish on his mother's side, and our son and daughter observe some of the Scandinavian traditions and make the Scandinavian food.

Editor's Note: Happily, the experience of Vorin and her family dispels the oft-told stories about competition and even supposed animosity between the Swedes and the Norwegians—at least in Jamestown!

LETTERS FROM SWEDEN TO ANDREW SANDBERG IN AMERICA

submitted by Sallie A. Olson

During a visit to my dad's cousin Betty Baron, I found an envelope full of letters written in Swedish to Andrew and Elisabeth Sandberg who arrived in America in March 1868 by various relatives in Sweden. The letters were handed down by Elisabeth Sandberg: first, to Elisabeth's daughter, Emma Sandberg Olson; then to Emma's daughter, Ruth Olson Ruggles Swanson; then to Ruth's daughter, Betty Ruggles Baron, my dad's cousin who kindly shared them with me.

My friend, Susan Friberg, is married to a Swedish professor, and he graciously translated the letters into English in 2010. They were translated so that Andrew Sandberg's posterity can enjoy them, learn from them, and appreciate the lives and sacrifices of their ancestors!

* * * * * *

EDITOR'S NOTE: These fifteen letters written to Andrew and Elisabeth Sandberg plus their last will and testament may seem long and at times repetitive. However, they are written by different people over a period of 18 years, from 1875 to 1893, and it seemed to me that they should be published in their entirety. Each letter carries a valuable piece of history, both in Sweden and in America during that period. Their writings not only tell about the emigrants but those who sometimes don't appear to be as prominent or important, those who were left behind. Each letter has a different story from a different perspective, and yet, there are several recurring themes: these people were deeply religious; health was of utmost importance;

they were farmers and they relate the joys and perils of farming in those days; and they were family—they missed each other enormously and longed to see each other face to face at least one more time. There was always the hope that the emigrants would return home, and often their relatives tried to entice them by telling them of a perfect piece of property just waiting for them to purchase at a very reasonable price.

This collection is a valuable piece of our Scandinavian heritage as seen by those who were left behind. The letters have been donated to the Fenton Historical Society Museum in Jamestown, New York. Interestingly, Sallie's great-grandfather was Frans Olson (originally Johanson), who had trained in Sweden to be a masonry artistan and was very talented. He emigrated as a young widower to Jamestown where Governor Reuben Fenton commissioned him to work on his mansion and other properties that he owned. Olson worked on the Opera House which later burned, and he worked on the Lutheran Church, and many other local buildings, as well. Sallie says that somewhere in the Sandberg family there was a marriage into the Fenton family. Sallie's grandmother was Lillian Soderquist Rowley. Her husband's grandfather was John Rowley who entered the Civil War at 13 years old, probably as a drummer boy. After he was discharged because of an injury, he married and had a son Bert who became a very good carpenter and built a church in Fentonville along with a Fenton family member. Sallie says that brings the two sides of her family full circle with a Fenton connection. Fascinating!

* * * * * *

Before you begin:

- There will be some words in italics. They are explanations for some phrases or words in Swedish, or an explanation about who a particular person is who is mentioned.
- Also notice that people in Sweden name their farm, so at the beginning of the letters it states a place and then

Sweden. That is the name of the farm from which the letter is written.
- Some letters talk about "charcoal stacks." In Sweden, they would cut a pile of wood, put a tarp over it and start a smoldering fire. It should not burn too fast, but just smolder. After a certain period of time, the wood would then be stacked into "charcoal stacks." The wood from these stacks would burn better and longer than regular wood.
- As of 2010, when calculating Swedish money into American dollars, divide the Swedish money by seven and you will get the dollar amount.

"Letters from Sweden"

Letter #1

25 March 1875, Snarn, Sweden. From his father, who dictated the letter to his grandson, C. W. Carlsson, the son of Carl August Larsson, who is the brother of Andrew Sandberg. C. W. Carlsson is the nephew of Andrew Sandberg.

Tenderly beloved grandchildren on a far away shore. I will now, after a long delay, write a few lines to you and let you know how we feel; that we enjoy health and feel well up to the moment of writing. And we wish you all the same. I will now tell you that in this country it is a cold winter. January 24th, the cold was so severe that they could not hold a service in the churches. It was colder than 48° *(minus 50°F)*. I will tell a little about the grain in this country. Oats cost 12-13 riksdalar *(money)*, barley and rye 18 riksdalar, wheat 24 riksdalar. But last fall they received 31 riksdalar per barrel for wheat. I will tell you that our way of counting money has been changed; 1 riskdalar is now called a krona, and we receive less for our work now than when you were here. A pig here, who is four weeks old, cost 10-12 riksdalar. We bought two pigs last spring, they cost 28 riksdalar a pair and they were reaching five weeks. We have three cows and one horse and one ewe who has got two lambs and two calves have we kept to grow if they will stay alive. The little son of Spabonnas, Johan, has started to walk now after Christmas and they all have good health and feel well up to the moment of writing. We send lots of regards from all relatives and acquaintances that they all enjoy health and feel well up to the moment of writing. There was about six feet of snow so the people had to shovel snow more than they could handle. In this country on the lake six farmers froze to death, two traveling salesman and a Colonel for the Grenaders was in the cold and storm and died. The Colonel, he stood dead at the sleigh. We ask you to send kind regards to Abramssons *(a family friend)* from us and grandmother would like very much to know how things are with them. Grandmother sends kind regards to Emma *(Emma Sandberg Olson)* and William *(William Andrew Sandberg)* and she would like to see them if possible. We give you regards from sister Anna, that she feels well and that she will now begin the third year at Fillinge. This letter, which I have dictated, the first time I have done so, so I suppose it can have faults both as regards to way of thinking and words. I ask that it is not given out, I only want to give it to you as a remembrance. Good bye for this time only a tender greetings to you all especially from father and mother. Grandmother sends greetings to Anders and Lovisa *(Lovisa/Louise is Andrew Sandberg's wife's sister, Anders is Lovisa's husband)*.

Signed by your nephew C. W. Carlsson

And I will tell you that Aunt and Uncle in Vaesteraas are dead. It was only seven months between them. Please send us a few lines in return. If Lovisa sends a letter, grandmother will pay. Anna greets her little cousins very much. She is feisty and talks about everything.

Letter #2

10 May 1875, Snarn, Sweden. From Jonas Persson and his wife Elisabeth and Andrew's nephew C. E. Carlsson

Our Lord Jesus Christ grace and peace. Dearly beloved children and your children on a far away and distant shore. I take the pen in my hand to write an answer to your dear letter which we received May 4th. We hear that you are in good health and feel well which is most important that God has created and we will also let you know that we have good health all the way up to the moment of writing. We wish from all our heart that you may enjoy the same blessed condition when this letter reaches you. We hear in your letter that you have been given a daughter *(Martha Sandberg)* and we wish her success and health which is most important in this life. We hear in your letter that Anders Wilhelm *(William Sandberg)* has become better and that was enjoyable for us to hear. We have lost a cow and one calf. The cow had problems in her legs so she could not stand up, so for three weeks we helped her stand up. The calf had to take care of himself. But now we have bought a cow from an auction in Garline which cost 86 riksdaler and she has four weeks left before she should have a calf. We hear that you are thinking of traveling here and that would be pleasant for us all to get to see you once more in this life, especially for grandmother and grandfather to see you but they are alive and there are certainly farms to buy both large and small for the one who has money.

That would be good now to buy but we can't decide because we don't know if you will come. Elsewise there are places to rent until you can find out about a suitable place. You can stay in our place until you can find somewhere to live. If you come traveling it would be best that you go to Arboga then we could fetch you there. The farmer at Spra *(farm)* has received a son who was born March 21, 1875 and his name is Anders Gustav and he is feisty and behaves well and all are enjoying good health and feel well until the moment of writing. And all relatives feel well and are in good health. Last year, Easter, we acquired a beehive and they swarm in the middle of the summer so then we had two bee swarms more than the old beehive that died. So we got four cans of honey. We are now building a new barn which will be larger so we will have both a horse and cows in the place and a shed in the same place. We have seeded one and a half barrels of oats and we seeded around one acre with beautiful wheat and it is beautiful and grows. Barley we have seeded. Uncle has leased a low lying land from Erik Ericsson in Fillinge which is located just below our meadow and it lasts for 10 or 12 years to cultivate in order to take four years of harvests and after that he takes it back again a small piece at a time. The spring is coming and the birches begin to be green and the grass grows again. Please be good to send greeting to Abramsons *(a friend who is a pastor in America)* from us. You would be well received when you come here anytime, especially as we have three fruit trees. When you come to Arboga then you should look up the merchant Olsson until we come and hence you can come whenever. There is one place to rent at Oesbo. Today we let out the cattle and grandfather took care of them the first day. The calf that we lost was four months old and that was the calf after the same cow who died and there are many who have lost cows. Some have broken their back when they have gone to the bull with them. We send greetings from little Anna that she should like to see her little cousins and that she would like to dance with them and she is forward and grows up. She is now as big as one should be on the fourth year and she talks about them almost constantly. Now I will write a few lines about myself that I just have received the holy sacrament in school and learned to know God and to obey his commandments and through that become forever happy. I go with the pastor since the second priest doesn't do anything so he can't go anywhere but someone is forced to take him and pastor. He receives 1200 riksdaler for each year. Now I have nothing to tell for this time only a dear greeting to all of you.

Signed: Jonas Persson and his wife Elisabeth and your nephew C. E. Carlsson

---

Letter #3

16 August 1876, Gibo, Sweden *(farm).* From his brother Carl August Larsson

God's grace and peace both over you and us all in the spirit of the Lord. I will now for the first time put down these lines with my pen some few well meant lines to you, my dear brother, and your family. I will first mention that I am in good health up to this writing moment and I wish you the same good condition and I wish these simple lines may reach you in good health. I believe it will, that it will be cheerful for you to see that I have not forgotten you even if I have not written lately. You should believe that I have not forgotten you. I will mention a little bit about the harvest here in Sweden as well as the weather. It has been an unusually dry summer here so the hay harvest has been small to an extent that it has not been so small in human memory, however, some is a little bit better than nothing. Then I will mention that I have been selected the second time this year to serve as a soldier and each of us has been over to the other side of Loaten to an estate by the name of Nagaala on a field maneuver. It was a kind of work that did not exactly appeal to me but if I don't have to do more of that, I will be glad. I have work in Ullbo Forest for the owner that I like better. I have two charcoal stacks for him and now I have this started and I will see what happens. Father will have one charcoal for them. We have been in Ullbo renovating a cottage for Enock Anders because he has got his house ready to move into. We get two kronor *(money)* a day each. So now I will tell you that I can feel good and I can tell you that I have it good now. But I cannot know how I will be in the future and nobody can tell that but if I live then I will tell you how I am in the future. I think it would be a great feeling in our blood if we should see each other in our bodily appearances and reach out a warm hand to each other. But I want to ask my dear brother if it would be a great loss to me if I moved to America. You can be kind and write how you feel since you know how it is. Perhaps I should see you once more in this life but if we never should see each other in this world, we will hope that we will meet again with Jesus in Heaven, that we there may be put on his right hand side, for I do not fear death, I will be united with you. It is with joy to be called over there in eternal grace. Now I want to ask you for a portrait of you and your wife and your children. I feel that would be my greatest joy to see if you still look like you did earlier because you did not recognize me when I sent you my picture. I will soon send a new one to you because I believe that you will find it enjoyable to see me even if it is just on paper, even if we never will see each other in reality. Now I will stop writing my short letter for this time with a prayer to the Lord when I think on people far away if we once more see each other it is something I don't know but now will you please be good and write to me as soon as possible and tell me how you feel.

Signed: Your dear brother Carl August Larsson

Write soon and don't forget me

Letter #4

17 June 1882, Harparboda, Sweden. From his brother Lars Larsson

God, peace be with us all. Now after a long wait, I will take the pen in my hand to let you know that I am still alive although not all days have been full of joy after I wrote to you. My wife has been ill for an entire year. Now she is on her way to get healthy again and that is a joy. Consider what it means to be healthy and what it is when you don't own health; because the gift of health is the most dear gift that we have received in our whole life; for that one we should praise and give thanks; for it is such a valuable gift. And we thank God to have reasonable health all of us, and I wish that these lines might reach you with the same. I hope that you might shed tears of joy one more time when you see your brothers handwriting. But consider my dear brother, Ander *(Andrew Sandberg)* if we once more in life were able to touch each others hands, then it would be the most touching joy that I cannot describe. Now we leave this subject. Now I will tell you how my life is at present. I cultivated one quarter of a hemman *(a piece of land)* after Swedish counting and pay one thousand kronor *(type of money)* in lease for every year. I can seed five to six barrels of rye and 25 barrels of oats. I am allowed to make two charcoal stacks in the woods every year and sell the charcoal wherever I want to. I have a meadow that I am in the process of cultivating so I have lots of work to do. I send tender greetings from brother Per Erick. He is with me working and he is healthy and feels well and lives alone. Still he talks about America almost every day but if he will ever travel he is not sure and perhaps he is wise not to do it because he has saved some money so he can buy himself a little house in Sweden if he wants to. I have heard that you have sold your estate. How did that happen? Did you not find it good to be a farmer in America, which is the country of heaven on earth for farmers? But perhaps you are better off now but tell me how you are, if you have a farm or a house that you own, or if you have some capital. Perhaps when you have gathered a sum of money then you can come back to Sweden and buy an estate and that would be a joy to see how all the acquaintances in America have it. Greet all of them that you know that I know. Hontorp *(name of farm)*, Larsson who is called Lasse, doesn't want to write. But if you see him, ask him to write a little letter to me. I have seen that you have three children and that they are healthy and Swedish/American. I have seen your portrait and it was a joy to see. We all send hearty greetings to you all on the other side, on the far away shore. We put our hope to our Lord, for without Him we are but a shadow and because of that we shall trust Him that He accompanies us to wherever He wants.

Signed from the heart tenderly to you, brother

Lars Larsson

Letter #5

2 April 1883 Faagelsjoemossen, Sweden *(a village or farm)*. From his father, Lars Larsson

In the name of the Lord, I am sending you a few words and simple lines to let you know how we are. That we have good health and feel good. We wish you the same good, which is the greatest treasure and wealth that we can own in this world. Now first and foremost, this is an answering letter to your heartily welcome letter that we got on March 17th in which we understand that you are in good health and are alive and it is a joy for us to find out how you feel. And now first, I ask you for forgiveness because I have not answered our welcomed letter which we have received from you and also may I thank you for your picture that you sent to me. You are very much like you have been although you have let your beard get longer. If I only could see you now and speak to you orally that would be a great joy. I should enjoy what we see in writing. You again have sold and shall move, it is sad to hear that you don't have a place to live but we hope that there is some way out. I hear that you think on your childhood home. It does not surprise me being so far away in a foreign country. We will never see and enjoy each other but I think that if I owned three thousand kronor then I shall not go to America instead you could have 3,000 kronor in your pocket when you come home to Sweden that you could buy a small and fine estate here and then I think and believe that you should surely like it better here than in America. I feel that it would be an enjoyable day for us to see you come here but I am afraid that it will never happen. Here there are estates for sale. Svansboaer *(farm)* just sold. I should mention a little bit about the weather here. There has been a lot of snow this winter. It started snowing in November but it has not been so cold and now it has thawed a little bit so it looks as it should be, a long spring. It was also a good harvest here last summer. So everything is going well in spite of everything. I can tell you that the price of cattle, one cow costs 100-200 kronor and a pair of oxen 400-500 and a horse 500-600 according to what condition they are. We have two cows and three sheep and one cat. I have gone to Ullbo Forest for two months and hewn and sawed lumber and there I made 1.50 kronor per day and Per Erik *(Andrew's brother)* also worked when close to Finnaakersby. He has made charcoal, 11 stacks this winter for the farmers and he has made good money. I send kindest regards from brother Lars in Harparboba *(farm)* that they are alive and have good health. During Easter, we were together at our old father in Gibo *(farm)* with all the brothers except you. Now I have to finish my short letter for this time. Please don't forget me but be kind and write soon. But most, remember your father that is healthy and spry. I include both us and you in God's mildness in whose protection I bid my most heartily farewell for this time.

Signed by our kind father, Lars Larsson

Letter #6

This letter is not signed or dated; however, with the information in the letter, it can be assumed that it is late 1884 or early 1885, and it is assumed that it is written by Carl August Larsson, since he included a message from his son, Little Carl. Little Carl that is referred to was born 18 November 1881 and died 27 May 1885, so if he was three, then it was after his birthday in November 1884, but before he died in May 1885. It says your cousin, Little Carl, so it can be assumed that the letter was sent to Andrew's children, who would be his cousins.

Gibo *(farm)*, Sweden

I send a little greeting from Anders Larsson in Little Ronningen *(village in Sweden)*. I visited with him and also with his son, Lasse, who has been to Koeping's market and bought himself a large mirror for 7 kronor which was really beautiful. He bought a wheel for the threshing machine which I will go there and help him mount the little wheel. It cost 8 kronor. Everyone is in good health and feels well. Now a tender farewell for this time. Anders Larsson told me that I should send greeting from him.

(Not signed)

Also, I add a little greeting from our little Carl. He grows and enjoys life among the flowers because he is both healthy and feisty and now he starts talking about anything and he recognizes his uncles and talks about them sometimes but you, he does not recognize. He is 3 years old and he is a great joy for his grandfather. They are really buddies. He carves little figures of humans and horses and toys of all kinds. I greet you all very much both friends and cousins.

Signed, full of friendship, your cousin, little Carl

Letter #7

18 February 1885, Gibo *farm),* Sweden. From his brother Carl August Larsson

God's grace and peace be with you in the name of the Lord. I take my pen in my hand in order to let you know how we are and how we live here in the old Sweden; that we thank God for good health until now although I wish you the same good gift for what we have to thank our highest beneficiary. I wish that these lines may reach you with that good hope and I wish with all my heart that these lines may give you so much pleasure to know that we live and feel well. I think many times that it should be extra fun to see you and talk to you but you are too far away in the world so it seems difficult to imagine such a visit. If the distance were not so far, I should come and see you and then I could come back here, but here there is much talk about the difficult times in America. How it really is, I don't know and if I get there then I don't believe I should like it very much there not as much as here. Now I will tell you what I am doing now. I have attempted to make a cabinet to have milk in and now I will make a new cart. Grandfather, he is in good health and spry and we put together milk containers in our workshop in the street house because there Jan Jansson created a carpenter shop and we are allowed to use it. I send regards from brother Per Erick *(Andrew's brother).* He will enter his farm this spring Finnaaker *(farm)* and he will stay there for a while hopefully. Brother Lars *(Andrew's brother),* from him I have not heard anything, but I hope he is well and healthy. I will also mention a little bit about the weather here. We have received lots of snow and unusually cold weather all the way to February. Then we had a thaw. So the deep snow has receded somewhat. The harvest is good in all parts so we will survive well. Nothing is now as expensive as it was in earlier times for clothing or food. One barrel of rye you can buy for 13 kronor and the daily wages is just like earlier so it is easier to get by here also as long as one can remain healthy. I can tell you that I have a plot of land to farm, in spite of the fact that I live in Gibo. I will lease this for 30 kronor per year. I have grown potatoes there and I can have half of the potatoes.

I have oats there. I receive four barrels of oats this summer and one barrel barley and one barrel rye. But the harvest of hay was small, just one wagon load. I have paid 60 kronor earlier for the land but it was too much for it and it was too much because I could only sell two barrels of oats. I can send you my warmest greeting from Per Jonsson in Spabo, that they are healthy. I ask you how far it is between you and Masongslasse *(he is asking if Andrew is a good friend of Masongslasse)*. I believe I have forgotten to write to Loaangbo *(farm)*. Now I have to finish and I send you a tender farewell for this time. When there is a deep love then nobody is far away. Please write as soon as possible so we will know if you are alive or dead. Live well.

Signed: Your dear brother, Carl August Larsson

(a piece of woven material was included in this letter)

Letter #8

21 November 1887, Snarve, Sweden. From Anna Ericsson, Andrew's niece

Beloved relatives, We now will write a few lines to you to let you know that we are alive and enjoy good health up to this letter and wish you all the same good. We should first thank you so much for the welcome letter and portrait we received from you in which we see that you have been traveling. It was nice to receive a small description about the great waterfall *(this was probably Niagara Falls since Jamestown is close to Niagara Falls)*. There is a little sad thing in this letter. Father *(Andrew's uncle)* has pain in one leg so he has not been able to work for three weeks and does not yet know when there will be significant improvements. But however it is, good that grandmother and grandfather are so much in good health as they are. Grandfather is now in the forest and makes charcoal but he has of course one assistant; otherwise he would not be able to handle it. He is right now home to have dinner, he is home from making charcoal and is covered with black charcoal. We will send you many greeting from all the relatives that they are in good health and that Ericssons in Hidda at Ervalla *(farm)* has bought a place at Koertinge for 1,600 kronor. There is three and a half acres of cultivated land and two acres forest of which some could be cultivated. An uncle gave him 1,000 kronor. So if you would like to come to Sweden there are surely places to buy, both large and small. Aunt Stina in Wettgerga has two children who married last fall, one boy and one girl, so now she has four of her many children married. We should mention that we have three cows and one small bull, one horse, one pig, one ewe, one year old pig that we slaughtered last week. Grandmother has forgotton how old your children are which she wants very much to know in your next letter. We want to know how things are with Lovisa. How many children they have and how they live. We never hear anything from them. Please send our best regards to them from us if you see them; they might write sometime also. It looks like they never think about Sweden since they never write or maybe they have become so rich they don't care to write letters home to their poor parents. The harvest has been reasonable this year. We got 8 barrels of rye, 20 barrels of oats, 30 barrels of potatoes, but the hay harvest was bad. Potatoes we got more than we need. I want to give my cousins a few photos as a memory of me, please receive it even if it is not much. I must finish for this time with a dear greeting from us all to all of you. Be kind to write when the occasion allows and let us hear how you feel.

Signed: Anna Ericsson

It is no good that we pay for the letter because then it doesn't reach you because as soon as we pay for them they don't reach you.

Letter #9

14 February 1889, Gibo, Sweden. From his brother Carl August Larsson

God's grace and peace be with us all. Dearly beloved brother and sister-in-law, far away in a foreign country. I for this time after a long wait sit down and write a few words and well meant lines to tell you that we all at present are alive and in good health until the moment of writing which is most important that we can have in this life on earth. I wish these simple lines may reach you with the same great advantage. Now for the first time I have to tell you and let you know what has happened and taken place in the house of our father *(Lars Larsson, Andrew's father)*. He has for the second time become a widower. October 20th our stepmother *(Lars Larsson's second wife, Joanna)* died and now she has reached a fine grave and her final goal in life. Oh the day of hope that clears the mist of our mortality. You come down to our earthly existence with a ray of light in our famine pain, and sorrow and earth disappear away like the shadows of night. And three weeks thereafter the old Stentorp *(farm)* woman also died and ended her earthly existence. And then I have to tell you what happened in Gibo *(farm)*. Our father must hold an auction on all that was left in the house in order to be able to exchange my inheritance for the children of our stepmother. They shall have half of what he owns and it will be difficult for us to accept this condition because she had nothing to bring to Gibo of any value and one can hardly perceive these children as humans but rather as wild animals in the woods which gathers for themselves as much as they possibly can because they were here for the auction as if they should own the whole of Gibo. I have to tell you that we have moved from Forgelssoemonen *(farm)* again and home to father in Gibo and we shall be close to him. He is now healthy and spry and is able to putter around doing some work. I will now tell you how many cows we have. We have 3 cows that are ours and father has one cow for himself and one pig so we have 4 cattle together and 3 sheep and 1 horse. I will tell you what kind fo work I have, I am in the woods and hew lumber in Svartkjaersnaaret and I get 5 ore *(100th of a* *krona)* for each measure of lumber and in addition I have had a charcoal stack this fall and when I finish this work I will start the seasonal steam threshing and then to Stentorp and build a grain separating machine and then I will start building a shed for the wagons and a separate barn for the horses and in addition I am here and there for anyone who needs my help. And I have to tell you that I still have Forgelssoemaassen but for next year I don't know how I will do. So now I have two places to work on so I have a lot to do. Kyndelsmess Day *(holiday in the fall)*, I and grandfather went to Harparboda *(farm)* and visited brother Lars. They live and are in good health and feel comfortable. They have got a little daughter by the name of Tilda, who is now 6 weeks old and was really well behaved. I send greetings from Per Erik *(Andrew's brother)*, he is in Finaakersby *(farm)* and hews and makes charcoal for the farmers over there. I will mention about the weather. Here we have had a beautiful summer so everything has grown very well except the potatoes that almost disappeared in the early summer. We have had so far an unusually beautiful winter and it has never been more than one foot deep of snow at any time. I must stop my simple letter for this time with a tender farewell in the peace of the Lord.

Signed in friendship from Carl August Larsson

Today I should go to Tuna *(farm)* for an auction then I shall put the letter into the mail on February 28th to let you know how we are and then please send a letter soon because it is a great joy.

Letter #10

20 September 1889, Snarn, Sweden. From his niece Anna Josefina Larsson Ericsson, daughter of Lars Larsson, brother of Andrew

Beloved relatives be always well, that is our daily wish. We may now tell you that all of us are in good health and feel well. We may also tell you that we already have finished picking the potatoes.

We got almost 30 barrels. It has been a good harvest this year with everything except hay and oats harvest. They were bad. We have now finished all outdoor activities. We have thrashed both oats and rye. It goes very fast for us because we now have our own thrashing machine so we can do the thrashing whenever we want to. Dad *(Lars Larsson, Andrew's brother)* has bought me a sewing machine so I can sew when I don't have so much else to do. There is a girl from Taeby *(farm)* who is home from America. She has been there for 5 years but now she is home and visiting but she will return this month. I have talked to her about you. She has never heard about Boonertown, New York *(that was the address on an envelope with all these letters)*. The city where she is in service *(works)* is St. Tjaalis *(this was very hard to read)*. She feels that it is so good in America so she does not want to remain in Sweden. So it could not be dangerous for someone like you to come here. Imagine how joyful it would be. We hope that someone soon will come. Emma *(Andrew's daughter)*, she can come soon so she then doesn't have to travel back alone. I am to send my picture but we have heard that there has been a large flood over there and you have even been able to move. So it is not worthwhile that I send the portrait before you write an answer. Then we write immediately and send the picture. We can greet you from all relatives that they are well both in Skavo, Writberga and Koestinge and all relatives. We must ask what kind of summer you have had. Here it has been a dry summer but it looks like we should get a wet fall. I dream very much about America. I dreamt one night that grandmother *(Anna's husband's grandmother)* and I traveled there and I could see clearly your house and Aunt Lisa. She was so much like as I saw her on her portrait. It would be great joy if I could see some of my relatives who are so far away. Please consider that you come soon. We have nothing more to write about for this time only many dear greetings from us everyone to everyone of you.

Signed in friendship, Anna Josefina Ericsson

Please tell how Aunt Lovisa *(Andrew's wife's sister)* is; if you have heard something from her or if you visit each other sometime.

Letter #11

19 November 1890, Snarn, Sweden. From Anna (Ericsson) Oedein, Andrew's niece, daughter of Per Erik Larsson, brother of Andrew

Beloved relatives, I write a few lines and thank you very much for the letter that we received. It was great joy to hear that you feel well and enjoy health which we also have, God be praised. But father had problems with his legs again but now he is better so they can continue to make charcoal. He was in the hospital close to four weeks so it is not so fun. But if he were not able to get out of bed it would be worse. But he is not careful enough against being hit when they work in the forest with such work. Elsewise, we are all healthy. Grandmother and Grandfather *(Anna's husband's parents)* are also healthy in spite of the fact that they are so old. Grandmother runs and jumps worse than any young girl. We were so happy when Pastor Abramsson came to us so we could talk with him and could hear about how things are in America. I now want to mention a little about the harvest; it has been exceptionally good. We have about 20 barrels of oats, 6 barrels rye. The hay harvest has also been good. We have 15 barrels of potatoes; but they were rather bad and some of us have not even got back the amount seeded. We can send regards from all relatives that they are well. Then I will tell you that I am married. I was a bride on the 9th of November. I became so anxious when I heard that Emma (Sandberg) was going to be married so I should hurry and compete with her. My husbands name is Per Adolf Odein. He is a husar *(special kind of soldier)* for Oppeby, Fellingsbro, Sweden. We expected Emma and her husband to come to visit us last summer, but in vain. But next summer we will wait impatiently and hope the wait is not in vain. Now I have to finish for this time with many tender greetings from us all to you all.

Sincerely, Anna Odein

Please send this letter to Abramsson's widow *(Abramsson the pastor)*. Please send greetings also from us.

Letter #12

11 May 1891, Snarn, Sweden. From P. A. Odein, husband of Anna Ericsson Odein, Andrew's niece

Beloved relatives. We thank you so very much for the letter that we received a long time ago. In it we saw that you have good health which is the best one can wish for in this world. We also have the joy to have good health, both old and young in this house. Except my father-in-law, he has weak legs but we thank God that he is not weaker. He is not so weak that he cannot work every day. Our parents are very perky for such a high age. The old girl spins and sews as she was just 20 years old. The old man is puttering with all kinds of things and now he will even have coal stacks. The summer has come here and the spring seeding has started. In spite of the expensive grain for seeding which is very high. The potatoes are very dear here because of the bad harvest last year. We have lots of work here. We are going to put up a new barn, we are going to have two charcoal stacks which we are working on, and we have to do our best to seed about 5 barrels of oats. We have now not less than 8 cattle, 5 sheep, 1 horse and 1 pig in our barn so the times have changed considerably since we saw each other last. It is good that one can work oneself in this world so one does not have to suffer to be in want. But it does not suffice to some extra decorations and that is okay. There is not much else to tell this time. I see in your letter that you wish to have a photo of me and I promise that will come but so far I have not taken a photograph of me but as soon as I find time we shall have one of all of us. I thank you so very much for the good wishes that you sent us and if God grants us good health, I hope that we shall work ourselves forward in this world also. I will take part in the military meeting in August.

We have a field maneuver that will take place around Falkoping and will last for 8 days. My wife asks Martha *(Andrew's daughter)* to send her a box of grapes. She thinks that would certainly be a feast here in Sweden. Also she asks if Emma *(Andrew's daughter)* is married now. We should send our best wishes and a good future and that she gets married soon because it is pleasant to be married. The old people thank you for the invitation to the New Year's festival but they say that they like it best in Snarn and that they will finish their days, if God so decides, here. Please send greetings to Abramsson's wife *(pastor friend's wife)* from her sister who wrote a long time ago and has received no answer, so she believes that the letter did not reach the address. We will now finish our letter with many tender greetings from us all both parents and relatives.

Signed, the soldier P. A. Odein

Greet Abramsson from Medaaker *(village)*, we will go there for summer vacation because it is a healthy climate there. Your children will receive a photograph as soon as possible. Please send one to me.

Signed, Anna Odein

Letter #13

15 November 1891, Snarn, Sweden. From P. A. Odein husband of Anna Ericsson, Andrew's niece

Beloved relatives, Be well is our daily wish. To begin with, we should tell you that we are in good health, all of us, both young and old. We also thank you for the invitation for the wedding *(Emma Sandberg and Frans Olson)*. It was nice to be invited to a wedding to such a distant country to where you anyhow can not go. The letter came here exactly 8 days after the wedding day so we did not have to arrange celebrations but we compensated anyhow by a big pot of coffee together to have some feeling about the wedding dinner. We have now received a little daughter and her name is Freda Matilda. She is healthy and feisty like a freshly opened flower and we will thank God who has given her so great advantage. I will now tell something about our harvest. We have had an ordinary harvest as far as hay is concerned. It was small because of the long drought in the beginning of summer. At about mid-summertime, a blessed rain came that gave water for the spring grain and the potatoes so those have received a rather significant amount. But down on the flat land they have had a bad harvest. So the grain prices are rather high. Oats cost 13 kronor for 100 kilo and the rye is 19 kronor with the same price for wheat as the rye. And now they say it will be even higher but famine we hope will not happen anyhow. We have now finished our new barn so now we are solidly settled and our pastor Brodin was here and blessed the building with a prayer and many people took part. We are prepared to start the charcoal stack. We will now work hard in the woods to be finished before the great Christmas holidays so we can be home and celebrate it together if God will allow us to have good health as we presently have. I will now on behalf of grandparents, uncles, cousins and all relatives congratulate Emma as a wife and we wish her entire house happiness and a comfortable life. So are the days of marriage as nice as the time of youth. Should it happen that the new couple is prepared to make a visit to their homeland, then they are very welcome here to Snarn and we shall do our best to make them feel at home and with as much comfort as possible. But now the fall has come here and chased away all the green in nature and its beauty and today the ground is covered with an inch of snow so now we have only the strong northerly winds to take into consideration. But old grandfather is still in such a good shape in spite of the fact that he is 90 years old that he can provide the women with fire wood so we don't need to freeze. Please give regards to Abramsson from Medaaker *(a family friend)*. I will now finish for this time with many dear greetings from all of us but first and last the greetings are from your old parents.

Signed friendly P. A. Odein

Merry Christmas wishes to you

Letter #14

7 July 1893, Medaaker and Snarn, Sweden. From P. A. Odein, husband of Anna Ericsson, Andrew's niece

We will now again send you a greeting and let you know how we are in Sweden. Now when it has become summer and warm, we have an acceptably good health both old and young and we wish the same good gift to you. I will now tell you that we expect a rather good harvest; if we can hope for as good as weather as we have had until today. Also I will tell you that we have bought a place although we have no money, but the price was so cheap, so we believe that it will be possible anyhow in the future if we can remain healthy. The land is about 70 acres of which 20 acres is cultivated soil, the rest is wooded land that can be cultivated and the price was 3,600 krona *(about $515)* of which 1,000 kronor was a mortgage that could be accepted. We made a down payment of 500 kronor and the rest has to be paid before March 14, 1894 so we will probably have to borrow some money for the time being. Also I will tell that we have got a new owner *(man who leases the land)* named Graaskanlar Lundborg in Arboga and he is well known. He bought Noss Ryby *(farm)* for 81,000 kronor *(about $11,600)* and has been here and looked over the small farms so we have new contracts *(leases)* also. My father-in-law *(Per Erik Larsson, Andrew's brother)* shall retain the little farm as long as the old couple is alive and he has accepted in spite of the fact that they have got an increase in the rental costs. Anna and I live at the new place which is located in Koestinge Himmita county. We thank you for the letter that we received a long time ago although we have not got down to answering because the old people think it is so nice to receive a greeting from their children who have been separated from each other and they feel that it should be a great joy once more in this life to see these children they saw in earlier days, have hugged to their breast so many times. They ask if you have an estate and if anyone will come to Sweden. They send a thousand greetings to your children and best wishes to them in every way. But they cannot work but they are rather healthy both of them. The old girl now walks on the floor and dictates to me what I am going to write and the old man, he is puttering around with this and that outdoors, but they are now more than 80 years old so we have to realize that it is not much to build on. I will now send you a greeting from all of your relatives here and they have recently been here practically each of them and they are healthy and perky and they get reasonably well forward in the world everyone in his job. In addition to the last, I will send you our greetings and may we wish you welcome here if any one of you should take themselves together and travel here. And no other news I have to tell you except that Johan Jansson in Fillinge has become a widower with many small children and that is difficult but my ways are not your ways, says the Lord. Please write soon asks grandfather and grandmother. Goodbye for this time.

Signed: P. A. Odein

Letter #15

3 October 1895, Gibo, Sweden. Letter found in an envelope addressed to Andrew Sandberg for the whole family, from Lars Larsson, Andrew's father. The envelope is dated 18 October 1895 with postage of ten cents.

Beloved son, daughter and children, may you be well, that is my daily wish and I am very well I say daily because I think very much on you and have many times told August *(Andrew's brother)* that he should write but he forgets so now, I send a few words. I hope he will write later. I have to tell you that I have not been well. I have spent the whole winter in bed but when spring came,

I became a little better so I have been up the whole summer so I have rested now in the fall. I have helped out with picking the potatoes. We have had a dry summer but the harvest has been good. The hay wasn't much but the corn was good and potatoes also. We have had a beautiful fall. We spoke and said that you should come home. I feel that it would be so great to see you coming home and have enough money to buy but I believe that you will not come home. We have to do with the photographs that you sent from your house in America. If I stood here I could even enjoy you and see you sometimes. August has also considered buying us a house, it is a piece of land close to the Ives Lake at the large peninsula. He will buy and he will build all of it himself and it will cost money but we need not very much as long as we can stay in Gibo but my time is soon over. I am now 80 years old. I have had my 80th birthday. Please write to me, I want very much to know how you are doing and if you come home anytime, perhaps in the spring; in winter it is too cold to visit. We had a cold winter with much snow. I send regards from August and Augusta and little Tilda. They are all well and feel good. I hope you all think about us, I will now finish my letter for this time with an old saying in Swedish *(translated)*—"goodbye to you."

LAST WILL AND TESTAMENT OF ANDREW SANDBERG AND ELISABETH SANDBERG

Ashville, New York
29 November 1912

"That they after one's death have the right to keep both solid and loose property and after the death of both, it falls to our children, Emma Olson, daughter and Andre Wilhelm Sandberg, son, and after their death, that it falls to their children. And that the undersigned has the right to manage all property as long as he is alive and if some carelessness should happen that he or she will be put under power of attorney.

(signed) Andrew Sandberg

Witnesses:
Carl Lindberg
Maria Lindberg

In the name of God, Amen.

AFTERWORD

I just finished reading all of these stories once more, and with each reading I've been impressed by the memories and insight of each author. As I read, I felt the authors' love for their ancestors and the pride in their heritage. I laughed with some of them and cried with others, and I've felt just a bit of the joy and the pain of our ancestors, both those who emigrated to this New World and of those who remained in the "Old Country." It's no mystery that so many of the pictures of our ancestors portray them as stern, unsmiling people. However, we know there must also have been many occasions for laughter and celebration—think of all the Sven and Ole jokes there are!

The authors whose stories you have just read are pleased to have been able to preserve their personal memories of their Scandinavian heritage and to honor those brave ancestors who left family and homeland to travel into an unknown future to try to make a better life for themselves and their families. The writers hope you have been stirred to ask questions while you have the opportunity and that you will be inspired to preserve your own family's heritage in writing for those who follow you.

Tack så mycket!

Barbara Ann Hillman Jones

ACKNOWLEDGMENTS

*O*ur *Scandinavian Heritage* was a group project, and there are many people who have had a unique and indispensable part in its development and successful completion. I'm extremely grateful to the following:

. . . first and foremost, to the many contributing authors who have searched their memories and family records to find and write the wonderful stories contained in this book. Each one is unique, and each story is an important part of not only their family history but the history of the Scandinavian community. And yet, throughout the book there is a unifying thread that binds us together.

. . . to Stephen E. Sellstrom, Honorary Consul of Sweden, for your very kind letter of appreciation and encouragement for this project. I am proud to include it in the book.

. . . to The Rev. Dr. Arland O. Fiske, my husband's long-time clergy colleague and our friend, for offering to me *carte blanche* use of his research and writings. They are a wonderful historical addition to our book, and I'm grateful, Arland!

. . . to Dr. Julie Lindblom Boozer, whose encouragement, ideas, and energy kept me going, especially during the times I wondered if this project would come to fruition.

. . . to The Norden Clubs of Jamestown, NY, for their sponsorship. A special thank you to Sandra Sandy, president of The Norden Women's Club, for her assistance and enthusiastic support.

. . . to my husband David whose help with the sometimes difficult and confusing technicalities of producing a book was invaluable. Thank you for your encouragement and the many cups of coffee—I promise to start cooking again!

. . . and, finally, I'm deeply indebted to Yvonne McNallie, vice president of The Norden Women's Club, for her untiring, uncomplaining willingness to do whatever it took to make the book a success. Her communications—and we've had many—were always encouraging and helpful. Yvonne is the one who did all the local follow-up and "leg work," and without her partnership, this project would have been virtually impossible. The best part is that as a result of sharing this project, we've become good friends. Yvonne, I can't thank you enough! Skol!

INDEX OF CONTRIBUTING AUTHORS

AUTHOR	PAGE NUMBER
Anderson, John A.	295
Anderson, John E.	215
Bilicki, Tanya Carlson	122
Boozer, Julie Lindblom	83, 160
Canfield, Karen Thorstenson	289
Carlson, Loren G.	221
Carlson, Rheba Brumberg	262
Chall, Russell N.	265
Cowles, Judith Erlandson	190
Erickson, Harold & Dorothy (Bush)	105
Erickson, Lynette	105
Erlandson, Tom	275
Faulk, Leonard Edward	71
Fiske, Arland O.	19, 47, 53, 69, 80, 87, 108, 117, 124, 140, 146, 156, 187, 192, 198, 211, 218, 233, 250, 257, 263, 282, 291, 303, 321, 328
Flynn, Karin Carlson	166
Garrison, Sharon Lofgren	120
Goldman, Barbara Lundine	254
Gustafson, Susann Sparrman	238
Holt, Cynthia Chall	265
Jackman, Dolores Carlson	213
Jackson, Chuck	60
Johnson, Carolyn Gustavson	208
Johnson, Donna Close	314
Johnson, Donna Nilsson	284
Johnson, Janice Ulander	246

Johnson, Newkirk L.	90
Johnston, Vorin Hansen	334
Jones, Barbara Hillman	62, 101, 132, 164, 206, 241, 272, 310, 332
Jones, Calvin David	260
Jones, Gregory	159
Kerns, Celeste Nelson	86
Kindberg, Carol Lind	110, 142, 189
Koplik, Larry	312
Lindner, Martha E.	50
Livsey, Karen E.	330
Lundine, Stan	254
Lynch, Margaret Mae Haglund	151
Mattson, Gordon Henry	111
McCullor, Lamae Ahlgren	129
McNallie, Yvonne Thorstenson	148, 324
Nelson, Nels John	78
Nichols, Denise	143
Nygaard, Julie Erickson	105
Oeffling, Karin Hillman	134, 306
Olsen, Sallie A.	337
Oster, Lois Jones	209
Peterson, Gladys Carlson	136
Peterson, Katie (Cathy)	85, 293
Quackenbush, Ann Nelson	279
Richetti, Elizabeth (Beth)	45
Samuelson, Jane	202
Sandy, Donald K.	97
Sandy, Sandra	65, 127
Seastedt, Jean W.	67, 200
Shevory, Joan Peterson	243
Shows, Dennis	56
Sorg, James (family of)	326
Stratton, Jay T.	168, 316
Swan, James	236

Thorsell, C. Philip	52
Thorstenson, Arthur (Pete)	267
Traynor, Maj-Britt	34
Volk, Carolyn Pearson	307
Waggoner, Norma Carlson	103, 194, 220
Wright, Carilyn Larson	252
Wright, Mary	195

BIBLIOGRAPHY

Fiske, Arland O., *The Scandinavian Heritage*. North American Heritage Press, Minot, ND, 1987.
   The Scandinavian World. North American Heritage Press, 1988.
   The Best of The Norwegian Heritage. North American Heritage Press, 1990.
   Stories from The Swedish Heritage. North American Heritage Press, 1992.
   The Best of The Norwegian Heritage, Volume II. North American Heritage Press, 1996.

Jones, Barbara Ann Hillman, *Recollections of a Jamestown Swede*. Xlibris Corporation, 2009.

Jones, Barbara Ann Hillman, *Cameos*. Xlibris Corporation, 2011.

Moe, M. Lorimer, *Saga From The Hills: A History of The Swedes of Jamestown*. Fenton Historical Society, Jamestown, New York, 1983.

CPSIA information can be obtained at www.ICGtesting.com
Printed in the USA
BVOW080005141112

305459BV00001B/4/P